PLANNING AT GRASSROOTS
Government's Participation in People's Plan

About the Authors

Ganapathy Palanithurai, Professor in Rajiv Gandhi Chair, Gandhigram Rural Institute, is an academic activist working with the people in rural areas for building the capacity of the leaders and people to reinvent sustainable grassroots democracy. He is heading the Department of Political Science and Development Administration, in Gandhigram Rural University, Tamil Nadu. His policy advocacy role at the governmental level is increasingly felt at present in all the three levels, namely, sub-regional, regional and national as he does more fieldwork than theorization. He has been associating himself with State Planning Commission of Tamil Nadu, Population Foundation of India, Rajiv Gandhi Foundation, CAPART, Ministry of Rural Areas and Employment and DANIDA (Danish-Indo Development Agency) in specific areas of activities in connection with empowerment of people. He is in the network of the Non-Governmental Organisations for Panchayat activities. He involves himself in capacity building exercise for local body of leaders. He has evolved training module and manual for local body leaders. He has to his credit forty-one books, Ninty-two articles in reputated journals, twenty-three working papers, twenty-seven monographs, eighteen review articles on three major areas, namely, Legislative Behaviour, Ethnicity and Panchayati Raj System. He was a recipient of Fellowship from Sastri Indo-Canadian Institute, New Delhi and World Academy of Art and Science, USA. He has visited the US and Canada, on academic assignments. He was a visiting fellow in the MiGill University, Canada in 1989. He is a life member of Indian Institute of Public Administration, Indian Association of Public Administration, Indian Association of Political Science, Indian Association of American Studies, and Indian Association of Canadian Studies. He is a member of the export commitee constituted by the Government of Tamil Nadu, to monitor the training programme for local body leaders.

M.A. Thirunavukkarasu, the Field Co-ordinator of The Hunger Project, Gandhigram Rural Institute, is an activist working with people at grassroots level. He, along with veteran Gandhigram activists Jegannathan and Krishnammal, participated in tillers movement. He is an expert in micro-planning and he has facilitated the Panchayat leaders to prepare micro plan document for their respective Panchayats. He associates himself in capacity building exercise for local body leaders and has assisted in evolving training module and manual for local body leaders training.

G. Uma presently works as the Co-ordinator of The Hunger Project in Gandhigram Rural Institute. As a Co-ordinator of the project for Tamil Nadu, she co-ordinated women leadership trainning programme for the elected women representatives, especially women presidents of Gram Panchayats. She has also developed a support structure to extend support to elected women representatives when they are in the field. She was instrumental in sensitizing the grassroots media to cover the struggle of the women leaders in the Panchayati Raj System.

PLANNING AT GRASSROOTS

Government's Participation in People's Plan
An Experiment

G. Palanithurai
M.A. Thirunavukkarasu
G. Uma

CONCEPT PUBLISHING COMPANY, NEW DELHI-110 059

Cataloging in Publication Data—DK
Courtesy: D.K. Agencies (P) Ltd. <docinfo@dkagencies.com>

Palanithurai, G. (Ganapathy), 1953-
Planning at grassroots : government's participation in people's plan : an experiment / G. Palanithurai, M.A. Thirunavukkarasu, G. Uma.
p. cm.
Studies on panchayati raj system in Tamil Nadu, India.
Includes bibliographical references (p.)
Includes index.
ISBN 13: 9788180695582
ISBN 10: 8180695581

1. Panchayat—India—Tamil Nadu. 2. Rural development—India—Tamil Nadu—Planning. 3. Rural development projects—India—Tamil Nadu—Citizen participation. 4. Tamil Nadu (India)—Economic policy. I. Thirunavukkarasu, M. A., joint author. II. Uma, G., joint author. III. Title.

DDC 307.141 209 541 2 22

ISBN-13: 978-81-8069-558-2
ISBN-10: 81-8069-558-1

First Published 2008

Published and Printed by
Ashok Kumar Mittal
Concept Publishing Company
A/15-16, Commercial Block, Mohan Garden
New Delhi-110059 (India)

Phones : 25351460, 25351794
Fax : 091-11-25357103
Email : publishing@conceptpub.com

To
THE DIVINE MOTHER

PREFACE

'Micro Plan' is a much debated subject in many fora after the enactment of the 73rd and 74th Amendments to the Constitution of India. Discussions and debates were on and on for some time on this subject even before the enactment of the two Amendments. But these discussions were more in theory than in practice. After the historic Amendments Kerala has produced substantial amount of literature on multilevel planning from below with the participation of people. A few other states have also produced such literature based on sporadic exercises on evolving micro plan with the help of development organizations.

Tamil Nadu is known for its voice in favour of State Autonomy and against Village Autonomy. Empowering grassroots institutions has not been on the agenda of the Government of Tamil Nadu as it has always sought only administrative solutions to the governance problems.

Against this background, we thought that micro plan can be considered as an instrument to make the government departments work in the people's plan. Planning exercises at the grassroots will bring a development culture, participatory culture and inclusive culture among the people. People will be mobilized for governance and development activities through this planning process. Micro plan can work for gradual devolution of powers.

An initiative has been taken in a few districts with the support of The Hunger Project, New Delhi to enable Panchayats to develop a plan. In this new venture a few non-negotiable principles have been stipulated as a pre-condition. They are : (a) the District Administration has to participate in the whole process of planning as partner; (b) the Gram Panchayat President should have the required commitment and enthusiasm; (c) the community should have participative resilience and they have to participate voluntarily in the plan preparation; and (d) the community should not have intensive conflicts. If the above conditions are met, we start work. But in the whole process of planning, we wished to be in the background and Panchayats are pushed in the front.

In Tamil Nadu we have started the planning exercise in Sivagangai District. Based on the experience in Sivagangai District we moved over to Pudukkottai District based on the invitation of the District Collector. With the rich experience of Pudukkottai, we got into Dindigul and Tuticorin Districts for preparation of micro plan, on invitation from the District Collectors of the respective districts. From Sivagangai to Tuticorin we have got rich experience, phase after phase. With the experience thus gained, we embarked upon the process of helping seventeen Gram Panchayats evolve a perspective plan to reconstruct the tsunami affected areas. In all the places after completing the plan preparation and getting the approval of Gram Sabha, dissemination workshops were conducted to sensitise officials, Panchayat leaders and media.

No doubt preparation of the micro plan was a major initiative and a difficult task. But still difficult is implementing the plan activities. For carrying out the plan activities, we have to stand with Panchayat leaders and help them contact the government departments. Making the officials work with Panchayat leaders is very difficult. This micro plan not only makes the officials work with leaders and also to spend funds on the prioritized activities of the people mentioned in the plan document. After one year a thorough evaluation is done. It provides rich insight into the planning process at the micro level. It will contribute richly to the Eleventh Five Year Plan preparation.

For the above exercise The Hunger Project has helped immensely. Ms. Rita Sarin the Country Director took personal interest in this exercise and she was with us in the whole enterprise. The five District Collectors evinced keen interest in getting the assignments done with the active participation of the community and the bureaucracy. Equally, the Panchayat leaders and the community leaders have also participated in the new exercise enthusiastically. The project staff of The Hunger Project and the

Rajiv Gandhi Chair for Panchayati Raj Studies were deeply involved in every action of the micro planning in the select Gram Panchayats. In the process of implementation, more specifically, the Project Officers of District Rural Development Agency of the said districts helped the Gram Panchayats. Media representatives have given wide coverage to the success and struggles of the exercises. Further the teaching staff of the Department of Political Science always proved to be a source of strength to all our project activities. The NGOs who have associated with this exercise in Sivagangai District and Nagapattinam District have keen an immense source of support in this exercise. We express our sincere thanks to all the above responsible individuals and organizations for their deep commitment, involvement and devotion to the cause.

G. Palanithurai
M.A. Thirunavukkarasu
G. Uma

CONTENTS

1

INTRODUCTION

"Planning" in India is believed by everyone to be an exercise that can be done only by top level bureaucrats and technocrats with the direction of the policy-makers for the development of the whole country. The concept of planning as an exercise and process which can be done at the lowest level in the hierarchy of governing structure with the involvement of the people has also been posited to the policy-makers ever since India adopted planning as a legitimate government exercise but it did not gain any support (Raj, 1984). Committees were constituted to probe more into the details of the process and as a result reports were submitted (K.V. Sundaram, 1977). In the beginning of 1970s the dominant thought of keeping planning at the top became flexible to some extent as such planning had not yielded the expected results to mitigate the problems of the poor, and initiatives at the provincial level that too at the sectoral level were allowed. It went still further in the 1980s with the initiative for planning being undertaken at the district level. The 1990s marked a historic departure from the conventional arrangements to achieve development so as to match globalization of economy and decentralization of powers. Planning at grassroots was made mandatory to achieve development and social justice with the participation of the people (K.C. Sivarama Krishnan, 2000). Though globalization gained currency and its operation in full swing, decentralization did not get that much of attention as the stakeholders of decentralization are weak. To make decentralization work, an array of support structures has to be created. Against this background, even for planning at grassroots one has to support the grassroots institutions. Though there were sporadic experiences in decentralized planning in the past, implementable strategies and devices could not be gained from all those experiments and experiences. (T.M. Thomas Issac with Richard W. Franke, 2000, 21-29). The new initiatives, following the 73rd and the 74th Amendments to the Constitution of India, have to take into cognizance the fact that the top-down planning has not addressed the felt needs of the people. It has removed people away from governance and participation in development. Development as an activity to be done exclusively by officials resulted in large scale corruption in rural development activities. This too has to be recognized while considering the new option. People were made the beneficiaries. Their self-respect was jeopardized as they were not seen as development participants (N. Narayansamy, M.P. Boraiyan and M.A. Jeyaraju, 2000). It is so not only in India but also in many developing countries. Bridging the gap between the people and the government is a difficult task in the Third World countries (Commonwealth Foundation, 1999). In this context, planning at the grassroots, initiated through the 73rd and the 74th Amendments to the Constitution of India, has to remove all the above stated obstacles and barriers in the process of development.

The Problem

Though the provision has been made in the Constitution for planning initiatives at the grassroots, to what extent steps are being taken at the State level and the Panchayat level to plan for development at the grassroots is a question to be probed. Further at what level initiatives gain momentum and how this can be sustained is yet another question to be examined.

Objectives and Methodology

This study has the following objectives:

(a) to study the efforts of the State Government in strengthening the planning process at the grassroots;
(b) to find out the extent planning initiated from below by the Panchayats with the participation of people;

(c) to examine how the planning process is initiated from the grassroots by the Panchayats and with whose support; and

(d) to estimate the implications of the intervention of the government and other agencies in the planning process at the grassroots.

The above stated objectives could be studied through documentary analysis and process analysis. The government's position on microlevel planning could be evaluated from the steps taken by the government. A process analysis can be made on the initiatives of planning at the grassroots by the Panchayat institutions with the support of the development organizations.

Context

There are two approaches to analyse decentralized planning. One is historical in nature and the other is contextual or critical analysis. Through the historical approach, ever since the concept of planning gained currency in India, discussions and deliberations had been conducted as to what alternative strategies have to be evolved to overcome the difficulties of centralized planning (James Manor, 1999). But all the discussions and deliberations were held against the backdrop of centralized planning. The issues and problems were looked at from the perspective of the centre and not from the perspective of the periphery. Macro economic activities through centralized planning did not mitigate the microlevel problems particularly those relating to the basic needs (G. Palanithurai, 2003). Hence the policy makers were compelled to think of planning units at different levels, namely the district and the block. Yet there was no conscious and deliberate decision to establish planning units below the State level. Even to establish a planning unit at the State level, it took nearly about two decades after independence. Such a kind of rigid centralization had been practiced in Indian politics and administration (Jayati Ghosh, 1998).

But the decentralized planning enunciated at present is totally different and it makes a real breakthrough as it has been incorporated in the Constitution itself. It is not an isolated event that took place in Indian planning. It is a corollary of a worldwide event which pushes the economy to cross the boundaries of the nations and into every segment of the society. Both in economy and polity an overhauling took place by which the paradigm of governance, administration and development has been totally altered (Ajit M. Banarjee and K.A. Chidambaram, 1996; Sofi Ali and Anita Rao, 2000; Olle Tornquist, 1999). A new paradigm has been developed by which new opportunities, which are uncommon, can be harnessed by enhancing the capacity of the stakeholders (International Commission on Peace and Food, 1990). Through this paradigm power is given to the people to determine their destiny (The World Bank, 2003). People have been projected as the major stakeholders and they have to decide their course of action in the process of development (Robert Chambers,1983). In the present context the concept "government" has been redefined. It is not a provider but a facilitator. The government takes a back seat and the community or the user group remains in the front to take development initiatives. Thus the concept of government is no longer relevant and it is only "governance" which is relevant at present (Rajesh Tandon and Ranjita Mohanty, 2002).

For the development of the community, activities have to be initiated through a new system of governance created at different levels below the State with the incorporation of the Amendments to the Constitution of India. Governance structures have been created at the village level, the block level and the district level, including towns, municipalities and corporations. To induce the people to participate in the development process, powers have been devolved to different levels and the planning mechanism had been incorporated into the Constitution itself. By doing so the trend of development activities has been altered from "supply-driven" to "demand-driven" mode (G. Palanithurai, 2000).

The major provisions and basic principles have to be conformed through an Act at the provincial level. Hence all the states have conformed to the bases of the Constitutional Amendments in State Acts. Tamil Nadu also has passed conformity Acts. Enacting a legislation is not a big task in a democracy since it is a representative democracy based on the principle of majority in Parliament and Legislative Assemblies. To pass a legislation the members of the decision-making body have to be managed through the established procedure. The difficult task lies in operationalizing the provisions of the Act which has to take place in the society among the people. In India there are a large number of key provisions in the Constitution which are still not operated effectively because of social conflict, social discrimination and illiteracy. Hence the focus should be on the operational part of the legislation. In the Tamil Nadu Panchayat Act due recognition was not given to the District Planning Committee and its responsibilities. The District Planning Committee and its functioning have to be seen and analyzed against the larger backdrop of devolution of powers in Tamil Nadu, because devolution of powers and planning at micro-level will alter the existing mode of governance (G. Palanithurai, 2003). To perform the above task, the State Government and its leadership should have sufficient will, because this initiative to devolve powers, functions, finance and functionaries will cripple the existing exploitative and corrupt nexus between the ruling elite and the inert bureaucracy. It will mobilize the people for strengthening democracy. People's perception has also to be changed as they regard themselves as beneficiaries instead of development participants having lost their self-confidence and self-respect. Further, people have to be conscientized and capacitated. The whole exercise has to be done with the backing of the Central Government.

Perception

To undertake the gigantic and uphill task, normally any leader will pursue the usual course of action. In the Indian context, this new exercise of democratic decentralization starts only from the State Government, and not from the Central Government. Normally, the term democratic decentralization is used in development literature to refer to the transfer of authority to plan, make decisions and manage public activities from the national level to any organization or agency at the sub-national level and down below. Decentralization in India refers to a situation in which the lower-ranking units below the State level acquire all powers and responsibilities from the State Government and also exercise sole control over the determination of their goals and targets.

Tamil Nadu's ethnic political culture demanded adequate powers to the State Government since independence. Now these political parties, which are coming to power alternatively, view decentralization as a threat to the power of the State Government. These political parties, namely both the Dravida Munnetra Kazhagam (DMK) and the All India Anna Dravida Munnetra Kazhagam (AIADMK), forcefully opposed the creation of the three-tier Panchayati Raj System as it would emerge as a countering political force. Hence, they have developed a strategy to keep the Panchayat system a weak instrument while appearing to conform to the major provisions of the 73rd Amendment to the Constitution of India (G. Palanithurai, 1999).

The Panchayat was created through the conformity legislation enacted during the period of the All India Anna Dravida Munnetra Kazhagam. The Act has many retrograde provisions (G. Palanithurai, 1998). The Act has not given any real power to Panchayats. The new Panchayati Raj was operationalized only during the period of the Dravida Munnetra Kazhagam. All the powers given to the Panchayati institutions are supervisory in nature and not of the decision-making kind. The powers given to Panchayats, however meagre, have not been given through any Act but through Government Orders. The ruling parties at the State level somehow or other have managed to keep the local bodies in their party fold as the ruling parties have to emerge victorious in the local body elections also. As a result most of the local body leaders never raise their voice against the State Government for more power, finance and functionaries to local bodies. Only the lowest units in the system, namely the Gram Panchayats, which are freed from political affiliations raise their voice against the State Government and demand powers to local bodies. The District Planning Committee was created and it was placed under the Chairmanship of the District Collector. After a prolonged fight the District Collector was replaced by the District Panchayat

Chairperson. Elections to District Planning Committee were conducted and now it is in position but no meaningful activity is undertaken by it.

Virtually, planning at multi-level exists only in concept and theory but not in practice. But the State Planning Commission had prepared a report, guidelines and a training module for multi-level planning (State Planning Commission, 1997). Both leaders and officials had been trained (G. Palanithurai, 2000). The elected representatives elected to the District Planning Committee have taken cognizance of the mandatory functions of the District Planning Committee. But there is no concerted effort to build up this process of planning from below and, as a result, the rural development activities are carried out still in the supply-driven mode and people are not involved in the development activities. More than that the felt needs of the people projected through the Gram Sabha are not met, but a variety of activities are being carried out through sectoral departments (G. Palanithurai, 2003).

In order to break the deadlock, an exercise was initiated with the intervention of The Hunger Project by which select Gram Panchayats in Sivagangai District, Pudukkottai District, Tuticorin District, Dindigul District and Nagapattinam District have been set up as model Panchayats in terms of planning at micro-level with the participation of the people who are willing to involve themselves in the preparation of plan for the development of the communities in the Panchayat area. The question might arise, why these Panchayats alone in these five districts? The leaders of these Panchayats evinced interest in this exercise and volunteered themselves while they were undergoing training. Further, these Presidents are supported by the respective District Collectors who have assured that they will extend all possible support and coordination to this exercise.

Initiatives of the Government

By going through the document entitled "Report of the Working Group on Decentralized Planning and Panchayati Raj" prepared by the Planning Commission, 1997, one can infer the poor interest evinced by the Government of Tamil Nadu in all the previous experiments. In the 73rd Amendment, while there was a discussion in the Parliament, the two major political parties, namely, the DMK and the AIADMK being in power in Tamil Nadu State alternatively, made a categorical statement that they had not imagined a structure for Panchayati Raj above the Block Panchayats. They wrote letters to the Government of India that the District Panchayat has to be abolished. With both these parties opposed to the district level structure what would have been the fate of the District Panchayat in Tamil Nadu? Further, when the District Planning Committee was formed, the District Collector was made the Chairperson of the District Planning Committee. After a prolonged negotiations the District Panchayat President was made the Chairperson of the District Planning Committee. To fulfil the Constitutional obligation, the District Planning Cell with a skeleton staff was created. It has to look after the day to day administration of the District Panchayats. Neither the State Government nor the District Planning Committee took any step with regard to the preparation of the District Development Plan. The State Planning Commission, though it took the initiative, did not have the backing of the State Government. As a result planning at the district level has not seen the light of the day.

But organizations and activists engaged in public affairs, seeing the apathy of the State Government in taking the measures for micro-level planning, became interested in taking the initiative. Except in West Bengal and Kerala, micro-level planning has been undertaken only at the initiative of the development organizations. In this context in Tamil Nadu State, The Hunger Project initiated the process of planning at Gram Panchayat level as Gram Sabha has got power to approve the plan document which becomes a legal and legitimate plan document. The Hunger Project has certain objectives, namely ending hunger through micro plan, mitigating malnutrition, empowering women and children through the micro plan, and working for social development through micro plan, all under women's leadership. But The Hunger Project realized the fact that in the context of weak devolution of powers to the local bodies, micro-level planning will be a meaningful exercise only when it is done with the partnership of the district administration as the sectoral departments are under the district administration. Since sectoral departments are not under the control of the Panchayati Raj System for implementing the plans of the Panchayats, the cooperation of the sectoral departments is imperative. Against this background, working with the district administration becomes inevitable. Further, though the State government is not interested in devolving powers, it is interested in achieving social development. This interest can be exploited to initiate micro-level planning. The Hunger Project in Tamil Nadu is taking a major lead in initiating micro-level planning at the Gram Panchayat level. Ten Gram Panchayats in Sivagangai District headed by women have planned and started working on the plan. Following Sivagangai District, in Pudukkottai District, 13 Gram Panchayats have been selected and planning is over. Another 30 Gram Panchayats have been selected for this exercise in Tuticorin District and Dindigul District. Wherever the district administration is taking initiative, The Hunger Project joins them as partner and initiates micro-level planning. Panchayats are selected for this planning on two conditions, namely the Gram Panchayat leader should have honesty, commitment and capacity and the Gram Panchayat should enjoy the support of the communities without any social and disharmony.

2

MICRO PLANNING METHODOLOGY

Till date since Independence our Central and State Governments have prepared ten Five Year Plans with the help of experts and government officials and carried out the same for the development of our people. Our governments have spent crores of rupees in our villages to implement these plans. Even then, all of us know that many of our basic needs have not been fulfilled. Not only that, our government have created an impression that achieving development is the duty of the government. Nowhere is it proved that government alone has brought development of the community. It can be brought only by the people synergizing the efforts of the government. The government can render a help to those who aspire for achievement and development. People who are in poverty have to struggle against it, for which the government can provide all possible assistance. It has been the practice in India that all development activities are carried out on supply driven mode and never on demand. The 73rd and 74th Constitutional Amendments have provided an opportunity reversing the trend. Though 74th Amendment has provisions for district level planning, in Tamil Nadu, this district level planning exercise was not carried out and so it was thought of preparing a plan at village level as an experiment. This methodology is devised on the basis of the planning exercises done in Sivagangai, Pudukkottai, Thoothukudi and Dindigul Districts, and the District Collectors of these districts helped this process as partners and also took part in the planning exercises and in plan execution by understanding the legal sanctity of the Village Panchayats.

This planning has got certain objectives. They are: (a) to reverse the trend of working on supply-mode to working on demand-mode; (b) making the people as participants in their development initiative; (c) making the government departments work on people's plan,

(d) making the people dream and envision for their development; and (e) planning is an instrument by which local self-governance can be strengthened.

I. Objectives of the Planning

According to Article 243G of the Constitutional Amendment and 240 and 257 of the Tamil Nadu Panchayats Act, the local body institution should prepare development plan to ensure economic development and social justice. Such plans should have the following objectives:

(A) Economic Development

The plan should be developed in such a way that it has to achieve economic development by increasing the production in agriculture, land reforms, small irrigation system, animal husbandry, dairy and poultry and fisheries. Economic development is the key in this process.

(B) Social Justice

The benefits of economic development should reach the various categories of the community, particularly, it should reach the poor and the socially weaker sections. Further, the plans should facilitate increased income by providing employment opportunities to the socially disadvantaged and the marginalized.

(C) Welfare

The plan should incorporate schemes for providing infrastructural facilities like road, water supply, housing, street lights, waste disposal, and also social welfare schemes like education, welfare of women, children and cultural activities.

(D) Environmental Protection

The plans should have the component to protect nature and

environment. It should not cause damage to the eco-system, flora and fauna. It should have devices to manage natural resource. It should aim for creating green, clean and thus eco-friendly villages.

(E) Coordination

The plan should ensure the total development and growth of the entire village by incorporating all the development plans of the concerned area, plans of the respective departments, schemes for individual benefits, schemes that are implemented by the government departments, schemes that are implemented by banks, NGOs and other development agencies.

(F) People's Involvement

The plan should be on the basis of collection of data, confirmation of the same, assessing the needs, evolving activities and prioritizing the same. At every level people have to be involved and people should own the plan.

II. Steps Followed in Planning Exercises

(A) Preparatory/Environment Building

1. *Meetings with District Administration* – Prior to the commencement of the exercise in the village, meetings with the district administration were to be held. This meeting was meant to ensure their cooperation not only for the preparation of the plan but also to implement the District Administration's cooperation as critical component for the preparation and implementation of the plan.
2. *Identification of Gram Panchayats* – Inputs from the District Administration helped the process of identifying the Gram Panchayats for planning exercises. Gram Panchayats were selected on the basis of certain conditions. They were, commitment of the Panchayat leader, cooperation of the community to the Panchayat and

willingness on the part of the Panchayat leader to follow the process.

3. *Memorandum with Gram Panchayats* – Once the *Gram Panchayats* were identified, a preliminary discussion with the representatives of the Panchayat was to be held in which objectives of the planning and clarifying the roles to be performed by different agencies were to be explained. The *Gram Panchayat* should subsequently pass a resolution committing its willingness to create a Panchayat level plan for its Panchayat.
4. *Orientation* – A day-long orientation for the Gram Panchayat members, representatives from SHG's, youth groups, and other opinion makers at the village level were held within the Panchayat. The orientation emphasised the importance of planning, the steps to be undertaken and the importance of the Panchayat owning the process.
5. *Gram Sabha Meetings* – Subsequently the Gram Sabha of the respective Panchayat should be apprised of the activities. There were five statutory committees that a Gram Panchayat must establish. If these committees had not been established then they must be set up in consultation with the Gram Sabha. The Appointment of Committees ensured greater participation in the planning process. There was a need to create a Planning Committee to oversee the entire process of preparation of the Panchayat Plan. If the number of committees at the Panchayat level is to be kept within a manageable limit, the Panchayat Council can take on the responsibilities of the Planning Committee with one co-opted, non-elected member from each of the five statutory committees (Appointment Committee, Development Committee, Agricultural and Watershed Committee, Works Committee and Education Committee). Periodical updates presented to the Gram Sabha assisted in a broad based participation in the process in order to ensure direction and coordination.
6. *Capacity-building* – A five-day workshop for elected representatives of these Panchayats—inclusive of council members—served as the base for further work. The

workshop consisted of a vision exercise as well as sessions on planning. Once the planning committee of the Panchayat was created, a three-day workshop on "Planning for Social Development" ensured that the focus of planning does not remain limited to infrastructure creation alone.

7. *Orientation of Committee Members* – The members of the committees required orientation and role clarification to take forward the plan creation process.
8. *Interface between elected representatives and the district administration* – At regular intervals from the inception onwards there was regular interaction between the elected representatives and the district administration. In the long run, this developed the capacity of the elected representatives to deal with the administration and the interest and commitment of the administration added value and lent credence to the plan creation and implementation exercise.
9. *Exposure* – Organizing brief exposure visits to witness innovations undertaken by other Panchayats in the State enabled the Panchayats to 'think out of box'. The fact that they do not have to limit themselves necessarily to only scheme-based activities but they could plan their own interventions was reinforced.
10. *Ward/Hamlet-level Meetings* – To generate interest amongst all sections ideally, meetings were held at the ward/hamlet level on the need for plans, the steps to be taken, committees to be constituted and the roles to be performed.
11. *Village-level Officials* – An opportunity for a meeting between members of the statutory committees, the Gram Panchayat and village level officials were created. This enabled the village level officials to give their inputs and facilitated participation of others in the plan preparation process.

(B) Data Collection

12. *Identification of Data needed* – In consultation with the members of the statutory committees and the Gram

Panchayat identification of data needed to be collected to develop the plan was undertaken. The sources of data and the processes by which the data could be verified were explored. Each committee took on the responsibility to collect the needed data on various aspects of development.

13. *Finalization of tool to collect the Data* – Tools to collect information were finalized. A well-formulated template prepared by the State Planning Commission was used.
14. *Identification and Orientation of Investigators* – The committees needed to enroll additional village level volunteers to assist in the data collection process. An orientation of those undertaking the responsibility to collect the data was organized to facilitate data collection.
15. *Review of Data and Collation* – Once the data were received and they were reviewed with the committee members and investigators and if there were any gap to be filled up it had to be attended to. The collected data should be compiled and collated.
16. *Presentation of Data for Confirmation* – The data that were collected were presented to the Gram Panchayat and Gram Sabha for their approval. An analysis accompanied the presentation of the information. Feedback and comments were obtained and incorporated.

(C) Community-Based Planning

17. *Hamlet Level Development Workshop* – A comprehensive hamlet level development workshop was conducted. At the hamlet level, a series of activities needed to be undertaken with an emphasis on enhancing the participation of families was undertaken.

    (a) *Identification of the Most Vulnerable* – Poor families, women-headed families, landless families, homeless families, families headed by a person with disability and no other/inadequate wage-earners, families headed by the aged. An attempt was made to explore the extent of benefits these families receive from existing social security and employment schemes and to try and verify the accuracy of the data. The data were also useful as the Panchayat can use them to monitor the extent of benefits they are able to get from the government;

(b) *Identification and Prioritization of Needs* – The needs emerging from each hamlet and the priorities were identified;

(c) *Solutions, Possible Costs and a Realistic Re-prioritization were done* – For each of the needs that were identified, potential solutions and the estimated costs were worked out. Once this information is available, it is possible that the hamlet may choose to re-prioritize its needs; and

(d) *Information Sharing and Review* – The collected data and analysis made should be shared with the members present at the hamlet meeting since it could enable discussions and assist in identifying needs and priorities.

In the past Venn diagrams, ranking of priorities, resource maps, and wealth ranking were used as tools. Even in the absence of any PRA technique being utilized, a sensitive and focused facilitator with an inquisitive mind could in a group situation cull out a wide variety of responses and achieve all of the above. The role of the facilitator for the group meetings is absolutely critical.

18. *Consolidation of Hamlet Plans* – The inputs emerging from the hamlet level meetings needed to be consolidated by the committees.
19. *Presentation and Approval of Gram Sabha* – The consolidated plans must be presented to a special Gram Sabha for its inputs, comments, feedback and approval. The plan was finalized only after approval of a special Gram Sabha.
20. *Panchayat Meeting* – The Gram Panchayat incorporated the suggestions made by the Gram Sabha and then prepared an action plan for the next steps to be taken and allocate responsibilities for each. The plan should ideally be broken up into realistic annual plans to make it more realistic for follow-up and monitoring.

21. *Identification of Potential Support Institutions/Departments*—The Gram Panchayat tried and identified potential sources of support both monetary or otherwise for specific components of the plan. These included sectoral departments, DRDA, MP-LAD, MLA-LAD, local NGOs, Banks etc.
22. *Proposal Creation* – Several components required to be converted into specific proposals that are then presented to either sectoral departments or the DRDA for support. Technical details wherever necessary were added to the proposals prior to their acceptance by departments.

(D) Implementation, Monitoring and Review

The statutory committees and the Gram Sabha must play a key role in the implementation, monitoring and review of the process of transforming the plan into reality. The easiest way to guarantee this is ensuring the ownership of each of the critical stakeholders in the Plan.

Key government officials and elected representatives – District Collector, Project Officer-DRDA, other key officials in DRDA, BDOs, Panchayat Union Councillors, District Councillors, MPs and MLAs involving in the process of implementation.

III. Templates to Collect Data for Planning

Profile of the Village Panchayat

Name of the Village Panchayat	:			
Panchayat Union	:			
Taluk	:			
District	:			
Total number of hamlets	:			
Total number of wards	:			
	SC/ST		*Others*	
	Male	*Female*	*Male*	*Female*
Name of the Ward Members				

Population Details

Sl. No.	Details	*1991 Census*		*2001 Census*	
		Male	*Female*	*Male*	*Female*
1.	Total Population				
2.	Literates				
3.	Scheduled Caste				
4.	Scheduled Tribe				
5.	Most Backward Class				
6.	Backward Class				
7.	Other Communities				

Financial Status of the Panchayat

Sl. No.	*Year*	*Particulars*	*A/c I*	*A/c II*	*A/c III*
1.		Income (Rs.) Expenditure (Rs.)			

Village Panchayat Fund

Sl. No.	*Details of Income*	*Amount (Rs.)*	*Details of Expenditure*	*Amount (Rs.)*
1.	House Tax		Salary	
2.	Library Tax		Presidents TA & Sitting Fees	
3.	Professional Tax		EB Charges for Panchayat buildings	
4.	Registration Fee		Maintenance of OHT	
5.	Stamp Duty		Maintenance of Street light	
6.	Bank Interest		Maintenance of Television	
7.	Local Cess		Group Insurance	
8.	SFC Grant		Transfer to A/c II	
9.	Other Subsidies		Maintenance of Road	
10.	Total Income		Funeral Grant	
11.	Opening Balance		Rainwater Harvesting	
12.	Total		Other Expenditure	
13.			Bank Commission	
14.			Installation of water supply equipments	
15.			Stationeries	
16.			Total	

Earmarked Fund

Sl. No.	*Details of Income*	*Amount (Rs.)*	*Details of Expenditure*	*Amount (Rs.)*
1.	Earmarked State Grant		Panchayat Building Maintenance	
2.	Fixed Deposit		Replacing motor by new one for drinking water	
3.	Income tax		Bank Commission	
4.	Sales Tax		Total	
5.	Chess			
6.	Bank Interest			
7.	Schedule			

Scheme Fund

Sl. No.	*Details of Income*	*Amount (Rs.)*	*Details of Expenditure*	*Amount (Rs.)*
1.				
2.				
3.				
4.				
5.				
6.				
Total Income			Total Expenditure	

Anganwadi Details

Sl. No.	*Village*	*Building Facilities*		*Need*	*Teachers' Toilet*	*Students' Toilet*			*Status of Water Supply*	*Details of Need*
		Sufficient	*Insufficient*			*Male*	*Female*	*General*		
1.										
2.										
3.										

Details about Anganwadi

Sl. No.	Village	Playground and Teaching Materials	No. of Teachers		Noon-Meal	
			Male	Female	Sufficient	Insufficient
1.						
2.						
3.						

Details of Children and Pregnant Women (till February 2004)

Sl. No.	Age details of Children (in months)	Chittrampatti		Vellayakoundanpatti		Meenaveli	
		Male	Female	Male	Female	Male	Female
1.	0-5						
2.	6-12						
3.	13-24						
4.	25-36						
5.	37-48						
6.	49-60						
7.	61-72						
	Pregnant Women						

Details of Educational Institutions

Sl. No.	Village	Type of School	Building Facilities		Details of Needs	Teachers' Toilet	Students' Toilet		
			Sufficient	Insufficient			Male	Female	General
1.									
2.									

Sl. No.	Status of Drinking Water	Details of Needs	Availability of Playground, Teaching Materials and Teaching Aids (Other needs)	No. of Students		No. of Teachers		Noon-Meal Centre	
				Male	Female	Male	Female	Sufficient	Needs
1.									
2.									

Details of Drinking Water

Sl. No.	Village	Overhead Tank		Mark 2 Hand Pump	Shallow Hand Pump	No. of Drinking Water Wells	Street Taps/ Pipes	Needs	
		No.	Capacity					Need	Place of Requirement
1.									
2.									
3.									
4.									
5.									
6.									

Details of Roads

Sl. No.	Village	Present condition of the road	Present Length	Proposed Length	Type of Road Needed	Place of Requirement
1.						
2.						
3.						
4.						
5.						
6.						

Details of Culverts and Small Bridges

Sl. No.	Village	Items	Number	Need & Place of Requirement

Details of Public Distribution System

Sl. No.	Village	PDS Shop		Place of Functioning		Electricity Facility		Improvement Needed	Existing No. of Family Cards	No. of New Cards Needed	
		Full Time	Part Time	Own Building	Rented Building	Yes	No			SC/ST	Others
1.											

No. of AAY Beneficiaries Other Details

Public Health

Location of PHC, distance in kms.

Location of Sub-centre

Is the Sub-centre Functioning

Details of Improvement Needed in Sub-centre

Details of the Functioning of VHN

Details of Public Health

Sl. No.	Village for	Public Toilet		Is it in Use Household		No. of of Toilets	Details Drainage	Needs	
		Male	Female	Male	Female			Public Toilet	Household Toilet
1.									
2.									
3.									

Needs of Drainage Facility	*Needs of Smokeless Chula*

Other Infrastructural Facilities

Sl. No.	*Particulars*	*Place of Availability*	*Distance in kms.*	*Needs*	*Place of Requirement*
1.	Bus Stand				
2.	Passengers Shelter				
3.	Community Hall				
4.	Threshing Floor				
5.	Library				
6.	TV Room				
7.	Police Station				
8.	Post Office				
9.	Public Telephone				
10.	VAO Office				
11.	SHG Building				
12.	Common Market				
13.	Medical Shop				
14.	Co-operative Bank				
15.	Nationalized Bank				
16.	Trade and Commercial Establishment				
17.	Industries				
18.	Burial Ground				
19.	Cremation Ground				
20.	Open Theatre				
21.	Cooperative Milk Producers Society				

Housing Details

Sl. No.	*Village*	*Total No. of Families*	*No of own Houses*	*No. of Families not Possessing House Sites*	*Not Possessing Patta*	*No of Families Availed Housing Through Government Schemes*
1.						
2.						
3.						
4.						
5.						
6.						

Details of Rural Industries

Sl. No.	Details	No of Persons		Status of Avocation Involved
		Male	Female	
1.	Handloom			
2.	Powerloom			
3.	Handicrafts			
4.	Carpentry			
5.	Pottery			
6.	Blacksmithy			
7.	Tannery			
8.	Khadi & Village Industries			
9.	Washer Men			
10.	Stone Metal			
11.	Service Sectors			
12.	Gem Cutting			
13.	Other Works			

Details of Employees

Sl. No.	Details	No. of Employees		Status of Avocation
		Male	Female	
1.	Agricultural Workers			
2.	Agricultural Labourers			
3.	Government Services			
4.	Non-Governmental Services			
5.	Village Craftmen			
6.	Traders			
7.	Other Workers			
8.	Unemployed			
9.	Seasonal Migration			
10.	Dependent on Products of Minor Forest			
11.	Cottage Industries			

Details of Self-Help Groups

Sl. No.	*Village*	*No. of SHGs*		*Total No. of Members*		*Details of Revolving Loan Availed*		*Details of Cash Credit Availed*	*Details of Economic Activities*
		Male	*Female*	*Male*	*Female*	*Male*	*Female*		
1.									
2.									
3.									
4.									
5.									

Name of the Facilitating NGO in SHG Activities

Sl. No.	*Name of the SHG Group and Village Training*	*No. of Persons Availed*	*Training Details*	*Initiatives taken after training*
1.				
2.				
3.				

Total Geographical Area

Sl. No.	*Details*	*Geographical Area (in Hectares)*
1.	Forest Area	
2.	Uncultivable Dry lands	
3.	Land used for Non-Agricultural purposes	
4.	Cultivable Wasteland	
5.	Permanent land used for grazing purposes	
6.	Land with Trees	
7.	Currently, Land lying Waste	
8.	Other Lands	
9.	Other Types	
10.	Net Cultivable Land	

Irrigation Details

Sl. No.	*Water Sources*	*Total Nos.*	*Length in Kms.*	*Total Geographical Area*
1.	Rain Water			
2.	Irrigation Canals			
	(a) Government Canals			
	(b) Private Canals			
3.	Ponds			
	(a) Big			
	(b) Small			
4.	River Irrigation			
	(a) Big & Medium			
	(b) Small			
5.	Well Irrigation			
	Total No. of Wells			
	No. of Wells got Electrification			
	Fitted with diesel engine			
6.	Ponds			
	(a) Lift Irrigation			
	(b) Minor Irrigation			
7.	Rain-fed Land			
8.	Other Types			

Details of Ponds

Sl. No.	*Village*	*Survey No.*	*Name of the*	*Area of the Pond*	*Area Under Pond*	*Type of the Pond Ayakkattu (PWD, Panchayat)*	*Need of Improvement (Union)*	*Other Details*
1.								
2.								
3.								
4.								
5.								

Details of Oorani

Sl. No.	*Village*	*Survey No.*	*Oorani Details*	*Area*	*Needs*
1.					
2.					
3.					
4.					
5.					

Agricultural Details

Sl. No.	*Village*	*Type of Cultivation*		*Area*	*Area of Cultivable Land*
		Dry Land	*Wet Land*		
1.					

Farmer's Details

Sl. No.	*Details*	*Total No. of Farmers*	
		SC/ST	*Others*
1.	Small Farmers		
2.	Marginal Farmers		
3.	Big Farmers		

Details of Livestocks

1. Location of veterinary dispensary, distance in kms:
2. Is the veterinary dispensary functioning effectively?

Sl. No.	*Species*	*Total*	*Details of Needs*
1.	Bullocks Cows Buffalos Sheep Goats Hens		

Number of Persons Living below Poverty Line as per the Panchayat Records

Sl. No.	*Village*	*Families living below poverty line*					*Families living above poverty line*				
		SC	*ST*	*BC*	*MBC*	*Others*	*SC*	*ST*	*BC*	*MBC*	*Others*
1.											
2.											
3.											

Marginalized Sector

1. Re-deemed bonded labourers –
2. People affected due to communal riots –
3. People who lost all possessions and belongings due to fire and floor –
4. Unable to earn, due to suffering from chronic diseases –
5. Families employing children as labourers –

Poor Widows

Sl. No.	*Name*	*Village*	*Age*	*Sex*	*Community*	*Present Avocation*	*Remarks*
1.							
2.							
3.							
4.							
5.							

Disabled Persons

Sl. No.	*Name*	*Village*	*Age*	*Community*	*Sex*	*Present Avocation*	*Other Details*
1.							
2.							
3.							
4.							
5.							

Traditional Craftsmen who are in acute Poverty

Sl. No.	*Name*	*Village*	*Age*	*Community*	*Sex*	*Present Avocation*	*Other Details*
1.							
2.							
3.							
4.							

Migration of Families Seeking Employment Opportunities

Sl. No.	*Name*	*Village*	*Age*	*Community*	*Sex*	*Present Avocation*	*Other Details*
1.							
2.							
3.							
4.							

List of Persons Eligible to Avail Housing from Government Schemes

Sl. No.	*Village*	*Name*	*Community*	*Total No. of Family Members*	*Other Details*
1.					
2.					
3.					
4.					

List of Eligible Persons to Receive House Site and Patta

Sl. No.	*Name*	*Village*	*Community*	*Needs*
1.				
2.				
3.				
4.				

Sl. No.	List of beneficiaries of various schemes	Total Members
1.	Eligible persons to get family ration card	
2.	Eligible persons to get IAY benefit	
3.	Enrollment in self-help group	
4.	Eligible persons to get health card	
5.	Eligible persons to get skill development training	
6.	Names to be enlisted in food for work scheme	
7.	Eligible persons to avail KISAN card	
8.	Eligible persons to get self-employment card	
9.	Eligible persons to get ID card	

List of Eligible Persons to Avail from SGRY – 22.5 percent Allocation Individual Benefit

Sl. No.	Name	Village	Community	Needs
1.				
2.				
3.				
4.				

List of Activities Proposed

Sl. No.	Plan Activities	Solving Strategy	Development Partners	Expected Outcome
I	Child Welfare			
1.				
2.				
3.				
4.				

Village Development Plan – Activities for People's Participation

Sl. No.	Activity	Responsibility	Methodology
1.			
2.			
3.			
4.			

IV. Draft Village Development Plan

The first part of the Draft Village Development Plan contained the following details: District Collector's forward, acknowledgement of the Panchayat President, what was going to be done in the Gram Panchayat through this plan, history of the Panchayat, available resources of the Panchayats, and available basic facilities. The second part of the document contained the present status of the available resources. The third part contained the need and the place of requirement. And the last part contained the sources of resources and how to augment these resources for the successful implementation of the development plan.

3

MICRO PLANS

SECTION-I

By following the methodological nuances developed by the State Planning Commission for the preparation of micro plan at village level, participatory materials have been used to collect data and activities were prioritized through PRA meetings conducted in each and every hamlet. Focused group discussions were conducted for difficult stakeholders to map the issues of the different segments. Consolidated plan was presented in the Gram Sabha and got the approval of Gram Sabha. The Gram Sabha approval document was endorsed by the District Collector of the respective districts. The plan documents became a legally valid plan of the people and the government departments will have to work on it.

The following are the details of the Gram Panchayats that prepared the plan document in four districts :

Table 3.1 : Model Panchayats for Community-Based Micro Level Planning in Sivagangai District

Sl. No.	*Panchayat*	*Union*
1.	1. Veppangulam	
	2. Nerpugapatti	
	3. Kalipuli	1. Kallal
2.	4. Velangudi	2. Tirupathoor
3.	5. Vaduvanpatti	
	6. Sevalpatti	
	7. Kozhikudipatti	3. Singampunari
4.	8. Urathupatti	
	9. Manaloor	
	10. Keelavayal	4. S.Pudur

Table 3.2 : Model Panchayats for Community-Based Micro Level Planning in Pudukkottai District

Sl. No.	*Name of the Panchayat*	*Panchayat Union*
1.	Merpanaikadu	Aranthangi
2.	Poovalur	Avudayarkoil
3.	Melathur	Thiruvarankulam
4.	Edaiyathimangalam	Manamelkudi
5.	Elaikadaividuthi	Karambakudi
6.	Melaputhuvayal	Kunandarkoil
7.	Parambur	Annavasal
8.	Nerijikudi	Ponnamaravathy
9.	Punakulam	Gandarvakottai
10.	Mookampatti	Pudukkottai
11.	Meenaveli	Viralimalai
12.	Virachilai	Tirumayam
13.	K.Rayavaram	Arimalam

Table 3.3 : Model Panchayats for Community-Based Micro Level Planning in Tuticorin District

Sl. No.	*Panchayat*	*Panchayat Union*
1.	Ottanatham	Ottapidaram
2.	Puthiamputhur	Ottapidaram
3.	Kodiyankulam	Ottapidaram
4.	Pattinamaruthur	Ottapidaram
5.	Tharuvaikulam	Ottapidaram
6.	Sriparangusanallur	Srivaikundam
7.	Siruthondanallur	Srivaikundam
8.	Thirupani Chettikulam	Srivaikundam
9.	Parakiramapandi	Srivaikundam
10.	Mukkani	Srivaikundam
11.	Mettilpatti	Puthur
12.	Mathalapuram	Puthur
13.	Kadalkudi	Puthur
14.	Thappathy	Puthur
15.	Iyanrajapatti	Puthur

Table 3.4 : Model Panchayats for Community-Based Micro Level Planning in Dindigul District

Sl. No.	*Panchayat*	*Panchayat Union*
1.	Sithargalnatham	Nilakkottai
2.	Kodanginaickenpatti	Nilakkottai
3.	Noothulapuram	Nilakkottai
4.	Karisalpatti	Reddiarchatram
5.	Pannaipatti	Reddiarchatram
6.	Kamatchipuram	Reddiarchatram
7.	Silvarpatti	Reddiarchatram
8.	Athoor	Athoor
9.	N. Panjampatty	Athoor
10.	Thevarappanpatty	Athoor
11.	Kallikkampatty	Athoor
12.	Anaipatty	Dindigul
13.	M.M. Koviloor	Dindigul
14.	Balakrishnapuram	Dindigul
15.	Mullipadi	Dindigul
16.	Thottanoothu	Dindigul

Following is the sample plan document of a Gram Panchayat in Pudukkottai district. All the fifty-four Gram Panchayats are having the same type of documents for their village development.

CASE – I

Village Development Plan

Meenaveli Village Panchayat - Viralimalai Panchayat Union
Pudukkottai District

Jatindra Nath Swain, I.A.S.,
District Collector
Pudukkottai

I am happy that the draft plan for the social and economic development of Meenaveli Panchayat in Viralimalai Panchayat Union has been prepared and, with the approval of the Gram Sabha, has taken shape as a plan document.

The commencement of planning from below marks a good beginning. Planning is an important basis of decentralization. I applaud the Panchayat President, the Panchayat Council Members and the Members of the Gram Sabha for making the necessary efforts.

The Rajiv Gandhi Chair for Panchayati Raj Studies of the Gandhigram Rural Institute and The Hunger Project, New Delhi, have together provided the assistance and the guidance needed for planning. I appreciate and thank them.

I wish your Panchayat success in coordinating the activities of all the departments engaged in rural development in Pudukkottai District in order to execute the plans specified in the plan document and thereby facilitating improvement in the life of the people at the lowest level. I assure your Panchayat that all the departments will function in unison with you in this coordinated venture of yours.

Signed
(JATINDRA NATH SWAIN)

ACKNOWLEDGEMENT

This document on the village development plan of Meenaveli Panchayat in Viralimalai Panchayat Union of Pudukkottai District has been prepared at the initiative and with the constructive suggestions of Shri Hitesh Kumar Makwana, I.A.S., the former District Collector of Pudukkottai District. It would not have been completed without his cooperation. We express our whole-hearted gratitude for his support in this endeavour. Shri Yatindranath Swain, I.A.S., the present District Collector of Pudukkottai District helped and motivated the Panchayat with his moral support and all the necessary facilities to complete this plan document. We place on record our debt to him.

The Project Officer, DRDA, Pudukkottai District, Mr. Selvarajan helped us by instructing all the officials to provide us the necessary information for this plan document. We express our thanks to him.

The role of The Hunger Project needs special mention. It is The Hunger Project which started this initiative for preparing the plan document. The Hunger Project motivated us and provided all the needed financial support for planning and implementing it. We acknowledge with gratitude the support of The Hunger Project.

The Rajiv Gandhi Chair for Panchayati Raj Studies of the Department of Political Science and Development Administration of Gandhigram Rural Institute, and its Coordinator, Dr. G. Palanithurai, provided us all the inputs and guidelines needed for preparing the document. Without his support and suggestions, this plan document could not have come out. The staff of the Department of Political Science and Development Administration provided unstinted support and guidance for completing this document. We acknowledge their service in this regard. We also acknowledge the valuable contribution of Shri K.M. Subramanian, B.D.O., who provided the required technical details.

For any plan to be meaningful, it should be implemented. To this end various institutions/organizations and departments have been approached and they will support us. We thank them also.

Finally, on behalf of the President, the Councillors, and the people of Meenaveli Panchayat, we thank all those who supported us in preparing this plan document.

V. Alagar
President/Executive Officer
Meenaveli Panchayat

What is going to be done in the Gram Panchayat through this plan?

- Enrolling all the children who have completed five years of age in school.
- Ensuring that the enrolled children continue their studies without dropping out.
- Conducting school annual day celebration to enable the students to display their creative potential.
- Providing basic amenities like drinking water, toilet, playground and vegetable garden in the school.
- Creating a sanitation and toilet among the students.

- Establishing reading rooms to encourage the desire to learn among the villagers and putting to use the Ayyan Thiruvalluvar Library.
- Providing toilet facility and playthings for children in the *anganwadi* and trimming their nails to ensure hygiene.
- Enrolling all the children who have completed two and a half years of age in the *anganwadi* and helping them to learn the habit of attending to their personal cleanliness.
- Ensuring the age-specific weight and the general health of children by providing them with appropriate balanced nutritious meal and ensuring the proper conduct of activities such as providing nutritious flour and noon meal under the integrated child welfare scheme.
- Preventing female infanticide by creating awareness among the villagers.
- Ensuring that all the children receive fully and properly the benefits of the immunization programme.
- Creating an environment free of child labour.
- Adopting measures to prevent child mortality.
- Creating awareness among the people about gender equality.
- Ensuring that all deliveries take place only in hospitals.
- Creating awareness among women about prenatal and postnatal care.
- Helping women to fully receive the benefits of the activities under the postnatal child welfare schemes.
- Helping pregnant women to properly receive benefits such as prenatal care, medical examination, immunization vaccines, nutritious flour and pregnancy assistance money.
- Providing the required minimum basic facilities in the sub-health centre.
- Helping the village health nurse to discharge her welfare functions well.
- Taking steps to ensure optimum utilization of the women's sanitary complexes.
- Ensuring that all the people get safe drinking water.
- Completely eradicating open air defecation.
- Arranging for common public toilets and their proper use.

- Removing waste in order to create a sanitary village.
- Creating awareness among the people about the dangers to the village from non-degradable substances like plastics and polythene and taking steps for their prohibition.
- Augmenting finances by converting public wastes into fertilizer.
- Planting, rearing and protecting saplings in public places to transform the village into a green village.
- Ensuring minimum basic amenities to all the habitations in the village.
- Installing solar lights on streets.
- Ensuring that all eligible families get ration cards.
- Arranging to issue pattas to those who own no house sites.
- Ensuring that essential commodities are properly available under the public distribution system.
- Building houses for houseless people.
- Eradicating untouchability and creating social harmony.
- Ensuring that the Adi Dravidar community gets all the benefits it is eligible for.
- Organizing poor women into self help groups and helping them to achieve social and economic upliftment.
- Making all the arrangements required to enable the self help groups to produce articles and to market them.
- Bringing together the village artisans into a federation, enhancing their manual skills and arranging for employment opportunities for them.
- Creating awareness to ensure that girls are married only after they complete twenty-one years of age.
- Observing the families of weak, destitute, elderly people, poor widows, poverty-stricken artisans and guaranteeing their livelihood.
- Identifying the disabled and reaching to them benefits that ought to reach them.
- Showing the way for male as well as female self help groups to function robustly.
- Motivating and guiding self help groups participating fully in public welfare activities and in Gram Sabha meetings.

- Repairing and maintaining water sources such as ponds, tanks, *ooranis* and *kanmois*, collecting rainwater in them and using them properly.
- Creating the right perspective among the people regarding the importance of water, water management and utilization of water.
- Developing natural resources and protecting them from damage and degradation.
- Creating awareness among the people to cultivate medicinal plans in public places in the village and in habitations and to use them.
- Creating awareness among the people to effect changes in agriculture to suit circumstances.
- Reclaiming common property resources from encroachment.
- Regulating common property resources and taking steps to augment the Panchayat income through them.
- Reorienting the Panchayat activities to a people-centred mode and carrying them out with people's participation.
- Transforming the Panchayat into an arena for people's action.
- Transforming the people into social citizens and making them participate in all Panchayat activities.
- Transforming the Gram Sabha into a forum for social upliftment instead of a forum for collecting grievances.
- Involving women and Dalits in a big way in all the activities of the village.
- Synergising the different organizations functioning in the village for development activities.

Village Development Plan
Meenaveli Village Panchayat
A Plan Document

Sl. No. *Title*

1. District Collector's Foreword
2. Acknowledgement of the Panchayat President

3. What is going to be done in the Gram Panchayat through this plan?
4. Introduction
5. Profile of the Village Panchayat
6. Details of Population
7. Panchayat Finance 2003-2004 / Income and Expenditure

Basic Details

8. Details of *Anganwadi*
9. Details of Children and Pregnant Women
10. Details of Educational Institutions
11. Details of Drinking Water Supply
12. Details of Road Facilities
13. Details of Culverts
14. Details of Public Distribution System
15. Details of Health Facilities
16. Other Infrastructural Details
17. Details of Households

Village Economy

18. Details of Rural Industries
19. Details of Rural Employees
20. Details of SHGs
21. Land Details
22. Details of Irrigation System
23. Details of Ponds and Tanks
24. Details of Agriculture
25. Details of Farmers
26. Details of Animal Husbandry
27. Details of BPL Families
28. Details of Marginalized Section
29. Village Development Plan — List of Needs

Introduction

Meenaveli Gram Panchayat is located in Illupur Taluk, Viralimalai

Union, in Pudukkottai District, Tamil Nadu. It is 40 kms south-west of the Trichy-Madurai National Highway and 4.6 kms east of Kovilpatti. The total geographical area is 920.06 hectares. The population is 3086 (male 1587 and female 1499). Perichipatti, Annayathoppu, Chittirampatti, Annathanapatti, Vellayankoundanpatti are the hamlets in Meenaveli Gram Panchayat.

The name Meenaveli was coined because the village is surrounded by ponds and other water sources teeming with fish. *Meenaveli* means "surrounded with fish". It is a multi-religious Panchayat with Hindus, Muslims and Christians and they are all living peacefully. Communal harmony is maintained. There is no discrimination on the basis of caste and there is no religious clash in the village. The inhabitants are mostly farmers and agricultural labourers. During non-season days people from this area migrate to Viralimalai, Kovilpatti and Manapparai for alternative sources of employment to generate income. The transport facility (bus) is limited to three trips a day. The youth have formed their own groups and work together. The NYK is guiding these groups for the development of the village. At present there are 20 SHGs, of which 14 are women groups and 6 are men groups. Most of the SHGs are awaiting bank loan and revolving fund from the government. One group has repaid the loan availed of from a bank. The groups have undergone training in tailoring, computer, composting and motor rewinding. Though they have undergone training in the above said activities there is no proper guidance for them to involve themselves in income generation programmes.

The Hunger Project attached to the Rajiv Gandhi Chair for Panchayati Raj Studies in the Department of Political Science and Development Administration of Gandhigram Rural Institute has been engaged in efforts to enable the Gram Panchayat to work for the development of the village through Micro Level Planning by involving the people of the village and to make the Panchayat a model Panchayat. Seven Statutory Committees and one Planning Committee have been constituted in the Panchayat. The profile of the village has been prepared out of the data collected from various departments, namely, education, health, agriculture, social welfare, and the village administrative office. The information collected has been tabulated to design a plan and the details are furnished as follows.

2a. Profile of the Village

Education

There is a primary school and a middle school. The primary school at Annathanapatti is under the management of ASSEFA, recognized by the Government of Tamil Nadu. The salary and the activities of the school are managed by the school itself. The villagers feel that the school is ensuring quality education. When there was a proposal to establish a school under the SSA scheme, the people said that there was no need for such an establishment. The infrastructural facilities of the school need to be improved. There is a water tank in the school.

In Meenaveli Village, there is a middle school headed by a headmaster residing in the same village. It is said that there has been remarkable improvement in the school after he joined the school. An amount of Rs.85,000 has been deposited in the bank, after collecting Rs.1,000 as donation from 85 persons. The PTA is functioning effectively and the school buildings have been constructed through government schemes. In order to increase the strength of teaching staff according to the student strength, three teachers have been appointed through the PTA. So, the strength of the teaching staff has increased to 8 (5 recruited by the government and 3 by the PTA). Lack of toilets for the students in the school is a major problem to be attended to immediately. Separate toilets should be constructed for boys and girls. Toilet facility for the teachers is available. The Village Panchayat has constructed a water tank in the school. In addition to all these the Panchayat has taken the initiative to remove encroachments. Trees have been planted on the school campus, the sides of the Panchayat road and other public places. SHG members are engaged in the protection of the saplings. Fencing work has been taken up at the school with stone posts and barbed wire.

For the past two years, the school enrollment is cent-per-cent and there has been no dropout during the past few academic years. The PTA, in collaboration with the Village Panchayat administration has taken efforts to sustain this status in the coming years also. It is learnt that the infrastructural facilities, particularly in terms of playground, teaching and learning equipments, are inadequate. It is felt that students need encouragement and motivation to involve themselves in various extra-curricular activities like dance, drama, and literacy activities. With regard to the academic quality of the students, it is said that 50 per cent to 60 per cent of passes is achieved. More concentration is needed in the subjects English, Tamil and Mathematics.

Anganwadi

In the villages of Meenaveli, Chittirampatti and Vellayankoundanpatti, *anganwadis* are functioning well. The *anganwadi* of Meenaveli Village is located in the community hall. Toilet facility is available in the *anganwadi*. Water is collected from the nearby public tap for *anganwadi* use. Children from Annathanapatti and Perichipatti, around 30 in number, have to come to the Meenaveli *anganwàdi*. But they do not come. Only the children belonging to the Meenaveli Village are attending the *anganwadi*. Facilities like play materials are not available. No separate toilet is available for the teachers.

In Chittirampatti *anganwadi*, the infrastructural facilities are sufficient. The children's toilet is in use and water facility is also available. It lacks only a playground for outdoor games. In Vellayankoundanpatti Village, the anganwadi is functioning in a rented building. A permanent building with toilet facilities has to be constructed. The Vice President of the Panchayat, who belongs to Vellayankoundanpatti Village, has supplied mats for the children's use. For the benefit of the children of Perichipatti and Annathanapatti villages, new *anganwadis* have to be sanctioned and separate buildings have to be constructed. In general, it is felt that the personal hygiene of the children is not properly attended to by the parents when they send their wards to the *anganwadi*.

Some of the parents have gone to places like Trichy, Thuvakudi and Erode in search of employment. The children (around ten) belonging to these families are not attending the *anganwadi*. Children below 3 years are eligible to avail of porridge freely supplied in the *anganwadi*. The parents of the children visit and collect the free porridge. From the distant villages, Perichipatti, Annayyanthoppu and Annathanapatti, the children are not able to attend the *anganwadi* and the porridge packets are distributed to the parents of the children once in a week. There is awareness among a few families, where the parents themselves prepare porridge for their children.

Training and orientation programmes for adolescent girls are being conducted in the anganwadi. The participation is satisfactory but, at the monthly meetings, there is poor attendance. After the completion of the 8th standard, adolescent girls prefer jobs to continuing their education. Pregnant women collect iron and folic tablets regularly. The adult women have habits like chewing tobacco, arecanut and betel leaf. Awareness on balanced and nutritional diet has to be created among the women. Monthly meetings for adolescent girls and children should be conducted regularly. Proper attention is needed to ensure maximum attendance at these meetings.

Panchayat Administration

The Panchayat administration is at present looked after by the Vice-President due to the sudden demise of the President in September 2003. The election for the post of President is yet to be conducted. The Panchayat meetings are held once a month and the accounts are displayed regularly. The income of the Panchayat has improved as a revision was made of the house tax. In the current financial year, the income is Rs.1,77,975, including SFC grant and stamp duty. With regard to expenditure, the electricity charge is more when compared to other items of expenditure. The total expenditure is Rs.1,88,982. From the earmarked fund, Rs.89,368 has been spent on maintenance of the Panchayat building and Rs.19,309 for replacing the motor pump of the drinking water supply system. The balance available in the account is Rs. 41,829. With regard to scheme funds there is Rs.2,58,598 in the SGRY scheme and the social forestry scheme. The opening balance in this account is Rs.1,13,764. The major activities under scheme funds are construction of threshing floor, tree planting under social forestry, construction of rainwater harvesting structures, and, improvement works in Kuppattan tank, carried out at a cost of Rs.2,25,564. The balance available in the account is Rs.1,46,798. Care is taken for the protection and maintenance of the saplings planted. It is expected that a considerable amount of income will accrue from the grown up trees in the future.

There is a possibility of planting saplings in the poramboke area and thereby income can be generated. Since Meenaveli is a remote village, there is no scope for a commercial complex to generate income. Some activities will be undertaken by the SHGs themselves to minimize the expenditure. Production of organic manure and marketing the same will be a means of augmenting income for the Panchayat. In Perichipatti Village, a building has been given to the SHGs and they are to undertake maintenance with their own funds.

Health and Sanitation

There is no sub-health centre in the Panchayat. So the people have to depend on the nearby sub-health centre in Akaraipatti Panchayat, which is 5 kms. away from Meenaveli. The PHC is located in Kodumpallur, 10 kms. away from Meenaveli. Since there is no proper transportation facility to the PHC, people are not making use of it regularly. It is said that the village nurse visits the Panchayat once a month, generally on Wednesdays, and provides services to the people. So there is an urgent need to construct a sub-health centre with a full time village nurse to look after the health needs of the villagers like vaccination for children and maternal care, prevention of contagious diseases, health care of adolescent girls and awareness on general health.

There are no proper drainage facilities in the Panchayat. Since the houses and streets are congested in the villages of Meenaveli, Chittirampatti and Vellayankoundanpatti, drainage facilities should be given priority. Awareness is given on the disadvantage of polythene use and people are educated to minimize the use of polythene. Awareness is to be generated on how waste can be recycled for profitable use.

Dustbins should be placed in important places in the Panchayat. Soak pits should be constructed in the needed places. The sanitary complex available at Chittirampatti is yet to be utilized fully. At present, the women make use of only the washing facility at the complex. There are 81 households, for whom sensitization is needed to construct household latrines. Moreover the available household latrines are not properly used. Users should be given awareness in this regard. The importance of smokeless *chula* is yet to reach this village. Necessary arrangements have to be made to create awareness in this regard as well as on non-conventional energy sources. There is a demand for around 500 smokeless *chulas*.

There are 6 OHTs under the drinking water supply system in this Panchayat. The OHTs are cleaned once a month but the chlorination is not done properly. Orientation to the OHT operators is needed in this regard. Further, environmental sanitation around the water points has to be upgraded.

Welfare of the Marginalized Sections

It is found that there are 193 persons living below poverty line. Agriculture is the main occupation and, due to limited employment opportunities in agriculture, several families are migrating and seeking employment opportunities elsewhere. Most of them are getting engaged in the construction industry and laying of roads in the nearby towns.

Many are engaged in gem cutting. In spite of poor income due to non-availability of any other source of income, many of the Christians in this village are working as carpenters. Mobilizing them by providing better tools and equipments through a centralized system of improved equipments will enhance their enterprise opportunities. Necessary steps have to be taken in this regard.

A cooperative milk producers society is functioning at V. Koundanpatti. Due to pending of loans, no new credit facility is available for the purchase of milch animals. Hence the milk production is very limited in the society. There is a possibility of extending credit facility to the eligible SHGs for purchasing milch animals. There are 131 widows, 19 disabled persons, 15 craftsmen and 8 destitute women living in poverty. The socio-economic development of the above mentioned individuals has to be planned for. The Public Distribution System shop at Meenaveli is not a full time one as the staff concerned have to look after another Public Distribution System shop in the nearby village. Of the 140 families who are eligible to avail of the new ration card 122 are below poverty line.

Profile of the Village Panchayat

Name of the Village Panchayat	: Meenaveli
Panchayat Union	: Viralimalai
Taluk	: Illuppur
District	: Pudukkottai
Total number of Hamlets	: 6 1. Meenaveli 2. Perichipatti 3. Annayanthoppu 4. Chittirampatti 5. Annadhanapati 6. Vellayankoundanpatti
Total number of Wards	: 4

SC/ST		Others	
Male	Female	Male	Female
4	—	3	2

Name of the Ward Members	Ward I – Mr. Muthukannu, Mr. Perumal, Ms.Ayeshabeevi Ward II – Mr. Alagarnayakkar, Ms. Chandra Ward III – Mr. Andiyakoundar, Mr. Nallu Ward IV – Mr. Alagar, Mr Chinnappan

Population Details

Sl. No.	Details	1991 Census		2001 Census	
		Male	Female	Male	Female
1.	Total Population	1379	1341	1587	1499
2.	Literates	670	395	830	560
3.	Scheduled Caste	450	426	493	432
4.	Scheduled Tribe	—	—	—	—
5.	Most Backward Class	625	586	689	616
6.	Backward Class	302	327	404	450
7.	Other Communities	2	2	1	1

Financial Status of the Panchayat

Sl. No.	Year	Particulars	A/c I	A/c II	A/c III
1.	2003-2004	Income (Rs.)	1,77,975	43,947	2,58,958
		Expenditure (Rs.)	1,88,982	19,309	2,25,664

Village Panchayat Fund

Sl. No.	*Details of Income*	*Amount (Rs.)*	*Details of Expenditure*	*Amount (Rs.)*
1.	House Tax	7123	Salary	33840
2.	Library Tax	713	Presidents TA & Sitting Fees	5610
3.	Professional Tax	4237	EB Charges for Panchayat Buildings	7686
4.	Registration Fee	170	Maintenance of OHT	25380
5.	Stamp Duty	91933	Maintenance of Streetlight	26622
6.	Bank Interest	1432	Maintenance of Television	28550
7.	Local Cess	3335	Group Insurance	3630
8.	SFC Grant	49348	Transfer to A/c II	19684
9.	Other Subsidies	19684	Maintenance of Road	4950
10.	Total Income	1,77,975	Funeral Grant	2000
11.	Opening Balance	42497	Rainwater Harvesting	8368
12.	Total	220472	Other Expenditure	12495
13.			Bank Commission	580
14.			Installation of Water Supply Equipments	7927
15.			Stationeries	1660
16.			Total	188982

Expenditure as on 29.02.2004 – Rs.188932
Balance – Rs.31490

Earmarked Fund (2003-2004)

Sl. No.	Details of Income	Amount (Rs.)	Details of Expenditure	Amount (Rs.)
1.	Earmarked State Grant	39368	Panchayat Building Maintenance	9990
2.	Fixed Deposit	2430	Replacing Motor by new one for Drinking Water	9249
3.	Income Tax	400	Bank Commission	70
4.	Sales Tax	400	Total	19309
5.	Chess	20		
6.	Bank Interest	799		
7.	Schedule	530		
Total Income till 29.02.2004		**43947**		

Opening Balance (01.04.2004) – Rs. 17191
Total – Rs. 61138
Expenditure – Rs. 19309
Balance – Rs. 41829

Scheme Fund

Sl. No.	Details of Income	Amount (Rs.)	Details of Expenditure	Amount (Rs.)
1.	Sampoorna Gramin Rozgar Yojana	120014	Threshing Floor Construction	34030
2.	Indra Awaas Yojana	10000	Returning the Fixed Amount	29480
3.	Social Forestry Tree Planting	119124	Social Forestry Tree Planting	119124
4.	Balance	3700	Rainwater Harvesting	18750

(Contd...)

(Contd...)

5.	Contribution to Employee's Fund	444	Bank Commission	420
6.	Bank Interest	5316	Upgradation of Kuppattam Pond	23760
Total Income		258598	Total Expenditure	225564

01.04.2003 Opening Balance – Rs. 113764
Total – Rs. 372362
Expenditure – Rs. 225564
Balance as on 29.02.2004 – Rs. 146798

Anganwadi Details

Sl. No.	*Village*	*Building Facilities*		*Need*	*Teachers' Toilet*	*Students' Toilet*			*Status of Water Supply*	*Details of Need*
		Sufficient	*Insufficient*			*Male*	*Female*	*General*		
1.	Meenaveli	Existing in the Community Hall	—	1	No	—	—	√	No	√
2.	Chittirampatti	√	—	—	No	—	—	√	√	—
3.	Vellayankoundanpatti	—	Rented Building	1	No	—	—	—	√	—

Details about Anganwadi

Sl. No.	Village	Playground Aids and Teaching Materials	No. of Teachers		Noon-Meal	
			Male	Female	Sufficient	Insufficient
1.	Meenaveli	No	—	2	√	—
2.	Chittirampatti	No	—	2	√	—
3.	Vellayankoundanpatti	No	—	1	√	—

Details of Children and Pregnant Women (till February 2004)

Sl. No.	Age details of Children (in months)	Chittirampatti		Vellayankoundanpatti		Meenaveli	
		Male	Female	Male	Female	Male	Female
1.	0–5	2	6	2	3	4	4
2.	6–12	8	7	3	6	4	3
3.	13–24	12	7	10	3	14	16
4.	25–36	20	8	6	8	7	8
5.	37–48	12	11	7	6	13	6
6.	49–60	7	8	9	6	10	7
7.	61–72	9	15	12	13	11	9

(Contd...)

(Contd...)

Pregnant Women			
I Para	14	7	9
II Para	5	2	4
III Para	3	3	2
IV Para	1	-	-
V Para	1	-	-
VI Para	1	-	-
No of Pregnant Women taking Porridge	8	4	-
Adolescent Girls	90	55	-

Details of Educational Institutions

Sl. No.	*Village*	*Type of School*	*Building Facilities*		*Details of Needs*	*Teacher's Toilet*	*Students' Toilet*		
			Sufficient	*Insufficient*			*Male*	*Female*	*General*
1.	Annathanapatti	Primary School (Sarva Seva Primary School, Recognized by the Government of Tamil Nadu)	—	—	1	—	—	—	—
2.	Meenaveli	Middle School	—	√	1	√	—	—	—

Sl. No.	Status of Drinking Water	Details of Needs	Availability of Playground, Teaching Materials and Teaching Aids (other needs)	No of Students		No of Teachers		Noon-Meal Centre	
				Male	Female	Male	Female	Sufficient	Needs
1.	Water is availed from the Panchayat tank	—	Playground is available Teaching aids are needed	63	48	3	-	-	√
2.	√	—	Playground is available Teaching aids are needed	335	300	5	(3 teachers recruited through PTA)	-	√

Details of Drinking Water

Sl. No.	Village	Overhead Tank		Mark 2 Hand-pump	Shallow Hand-pump	No of Drinking Water Wells	Street taps/ pipes	Needs	
		No.	Capacity					Need	Place of Requirement
1.	Meenaveli	1	30,000	5	-	4 (one is in use and the other three are not in use)	24	Extension of Pipeline	Meenaveli SC Street 500

(Contd...)

(Contd...)

2. Perichipatti	1	30,000	3	—	1 (not in use)	14	Mark 2 hand pump –1 Extension Pipeline	Perichipatti – 1 Perichipatti SC and BC Street – 75 metres
3. Annayan-thoppu	Water supply is from Perichipatti	—	1	—	—	2	Extension of Pipeline	Annayanthoppu – 30 metres
4. Chittirampatti	1	30,000	3	—	2 (not in use)	2	OHT –1	Chittirampatti Village
							Mask 2 Handpump – 2	Chittirampatti Melakalam – 800 metre
							Extension of Pipeline	Chittirampatti SC, Kounder Street – 100 metre
5. Annathanapatti	1	30,000	2	-	1 (not in use)	14	Extension of pipeline	Konar, Kounder Street – 175 metre
6. Vellayankoundan-patti	1	30,000	7	-	2 (desilting is to be made for the well near the temple. The other well is dry)	15	Mask 2 Handpump – 1 Extension of Pipeline	V. Patti SC Street 350 metre

Details of Roads

Sl. No.	Village	Present condition of the Road	Present Length	Proposed Length	Type of Road Needed	Place of Requirement
1.	Meenaveli	Metal Road	2 km	2 km	Pitumen (Thar) Road	Annayanthoppu – 1 km, Perichipatti – 1 km
		Pitumen Road	7 m	2 km	Extension of Pitumen road	Meenaveli to Perichipatti road
		Gravel Road	100 m	1200 m	Cement concrete Road	Meenaveli SC Street – 1000 m Muslim Street – 100 m Melatheru – 100 m
2.	Perichipatti	Gravel Road	50 m	50 m	CC Road	SC Street – 50 m
3.	Annayanthoppu	Gravel Road	50 m	50 m	CC Road	SC street – 50 m
4.	Chittirampatti	Gravel Road	1300 m	1300 m	CC Road	SC street – 400 Vadakkutheri – 300 m Therkutheru – 500 m Melatheru – 100 m
5.	Annathanapatti	Gravel Road	900 m	900 m	CC Road	Therkkutheru – 900 m
6.	Vellayankoundan-patti	Gravel Road	1250 m	1250 m	CC Road	SC Street – 500 m Therkkutheru – 250 m Vadakkutheru – 300 m Nadutheru – 200 m

Details of Culverts and Small Bridges

Sl. No.	Village	Items	Number	Need and Place of Requirement
1.	Meenaveli	Small Bridges	7	4 Meenaveli (near Sivankoil–1), Near Nithyakaliamman koil– 1, Near chavadi – 1, Muslim street –1
		Retaining Wall	55 m	490 m – Near Nithyakaliamman koil–100 m, Near Sivan koil – 50 m, SC street – 30 m, Near Mask – 30 m, Kilakku Christian street – 30 m, Middle School – 250 m
		Bunding Wall	—	200 m – Meenaveli Maaoorani karai – 200 m
2.	Perichipatti	Small Bridge	4	2 Perichipatti Road – 2 (3 bridges need to be maintained)
		Footpath Bridges	—	1 Thenoor salai –2, acrodd the Vellalar – 300 m
		Retaining Wall	—	800 m – Perichipatti salai turning
		Bunding Wall	—	1200 m – Perichipatti Vellalar Vadakarai–1000 m, Therkkukarai – 200 m
3.	Annayanthoppu	Small Bridge	—	3 Annayanthoppu Road – 2, Across Vellalar pallam – 1
4.	Chittirampatti	Small Bridge	4	4 SC Street – 1, Melathur – 1, Graveyard road - 2
		Retaining Wall	—	180 m – Near SC street – 100 m, Near Merkkutheru – 30 m, Near Villakkusalai – 50 m
5.	Annathanapatti	Small Bridges	1	—
		Bunding Wall	—	50 m – Annathanapatti Ooranikarai
6.	Vellayankoundanpatti	Small Bridges	6	9 Vadakkutheru – 1, SC Street – 2, Therkkutheru – 1, Nadutheru – 1, Nedunjchalai – 4 (2 small bridges need to be maintained)
		Retaining Wall	—	250 m near graveyard 100 m, Iyyan Ooranisalai – 100 m, near SC street – 50 m
		Bunding Wall	—	100 m Ooranikarai

Details of Public Distribution System

Sl. No.	Village	PDS Shop		Place of Functioning		Electricity Facility		Improvement Needed	Existing No of Family cards	No of new cards needed	
		Full Time	Part Time	Own Building	Rented Building	Yes	No			SC/ST	Others
1.	Meenaveli	—	1	√	—	—	√	Part time functioning of the shop should be made full time. A permanent building is needed.	563	80	60

No. of AAY beneficiaries

30

Other Details

H identification not yet stamped – 18

Cards not yet renewed – 23

Rice – 11476 kg

Sugar – 1058 kg

Kerosene – 1069 lt

Note :
* Part-time Public Distribution System in Meenaveli is open on Saturdays, Tuesday and Thursday.
* The present Public Distribution System shop is constructed by the community.

Details of Public Health Facilities

Location of PHC, distance in kms	Kudumpathur, 10 kms
Location of sub-centre	Akaraipatti, 5 kms
Is the sub-centre functioning	Yes
Details of improvement needed in sub-centre	A sub-centre is needed (Meenaveli)
Details of the functioning of VHN	Visits once in a month (probably on Wednesdays)

Details of Public Health Facilities

Sl. No.	*Village*	*Public Toilet*		*Is it in Use*		*No of Household Toilets*	*Details of Drainage*	*Needs*	
		Male	*Female*	*Male*	*Female*			*Public Toilet*	*Household Toilet*
1.	Meenaveli	—	—	—	—	3	No	2	130
2.	Perichipatti	—	—	—	—	23	No	2	62
3.	Anayanthoppu	—	—	—	—	20	No	1	6
4.	Chittirampatti	—	1	—	—	7	25m	—	220
5.	Annathanapatti	—	—	—	—	1	No	—	70
6.	Vellayankoundanpatti	—	—	—	—	—	—	—	203

Needs of Drainage Facility	**Needs of Smokeless Chula in Numbers**
300 m	90
200 m	50
100 m	5
300 m	200
Needed	50
Needed	105

* The Household Toilets are not in proper use.

Details of Other Infrastructural Facilities

Sl. No.	Particulars	Place of Availability	Distance in kms	Needs	Place of Requirement
1.	Bus Stand	Viralimalai Manapparai	20 kms 20 kms	—	—
2.	Passengers' Shelter	—	—	9	Vellayankoundapatti –1 Meenaveli –2 Chittirampatti –2 Perichipatti – 1 Annathanapatti – 1 Vellailakkulam – 1 Annayanthoppu – 1
3.	Community Hall	Meenaveli	—	1	Marriage hall –1 (Meenaveli)
4.	Threshing Floor	Meenaveli	—	4	Perichipatti – 1 Chittirampatti – 1 Vellayankoundpatti – 1 Annadhanapatti – 1
5.	Library	Meenaveli (1) (Panchayat Library)	—	1	Meenaveli (the building for library is in Annadhanpatti village. It is not used properly SHG meetings are conducted in that building)
6.	TV Room	Meenaveli–2 (SC-1) Perichipatti–3(SC-1) Annayanthoppu–1(SC) Chittirampatti–4(SC-1) Annadhanapatti –2 Vellayankoundanpatti–3 (SC-1)	—	2	Vellayankoundanpatti – 1 Meenaveli – 1
7.	Police Station	Viralimalai	20 kms	—	—

(Contd...)

(Contd...)

8. Post Office	Meenaveli	—	—	Meenaveli – 1 (building)
9. Public Telephone	—	—	34	Meenaveli – 5 Vellayankoundanptti – 5 Annadhanapatti – 2 Perichipatti – 2 Chittirampatti – 20
10. VAO Office	Meenaveli	—	—	—
11. SHG Building	Perichipatti	1 ½ kms (no EB connection)	5	Chittirampatti – 1 Meenaveli – 1 Annadhanapatti – 1 Vellayankoundanpatti – 1
12. Common Market	Kovilpatti Manapparai	6 kms 20 kms	—	(There is a scope for organizing daily market in Chittirampatti)
13. Medical Shop	Kovilpatti	6 kms	—	—
14. Co-operative Bank	Kodumpallur	10 kms	—	—
15. Nationalized Bank	Viralimalai	20 kms	—	—
16. Trade and Commercial Establishment	Kovilpatti (Trichi District) Viralimalai	6 kms 20 kms	—	—
17. Industries	Viralimalai	20 kms	—	—
18. Burial Ground	In all the six hamlets of Meenaveli Panchayat	—	—	(Platform and roof are needed to all the six burial grounds)
19. Cremation Ground	In all the six hamlets of Meenaveli Panchayat	—	—	Hand pump – 6
20. Open Theatre	Chittirampatti Perichipatti	1 km 15 kms	3	Meenaveli – 1 Vellayankoundanpatti –1 Annadhanapatti – 1
21. Cooperative Milk Producers' Society	Vellayankoundanpatti	—	—	Infrastructural facility is needed

Housing Details

Tiled House – 381, Hutments – 158, RCC Roof – 203

Sl. No.	*Village*	*Total No. of Families*	*No of own houses*	*No. of families not possessing house sites*	*Not possessing patta*	*No of families availed housing through government schemes*
1.	Meenaveli	175	155	20	45	30
2.	Perichipatti	78	75	3	10	21
3.	Annayanthoppu	23	23	–	–	20 (3 families from the joint-family system came out, house site is needed for them)
4.	Chittirampatti	236	221	15	40	7
5.	Annathanapatti	64	60	4	10	1
6.	Vellayankoundanpatti	177	162	15	20	17 (out of 30 houses provided by the government only 17 are existing 13 houses is dilapidated condition – unfit to occupy)

Details of Rural Industries

Sl. No.	Details	No of Persons Involved		Status of Avocation
		Male	Female	
1.	Handloom	—	—	—
2.	Powerloom	—	—	—
3.	Handicrafts	—	—	—
4.	Carpentry	12	—	Good – central work sheds are needed
5.	Pottery	1	1	Poor
6.	Blacksmith	3	—	Better
7.	Tannery	—	—	—
8.	Khadi & Village Industries	—	—	—
9.	Washerman	10	15	No water resources. Need of a Dhobi Ghana
10.	Stone Metal	—	—	—
11.	Service Sectors	—	—	—
12.	Other Works	6	—	VAO – 1 Conductor – 1 Driver – 1 In Military Service – 2
13.	Gem Cutting	Male and Female – 70		

Details of Employees

Sl. No.	Details	No of Employees		Status of Avocation
		Male	Female	
1.	Agricultural Workers	410	370	780
2.	Agricultural Labourers	180	195	375
3.	Government Services	7	–	7
4.	Non-Governmental Services	3	–	3
5.	Village Craftmen	56	15	71
6.	Trade	55	5	60
7.	Other Workers	5	–	5
8.	Unemployed	10	5	15
9.	Seasonal Migration	150	60	210
10.	Dependent on Products of Minor Forest	10	10	20
11.	Cottage Industries	56	52	108

Details of Self-Help Groups

Sl. No.	*Village*	*No. of SHGs*		*Total No. of Members*		*Details of Revolving Loan Availed*		*Details of Cash Credit Availed*	*Details of Economic Activities*
		Male	*Female*	*Male*	*Female*	*Male*	*Female*		
1.	Meenaveli	2	4	35	92	—	1 group	15000	Internal Credit
2.	Perichipatti and Annayanthoppu	1	2	17	29	—	1 group	Loan availed and repaid	Internal Credit
3.	Chittirampatti	1	2	20	33	—	—	—	—
4.	Annathanapatti	1	2	25	40	—	—	Women group has availed the loan	Internal Credit
5.	Vellayankoundanpatti	1	4	20	79	—	—	1 group	Internal Credit

Name of the Facilitating NGO in SHG Activities

1. Grama Seva Sangam, 2. ICICI Bank, 3. POWER (NGO)

Sl. No.	*Name of the SHG Group and Village*	*No. of Persons Availed Training*	*Training Details*	*Initiatives taken after training*
1.	Malligai Group (Vellayankoundanpatti)	2	Tailoring	(One of the member is doing business production and sales of washing blue, coconut thatches)
2.	Vivekananda Group (Perichipatti)	1	Computer Offset Printing	(Involved in other economic activities)
3.	Nethaji Group (Meenaveli)	2	Computer Offset Printing Motor Winding	(Involved in some other economic activities)

Total Geographical Area: 920.36.0 (hectare)

Sl. No.	*Details*	*Geographical Area (in Hectares)*
1.	Forest Area	—
2.	Uncultivable Dry Lands	—
3.	Land used for Non-Agricultural purposes	350.84.0
4.	Cultivable Waste Land	—
5.	Permanent land used for grazing purposes	33.42.0
6.	Land with trees	—
7.	Currently, land lying waste	—
8.	Other lands	344.87.0
9.	Other waste lands	7.54.0
10.	Net cultivable land	183.69.0

Irrigation Details

Sl. No.	*Water Sources*	*Total Nos.*	*Length in Kms*	*Total Geographical Area*
	Rain Water			
1.	Irrigation Canals			
	(a) Government Canals	4	—	—
	(b) Private Canals	—	—	—
2.	Ponds			
	(a) Big	1 (PWD)	—	34.92.0
	(b) Small	25	—	61.72.0
3.	River Irrigation			
	(a) Big & Medium	—	—	—
	(b) Small	—	—	—
4.	Well Irrigation			
	Total No. of Wells	195	—	—
	No. of wells got electrification	143	—	—
	Fitted with diesel engine	—	—	—
5.	Ponds			
	(a) Lift Irrigation	—	—	—
	(b) Minor Irrigation	—	—	—
6.	Other types	—	—	—
7.	Rainfed Land	—	—	183.69.0

Details of Ponds

Sl. No.	Village	Survey No.	Name of the Pond	Area of the Pond	Area Under Ayakkattu	Type of the Pond (Union, PWD, Panchayat)	Need of Improvement	Other Details
1.	Annathanapatti	15-1	Periyakalli Enthal	21.22.5	16.78.0	Union Pond	Desilting	
2.	Vellayankoundanpatti	50.2	Manthipallam	3.99.5	2.79.0	Panchayat	Desilting	
3.	Chittirampatti	52	Soman Enthal	5.15.5	3.91.0	Panchayat	Desilting	
4.	Chittirampatti	63-1	Bhiman Enthal	1.20.5	0.86.5	Panchayat	Desilting	
5.	Annathanapatti Chittirampatti	125	Mannaikadayan Enthal	8.18.5	10.9.0	Union	Desilting	
6.	Chittirampatti Annathanapatti	129-1	Kannapattankulam	26.7.5	23.56.5	Union	Desilting	
7.	Meenaveli	149-5	Periyakulam	110.17.0	92.44.0	PWD	Desilting	
8.	Meenaveli	282	Karukulam	18.47.5	31.12.0	PWD	Desilting	
		71-2	Karukulam	1.11.0				
9.	Perichipatti	166.1	Ethirillakulam	4.73.5	1.58.0	Panchayat	Desilting	
10.	Perichipatti	167.1	Kuppakoundan Kulam	3.98.0	4.7.0	Panchayat	Desilting	
11.	Perichipatti	179	Kadaikonenthal	2.63.0	3.72.5	Panchayat	Desilting	
12.	Vellayankoundanpatti	235.6 372.2	Nallampillai Kulam	11.8.5	14.21.0	Union	Desilting	

(Contd...)

(Contd...)

13. Vellayankoundanpatti	343	Panagkudi Kulam	7.97.5	8.38.5 6.84.0	Union	Desilting
14. Annayanthoppu	237	Kaduvetti Enthal	6.10	7.10.0	Union	Desilting
15. Chittirampatti	23.10	Adaikakoundan Enthal	1.31.5	0.92.5	Individual Maintenance Pond	Desilting
16. Vellayankoundanpatti	239	Kanakkan Enthal	2.19.0	0.95.5	Pvt Pond	Desilting
17. Vellayankoundanpatti	335-2	Konnai Enthal	0.90.5	1.46.5	Pvt Pond	Desilting
18. Vellayankoundanpatti	234-4	Perumakoundan Enthal	0.11.5	0.11.0	Pvt Pond	Desilting
19. Meenaveli	273-22	Parayan Enthal	0.43.5	0.61.5	Pvt Pond	Desilting
20. Vellayankoundanpatti	252	Kattapurikulam	4.14.0	—	Pvt Pond	Desilting
21. Perichipatti	160-1	Chulaikal Enthal	1.38.5	1.97.0	Pvt Pond	Desilting
22. Annathanapatti	—	Mathiaykkan Enthal	—	0.9.0	—	-

Details of Oorani

Sl. No.	Village	Survey No.	Oorani Details	Area	Needs
1.	Annathanapatti	6	Alaganchetti Oorani	1.05.0	—
2.	Chittirampatti	37	Muthan Oorani (A) Mathanda	0.38.5	Desilting
3.	Meenaveli	72.1	Maaoorani	7.22.5	Desilting and Bathingaghat
	Meenaveli	72.1	Kakoorani		
4.	Chittirampatti	30.1	Palaoorani	0.61.0	Desilting
5.	Chittirampatti	42	Sevvoorani	1.18.0	Desilting
6.	Perichipatti	160.2	Alagankoundan Oorani	0.34.0	Desilting
7.	Vellayankoundanpatti	319	Iyyan Oorani	4.28.0	Desilting
8.	Vellayankoundanpatti	335-2	Konnaienthal	0.90.5	1.46.5

Agricultural Details

Sl. No.	Village	Type of Cultivation		Area	Area of Cultivable Land
		Dry Land	Wet Land		
1.	Meenaveli	233.54.5	294.88.5	528.43.0	183.69.0

Farmer's Details

Sl. No.	*Details*	*Total No. of Farmers*	
		SC/ST	*Others*
1.	Small Farmers	16	150
2.	Marginal Farmers	72	320
3.	Big Farmers	–	15

Details of Animal Husbandry

1. Location of veterinary dispensary, distance in kms: Viralimalai 20 kms
2. Is the veterinary dispensary functioning effectively?

The post of Veterinary Assistant is vacant. The veterinary dispensary is not in use. Need of veterinary dispensary in Meenaveli.

Sl. No.	*Species*	*Total*	*Details of Needs*
1.	Bullock	300	Need of a veterinary sub-centre in Meenaveli (or)
	Cow	305	Veterinary Dispensary – 1 (or)
	Buffalo	20	Mobile Dispensary
	Sheep	1500	*Note*: Veterinary camps are not organized.
	Goat	1700	
	Hen	600	

Number of Persons Living below Poverty Line as per the Panchayat Records

Sl. No.	Village	Families living below the poverty line					Families living above the poverty line				
		SC	*ST*	*BC*	*MBC*	*Others*	*SC*	*ST*	*BC*	*MBC*	*Others*
1.	Meenaveli	50	-	-	25	-	60	-	10	30	1
2.	Perichipatti	7	-	-	20	-	19	-	6	20	-
3.	Anayanthoppu	16	-	-	-	-	10	-	-	-	-
4.	Chittirampatti	15	-	25	35	-	15	-	80	48	-
5.	Annadhanapatti	-	-	-	10	-	-	-	10	51	-
6.	Vellayankoundanpatti	15	-	-	25	-	12	-	2	136	-
	Total	103	-	25	115	-	116	-	108	285	1

Marginalized Sector

1. Re-deemed from bonded labour – Nil
2. People affected due to communal riots – Nil
3. Those who lost all possessions and belongings due to fire and flood – Nil
4. Unable to earn, due to suffering from chronic diseases – Nil
5. Families of child labour – Nil

Details of Poor Widows

Sl. No.	*Name*	*Village*	*Age*	*Community*	*Present Avocation*	*Remarks*
1.	Lakshmi W/o Mookan	Meenaveli	30	SC	Labourer	
2.	Ammaponnu W/o Nallu	Meenaveli	30	SC	Labourer	
3.	Karuthakannu W/o Palaniappan	Meenaveli	35	SC	Labourer	
4.	Palaniyayee W/o Nallu	Meenaveli	30	SC	Labourer	
5.	Karuthamani W/o Shanmugam	Meenaveli	40	SC	Labourer	
6.	Chinnaponnu W/o Murugan	Meenaveli	35	SC	Labourer	
7.	Mari W/o Andiyappan	Meenaveli	45	SC	Labourer	
8.	Palaniyayi W/o Sankan	Meenaveli	55	SC	Labourer	
9.	Mookayee W/o Raman	Meenaveli	47	SC	Labourer	
10.	Alagammal W/o Kuttayan	Meenaveli	60	SC	Labourer	

(Contd...)

(Contd...)

11. Parvathy W/o Silamban	Meenaveli	50	SC	Labourer
12. Gundumani W/o Thiruvan	Meenaveli	55	SC	Labourer
13. Nachammal W/o Adaikkan	Meenaveli	60	SC	Labourer
14. Sadachi W/o Adaikkan	Meenaveli	55	SC	Labourer
15. Periyakkal W/o Karuppan	Meenaveli	50	SC	Labourer
16. Karuppayee W/o Sangili	Meenaveli	60	SC	Labourer
17. Mariyayi W/o Paramadass	Meenaveli	48	SC	Labourer
18. Arokiammal W/o Manikkam	Meenaveli	46	Others	Labourer
19. Thangamma W/o Arokiyasami	Meenaveli	35	Others	Labourer
20. Pappathi W/o Shet	Meenaveli	49	Others	Labourer
21. Vellayammal W/o Murugan	Meenaveli	26	SC	Labourer
22. Chinnappillai	Meenaveli	60	Others	Labourer
23. Vaavu	Meenaveli	35	Others	Labourer

(Contd...)

(Contd...)

24. Chellammal W/o Ramasamy	Meenaveli	40	Others	Labourer	
25. Pappammal W/o Perumal	Meenaveli	55	Others	Labourer	
26. Achammal W/o Samirasu	Meenaveli	60	Others	Labourer	
27. Saroja W/o Rengaraj	Meenaveli	45	Others	Labourer	
28. Achammal W/o Kannan	Meenaveli	40	Others	Labourer	
29. Ramakkal W/o Gopal	Meenaveli	49	Others	Labourer	
30. Periyakkal W/o Soori	Meenaveli	37	Others	Labourer	
31. Vellayammal W/o Soor	Meenaveli	50	Others	Labourer	
32. Cehllammal W/o Rengaraja	Meenaveli	60	Others	Labourer	
33. Gandhimathi W/o Sethuraman	Meenaveli	60	Others	Labourer	
34. Chinnammal W/o Nallakoundar	Meenaveli	55	Others	Labourer	
35. Lakhsmi	Anayanthoppu	55	SC	Labourer	Handicapped
36. Azhagi W/o Pambayin	Anayanthoppu	45	SC	Labourer	

(Contd...)

(Contd...)

37. Savithiri W/o Chinnayya	Anayanthoppu	45	SC	Labourer
38. Magubeevi W/o Sheik Bai	Meenaveli	52	Others	Labourer
39. Lakshmi W/o Selvam	Vellayankoundanpatti	35	Others	Labourer
40. Chinnammal W/o Vellaichamy	Vellayankoundanpatti	50	Others	Labourer
41. Puravayee W/o Duraisamy	Vellayankoundanpatti	55	Others	Labourer
42. Karuthamani W/o Kannusamy	Vellayankoundanpatti	55	Others	Labourer
43. Sevathamani W/o Palanisamy	Vellayankoundanpatti	60	Others	Labourer
44. Nallammal W/o Chinnachamy	Vellayankoundanpatti	45	Others	Labourer
45. Rengammal W/o Raju	Vellayankoundanpatti	50	Others	Labourer
46. Mariapushpam W/o Arokiam	Vellayankoundanpatti	48	Others	Labourer
47. Nallammal W/o Nallan	Vellayankoundanpatti	55	Others	Labourer
48. Arokiammal W/o Appavu	Vellayankoundanpatti	45	Others	Labourer

(Contd...)

(Contd...)

49. Chinnathayee W/o Arokiam	Vellayankoundanpatti	40	Others	Labourer
50. Nayagathammal W/o Savarimuthu	Vellayankoundanpatti	50	Others	Labourer
51. Chellam W/o Allakannu	Vellayankoundanpatti	50	Others	Labourer
52. Sevathamani W/o Ponnan	Vellayankoundanpatti	60	Others	Labourer
53. Muthammal W/o Mariappan	Vellayankoundanpatti	50	SC	Labourer
54. Adakki W/o Mariappan	Vellayankoundanpatti	55	SC	Labourer
55. Vellayappan W/o Mariappan	Vellayankoundanpatti	45	SC	Labourer
56. Nallammal W/o Mammakoundar	Vellayankoundanpatti	50	BC	Labourer
57. Sadachi W/o Chinnayyakoundar	Vellayankoundanpatti	50	BC	Labourer
58. Chinnammal W/o Alagan	Vellayankoundanpatti	40	BC	Labourer
59. Chinnammal W/o Perumal	Vellayankoundanpatti	50	BC	Labourer
60. Selvam W/o Perumal	Vellayankoundanpatti	35	BC	Labourer

(Contd...)

(Contd...)

61. Chinnammal W/o Chidambaram	Vellayankoundanpatti	55	BC	Labourer
62. Periyammal W/o Palanisamy	Vellayankoundanpatti	46	BC	Labourer
63. Karuthamani W/o Palanisamy	Vellayankoundanpatti	50	BC	Labourer
64. Sevathamani W/o Ponnusamy	Sithirampatti	50	BC	Labourer
65. Deivanai Achi W/o Valvan Chettiar	Sithirampatti	60	BC	Labourer
66. Vellamani W/o Palaniyandi	Sithirampatti	55	BC	Labourer
67. Parvathi W/o Ponnusamy	Sithirampatti	55	BC	Labourer
68. Pappayee W/o Ramanathan Chettiar	Sithirampatti	62	BC	Labourer
69. Pappayee W/o Duraisamy	Sithirampatti	75	BC	Labourer
70. Pappayee W/o Manikkam Chettiar	Sithirampatti	70	BC	Labourer
71. Chinnatchi W/o Kanthayya Chettiar	Sithirampatti	75	Others	Labourer
72. Dhanam W/o Natarajan	Sithirampatti	55	Others	Labourer

(Contd...)

(Contd...)

73. Alamelu W/o Chidambaram	Sithirampatti	60	Others	Labourer
74. Rajamani W/o Perumal	Sithirampatti	55	Others	Labourer
75. Pappayee W/o Muthiah	Sithirampatti	70	Others	Labourer
76. Rajamani W/o Perumal	Sithirampatti	40	Others	Labourer
77. Silambayee W/o Silamban	Sithirampatti	50	SC	Labourer
78. Anchalai W/o Silamban	Sithirampatti	45	SC	Labourer
79. Alagammal W/o Kunnudayan	Sithirampatti	50	SC	Labourer
80. Periyammal W/o Azhagan	Sithirampatti	45	SC	Labourer
81. Mookayee W/o Arumugam	Sithirampatti	40	SC	Labourer
82. Ponnammal W/o Maadhan	Sithirampatti	75	SC	Labourer
83. Chinnathayee W/o Arumugam	Sithirampatti	75	SC	Labourer
84. Pappammal W/o Baghyam	Sithirampatti	70	SC	Labourer

(Contd...)

(Contd...)

85. Jegathambal W/o Karuppillai	Sithirampatti	65	BC	Labourer
86. Bhagyam W/o Manikkampillai	Sithirampatti	50	BC	Labourer
87. Angammal W/o Azhagan	Sithirampatti	50	BC	Labourer
88. Chellamm W/o Velu	Sithirampatti	35	BC	Labourer
89. Angammal W/o Perumal	Sithirampatti	75	Others	Labourer
90. Pechiyayee W/o Ramasamy	Sithirampatti	75	Others	Labourer
91. Angammal W/o Ramasamy	Sithirampatti	60	Others	Labourer
92. Maruthayee W/o Aandi	Sithirampatti	60	Others	Labourer
93. Veerammal W/o Yagappan	Sithirampatti	60	Others	Labourer
94. Chittupillai	Perichipatti	60	Others	Labourer
95. Chinnapillai W/o Azhagan	Perichipatti	65	Others	Labourer
96. Athammal W/o Mookkan	Perichipatti	40	Others	Labourer
97. Nallammal W/o Appachi	Perichipatti	65	Others	Labourer

(Contd...)

(Contd...)

98. Saroja W/o Chinnappa	Perichipatti	45	Others	Labourer
99. Pappayyee W/o Andiyakoundar	Perichipatti	60	Others	Labourer
100. Alagammal W/o Velayudham	Perichipatti	45	Others	Labourer
101. Poravayee W/o Chiannappa	Perichipatti	60	Others	Labourer
102. Sevanthiyammal W/o Mookkakonar	Perichipatti	50	Others	Labourer
103. Arayee W/o Karuppan	Perichipatti	55	SC	Labourer
104. Pappayee W/o Gopal	Perichipatti	60	Others	Labourer
105. Mookayee W/o Chinnu	Perichipatti	48	Others	Labourer
106. Sevanthimani W/o Perumal	Perichipatti	67	Others	Labourer
107. Pichayammal W/o Solaimalai	Vellayankoundampatti	55	Others	Labourer
108. Chellam W/o Palanichamy	Vellayankoundampatti	60	Others	Labourer
109. Mariyayyee	Vellayankoundampatti	55	Others	Labourer
110. Chellam W/o Duraisamy	Vellayankoundampatti	55	Others	Labourer

(Contd...)

(Contd...)

111. Pappayee W/o Ponnandi	Vellayankoundampatti	70	Others	Labourer
112. Perumayee W/o Duraisamy	Vellayankoundampatti	60	Others	Labourer
113. Chinnammal W/o Rengakonar	Annathanapatti	55	Others	Labourer
114. Nallammal W/o Ponnakol	Annathanapatti	45	Others	Labourer
115. Chinnamani W/o Palanichamy	Annathanapatti	30	Others	Labourer
116. Chellam W/o Vellayakol	Annathanapatti	50	Others	Labourer
117. Lakshmi W/o Adaikkakol	Annathanapatti	51	Others	Labourer
118. Chinnammal W/o Adaikkakol	Annathanapatti	50	Others	Labourer
119. Renganayagi W/o Krishnakoundar	Annathanapatti	70	Others	Labourer
120. Sevanthamani W/o Rengasamy	Annathanapatti	70	Others	Labourer
121. Ragammal W/o Ariakoundar	Annathanapatti	65	Others	Labourer
122. Kalyani W/o Velu	Annathanapatti	47	Others	Labourer

(Contd...)

(Contd...)

123. Sevatha W/o Karupayyakoundar	Annathanapatti	60	Others	Labourer
124. Perichiammal W/o Mannayakoundar	Annathanapatti	80	Others	Labourer
125. Chinnammal W/o Mannayyakoundar	Annathanapatti	79	Others	Labourer
126. Ponnammal W/o Vellaichamy	Annathanapatti	45	Others	Labourer
127. Muthulakshmi W/o Subramani	Chithirampatti	40	Others	Labourer
128. Chellammal W/o Karuppan	Chithirampatti	60	Others	Labourer

Details of Disabled Persons

Sl. No.	Name	Village	Age	Community	Sex	Present Avocation	Other Details
1.	Murugesan S/o Raman	Meenaveli	18	SC	Male	Labourer	Lame in leg
2.	Rajkumar S/o Rangaraja	Meenaveli	23	BC	Male	Labourer	Lame in leg
3.	Lakshmi D/o Mookan	Meenaveli	25	SC	Female	Labourer	Mentally retarded
4.	Kalaiselvi D/o Karuppan	Meenaveli	16	SC	Female	Labourer	Mentally retarded
5.	Vellaiammal W/o Nallu	Meenaveli	35	SC	Female	Labourer	Mentally retarded
6.	Chinnaponnu W/o Vadivelu	Meenaveli	36	SC	Female	Labourer	Lame in leg
7.	Nallammal S/o Kulandaisamy	Vellayankoundanpatti	35	BC	Female	Labourer	Lame in leg
8.	Nallappan S/o Karuppan	Vellayankoundanpatti	50	SC	Male	Labourer	Lame in leg
9.	Chinnthambi.	Vellayankoundanpatti	55	SC	Male	Labourer	Lame in leg
10.	Swaminathan S/o Periannan	Chittirampatti	22	BC	Male	Labourer	Lame in leg
11.	Angamuthu S/o Thandavanayakan	Chittirampatti	22	BC	Male	Labourer	Lame in leg

(Contd...)

(Contd...)

12. Ragupathy S/o Palanyandi	Chittirampatti	17	BC	Male	Labourer	Lame in leg
13. Murugesan S/o Andinayakar	Chittirampatti	22	BC	Male	Labourer	Blind
14. Pandian S/o Arumugam	Chittirampatti	32	BC	Male	Labourer	Deaf
15. Palanisamy S/o Adaikakoundar	Vellayankoundanpatti	45	BC	Male	Labourer	Lame in leg
16. Karuppaiah S/o Gangakoundar	Vellayankoundanpatti	37	BC	Male	Labourer	Lame in hand
17. Karuppan S/o Murugesan	Meenaveli	42	SC	Male	Labourer	Lame in leg
18. Malaikannu S/o Perumal	Perichipatti	45	BC	Male	Labourer	Lame in leg
19. Lakshmi W/o Chinnaiah	Anayanthoppu	50	SC	Female	Labourer	Lame in leg

Traditional Craftsmen who are in Abject Poverty

Sl. No.	Name	Village	Age	Community	Sex	Present Avocation	Other Details
1.	Vellanganni S/o Savarimuthu	Meenaveli	42	BC	Male	Carpenter	
2.	Velanganni S/o Paranjothi	Meenaveli	38	BC	Male	Carpenter	
3.	Rayappan S/o Sunthiyagu	Meenaveli	47	BC	Male	Carpenter	
4.	Savarimuthu S/o Sebastian	Meenaveli	47	BC	Male	Carpenter	
5.	Arokiasamy S/o Arulappan	Meenaveli	40	BC	Male	Carpenter	
6.	Chinnan S/o Kamatchi	Chittrampatti	52	BC	Male	Carpenter	
7.	Pootchivelar S/o Alagar	Chittrampatti	60	BC	Male	Carpenter	
8.	Savarimuthu S/o Arokiam	Vellayankoundanpatti	35	BC	Male	Carpenter	
9.	Aruldas S/o Arokiam	Vellayankoundanpatti	30	BC	Male	Carpenter	
10.	Arokiasamy S/o Savarimuthu	Vellayankoundanpatti	32	BC	Male	Carpenter	
11.	Manickam S/o Arokiam	Vellayankoundanpatti	45	BC	Male	Carpenter	

(Contd...)

(Contd...)

12. Irudayaraj S/o Ayyakannu	Vellayankoundanpatti	35	BC	Male	Carpenter
13. Sebastian S/o Savarimuthu	Vellayankoundanpatti	42	BC	Male	Blacksmith
14. Ezhumalai S/o Rangan	Vellayankoundanpatti	38	SC	Male	Cobbler

Details of Migrated Families Seeking Employment Opportunities

Sl. No.	Name	Village	Age	Community	Sex	Present Avocation	Other Details
1.	Arumugam S/o Kalangan	Meenaveli	29	SC	Male	Construction Worker	
2.	Alagar S/o Karuppan	Meenaveli	32	SC	Male	Construction Worker	
3.	Chinnaiah S/o Kuttaiyan	Meenaveli	35	SC	Male	Construction Worker	
4.	Arunachalam S/o Palaniappan	Meenaveli	29	SC	Male	Construction Worker	
5.	Murugan S/o Palaniappan	Meenaveli	27	SC	Male	Construction Worker	
6.	Ponnusamy S/o Palaniappan	Meenaveli	32	SC	Male	Construction Worker	
7.	Samikannu S/o Pitchan	Meenaveli	25	SC	Male	Construction Worker	
8.	Samikannu S/o Pitchan	Meenaveli	33	SC	Male	Construction Worker	
9.	Vadivelu	Meenaveli	40	SC	Male	Construction Worker	
10.	Palanisamy S/o Thiruvan	Meenaveli	38	SC	Male	Construction Worker	
11.	Ravi S/o Mohan	Meenaveli	18	SC	Male	Construction Worker	

(Contd...)

(Contd...)

12. Kumar S/o Mookan	Meenaveli	22	SC	Male	Construction Worker
13. Natesan S/o Karuppan	Meenaveli	20	SC	Male	Construction Worker
14. Murugesan S/o Tunwan	Meenaveli	28	SC	Male	Construction Worker
15. Chidambaram S/o Karuppan	Meenaveli	32	SC	Male	Construction Worker
16. Ammasi S/o Karuppan	Meenaveli	30	SC	Male	Driver
17. Chinnappan S/o Murugan	Meenaveli	27	SC	Male	Driver
18. Karuppaiah S/o Mookan	Meenaveli	27	SC	Male	Driver
19. Alagar S/o Sangili	Meenaveli	35	SC	Male	Driver
20. Chinnakannu S/o Karuppan	Meenaveli	33	SC	Male	Driver
21. Selvaraj S/o Karuppaiah	Meenaveli	27	SC	Male	Construction Worker
22. Chinnappan S/o Karuppaiah	Meenaveli	25	SC	Male	Driver
23. Das S/o Raman	Meenaveli	28	SC	Male	Construction Worker

(Contd...)

(Contd...)

24. Arumugam S/o Raman	Meenaveli	25	SC	Male	Construction Worker
25. Kumar S/o Palanisamy	Meenaveli	20	SC	Male	Construction Worker
26. Venkatesan S/o Velu	Meenaveli	20	SC	Male	Construction Worker
27. Palaniappan S/o Mookan	Meenaveli	50	SC	Male	Construction Worker
28. Perumal S/o Ponnusamy	Perichipatti	28	BC	Male	Vendor
29. Alagar S/o Perumal	Perichipatti	28	BC	Male	Vendor
30. Baskaran S/o Chinnakannu	Perichipatti	20	BC	Male	Vendor
31. Murugesan S/o Chinnu	Perichipatti	21	BC	Male	Vendor
32. Kandasamy S/o Chinnappa	Perichipatti	20	BC	Male	Vendor
33. Rajendran S/o Solaimalai	Perichipatti	21	BC	Male	Vendor
34. Sivaji S/o Chinnaiah	Perichipatti	27	BC	Male	Vendor
35. Ravi S/o Velayudam	Perichipatti	24	BC	Male	Tailor

(Contd...)

(Contd...)

36. Shanmugam, S/o Pitchan	Perichipatti	23	SC	Male	Tailor
37. Nallathambi S/o Saravanan	Perichipatti	22	SC	Male	Tialor
38. Logambal S/o Velu	Chittirampatti	18	SC	Female	Construction Worker
39. Dhanalakshmi	Chittirampatti	16	SC	Female	Construction Worker
40. Manikandan S/o Periyannan	Chittirampatti	25	SC	Male	Vendor
41. Vadivel S/o Alagakoundar	Annadhanapatti	32	BC	Male	Vendor
42. M.Chinnappa S/o Mayandithevar	Annadhanapatti	26	BC	Male	Vendor
43. Palani S/o Ramasamy	Annadhanapatti	39	BC	Male	Vendor
44. Druasamy S/o Chittirakoundar	Annadhanapatti	48	BC	Male	Vendor
45. Periyasamy S/o Sodayakoundar	Annadhanapatti	37	BC	Male	Vendor
46. Malaisamy S/o Duraisamy	Annadhanapatti	32	BC	Male	Vendor
47. Rajendran S/o. Algakoundar	Annadhanapatti	28	BC	Male	Vendor
48. Selvam S/o Alagakoundar	Annadhanapatti	28	BC	Male	Vendor

(Contd...)

(Contd...)

49. Perumal S/o Chittrayakoundar	Annadhanapatti	27	BC	Male	Vendor
50. Palani S/o Chinnakalai	Annadhanapatti	40	BC	Male	Vendor
51. Dhanapal S/o Krishnakoundar	Annadhanapatti	30	BC	Male	Vendor
52. Dhanapal S/o Alagakoundar	Annadhanapatti	30	BC	Male	Vendor
53. Chinnappan S/o Vellaisamy	Annadhanapatti	40	BC	Male	Vendor
54. Arumugam S/o Chinnu	Annadhanapatti	29	BC	Male	Vendor
55. Chinnappan S/o Kulandaivel	Annadhanapatti	37	BC	Male	Vendor
56. Tirupathi S/o Moorthy	Annadhanapatti	24	BC	Male	Vendor
57. Murugesan S/o Adaikalakoundar	Annadhanapatti	30	BC	Male	Vendor
58. Periasamy S/o Porappakonar	Annadhanapatti	40	BC	Male	Vendor
59. M.Nallusamy S/o Mangadikonar	Annadhanapatti	30	BC	Male	Vendor

List of Persons Eligible for Housing Grants

Sl. No.	Village	Name	Community	Total No. of Family Members	Other Details
1.	Meenaveli	Chinnanthal	SC	5	Labourers
		Muthukannu	SC	4	Labourers
		Karuthamani	SC	1	Labourers
		Nallammal	SC	4	Labourers
		Anjalai	SC	3	Labourers
		Pappa	SC	4	Labourers
		Mala	SC	3	Labourers
		Natchikannu	SC	4	Labourers
		Ammaponnu	SC	3	Labourers
		Selvaraj	SC	2	Labourers
		Kadar Ibrahim	SC	7	Labourers
		Bhooma	SC	3	Labourers
		Lakshmi	SC	4	Labourers
		Alagumani	SC	4	Labourers
2.	Chittirampatti	Chinnaiah	SC	5	Labourers
		Mani	SC	3	Labourers
		Silamban	SC	5	Labourers
		Palaniyandi	SC	5	Labourers
		Rajappan	SC	4	Labourers
		Rasu	SC	5	Labourers
		Mamundi	SC	2	Labourers
		Velu	SC	7	Labourers

(Contd...)

(Contd...)

		Srinivasan	SC	3	Labourers
		Surasu	SC	2	Labourers
		Mookariah	SC	4	Labourers
		Ganesan	SC	6	Labourers
		Murugesan	SC	4	Labourers
3.	Perichipatti	Raman	BC	4	Labourers
		Baskaran	BC	3	Labourers
		Vellaiammal	BC	3	Labourers
		Karuthakkannu	BC	2	Labourers
4.	Annathanapatti	Chinnakannu	BC	4	Labourers
		Manimaran	BC	3	Labourers
		Chinnaiah	BC	3	Labourers
		Raman	BC	2	Labourers
5.	Vellaiyankoundanpatti	Ganesan	BC	4	Labourers
		Mani	BC	4	Labourers
		Karuppaiah	BC	3	Labourers
		Alagarsamy	BC	4	Labourers
		Palaniappan	BC	4	Labourers
		Murugesan	BC	3	Labourers

List of Eligible Persons to Receive Housing House site and Patta

Sl. No.	Name	Village	Community	Needs
1.	Ammaponnu W/o Nallu	Meenaveli	SC	Housing, house site and patta
2.	Karuthamani W/o Shanmugam	Meenaveli	SC	Housing
3.	Mari W/o Andiyappan	Meenaveli	SC	Housing, house site and patta
4.	Kadatchi W/o Adaikan	Meenaveli	SC	Housing, house site and patta
5.	Arokkiammal W/o Manikam	Meenaveli	BC	Housing, house site and patta
6.	Pappathi W/o Settu	Meenaveli	BC	Housing, house site and patta
7.	Vellaiammal W/o Murugan	Meenaveli	SC	Patta, housing
8.	Chinnapillai	Meenaveli	SC	Housing, house site and patta
9.	Chellammal W/o Ramasamy	Meenaveli	SC	Patta, housing
10.	Ramakkan W/o Gopal	Meenaveli	SC	Patta, housing
11.	Periyakkal W/o Suri	Meenaveli	SC	Patta, housing

(Contd...)

(Contd...)

12. Chinnammal W/o Nallikoundar	Meenaveli	SC	Housing, house site and patta
13. Lakshmi W/o Chinnaiah	Annayanthoppu	SC	Housing, house site and patta
14. Mariapushpam W/o Arokiam	Vellaiyankoundanpatti	BC	Housing, house site and patta
15. Nayakkathammal W/o Arokkiam	Vellaiyankoundanpatti	BC	Housing, house site and patta
16. Sevathamani W/o Poonar	Vellaiyankoundanpatti	BC	Housing, house site and patta
17. Muthammal W/o Mariappan	Vellaiyankoundanpatti	BC	Housing, house site and patta
18. Nallammal W/o Manmathakoundar	Vellaiyankoundanpatti	BC	Housing, house site and patta
19. Selvam W/o Perumal	Vellaiyankoundanpatti	BC	Housing, house site and patta
20. Dhanam W/o Natarajan	Chittirampatti	BC	Housing
21. Silampayee W/o Silamban	Chittirampatti	SC	Housing, house site and patta
22. Anjalai W/o Silamban	Chittirampatti	SC	Housing, house site and patta
23. Ponnammal W/o Madhan	Chittirampatti	SC	Housing, house site and patta

(Contd...)

(Contd...)

24. Chinnathai W/o Arumugam	Chittirampatti	SC	Housing, house site and patta
25. Pappammal W/o Bhagyam	Chittirampatti	SC	Housing, house site and patta
26. Jegathambal W/o Karuppapilai	Chittirampatti	SC	Housing, house site and patta
27. Maruthayee W/o Aandi	Chittirampatti	SC	Housing, house site and patta
28. Veerammal Nagappan	Chittirampatti	SC	Housing, house site and patta
29. Chinnapillai W/o Alagar	Perichipatti	SC	Housing and patta
30. Aathammal W/o Mookan	Perichipatti	SC	Housing and patta
31. Saroja W/o Chinnappa	Perichipatti	SC	Housing and patta
32. Pappayee W/o Aandiyakoundar	Perichipatti	SC	Housing and patta
33. Poravayee W/o Chinnappa	Perichipatti	SC	Housing and patta
34. Alagammal W/o Velayutham	Perichipatti	SC	Housing and patta
35. Pappayee W/o Gopal	Perichipatti	SC	Housing and patta

(Contd...)

(Contd...)

36. Rasammal W/o Aariyakoundar	Anthanapatti	SC	Housing and patta
37. Sevitha W/o Surutaiyakoundar	Anthanapatti	SC	Housing and patta
38. Ponnammal W/o Vellaisamy	Anthanapatti	SC	Housing and patta
39. Muthulakshmi W/o Subramanian	Chittrampatti	SC	Housing and patta
40. Chellammal W/o Karuppan	Chittrampatti	SC	Housing, house site and patta

ABSTRACT

Sl. No.	Particulars	Total Members
1.	Eligible persons to get family ration card	122
2.	Eligible persons to get IAY benefit	55
3.	Enrollment in self-help group	48
4.	Eligible persons to get health card	16
6.	Eligible persons to get skill development training	36
7.	Names to be enlisted in food for work scheme	168
8.	Eligible persons to avail KISAN card	70
9.	Eligible persons to get self-employment card	42
10.	Eligible persons to get ID card	20

List of Persons Eligible to Avail SGRY -- 22.5 Per Cent Allocation Individual Benefit

Sl. No.	*Name*	*Village*	*Community*	*Needs*
1.	Murugesan S/o Raman	Chittirampatti	BC	Blind
2.	Swaminathan S/o Periannan	Chittirampatti	BC	Lame in leg
3.	Lakhsmi W/o Chinnaiah	Annayanthoppu	SC	Handicapped
4.	Rajkumar S/o Rengaraj	Meenaveli	BC	Lame in leg
5.	Murugesan S/o Raman	Meenaveli	SC	Lame in leg
6.	Palaniammal D/o Chinnaiah	Perichippati	BC	—

List of Activities Proposed

Sl. No.	Plan Activities	Solving Strategy	Development Partners	Expected Outcome
I.	**Child Welfare Activities**			
	1.Meenaveli–New Building for Anganwadi	SGRY	Village Panchayat, Union Panchayat, District Panchayat	Enough space, improvement in activities
	2. Sintex tank – 1	Village Panchayat Fund	Village Panchayat & Village Education Committee	Protected water supply
	3. Play materials and mats for three *Anganwadis*	Public Contribution	Village Panchayat & Village Education Committee	Improvement in IQ
	4.Awareness to creation on child rearing practices for mothers	Monthly meeting and special meetings in each habitation	EO (SW), VHN Women and Child Welfare Committee	Improvement in Children's Health status
II.	**Educational Improvement**			
	1. Additional Building for middle school – 1	SGRY	Union	Sufficient classroom, conducive environment for learning
	2. Additional Building for Primary School	SGRY, MLA local area Development Fund	Union	Sufficient classroom, conducive environment for learning
	3. Play Material for Middle and Primary School	Public Contribution and SSA	Village Panchayat, Village Education Committee, PTA	Students involvement in plays and games will be activated

(Contd...)

(Contd...)

4. Noon-meal Centre for Middle School	SGRY	Village Panchayat, Union Panchayat, Women and Child Welfare Committee	Convenient space and building, clean food preparation
5. Toilet for girls and boys in the middle school	SGRY	Village Panchayat, Union Panchayat, Women and Child Welfare Committee	Personal hygiene improves, environment protection
6. Encouraging girl children for secondary and higher secondary education	Individual counseling to concerned children and their parents, support facilities for educational expenses	Village Education Committee, PTA Village Panchayat and NGO	Enrollment of girl children in high school improves
7. Arrangements for extra–curricular activities	Organizing periodical orientation by the school teachers as well as youth volunteers	Village Panchayat, PTA and NGO	Annual day celebration — children's participation will be more
8. Special classes for middle school students	Organizing evening coaching classes by the school teachers and youth volunteers	Village Panchayat, PTA and NGO	Improvement in the percentage of pass
III. Health and Sanitation Improvement			
1. Getting sanction to construct a sub-health centre	Sending proposal by the Village Panchayat	Village Panchayat and Village Women and Child Welfare Committee	Increase in the infrastructural facilities for improved health status.

(Contd...)

(Contd...)

2. Strengthening the service of the VHN	Ensuring maximum attendance for PNC/ANC and children immunization 100% coverage	Village Panchayat, Village Women and Child Welfare Committee, SHG, *Anganwadi* Teachers	Improvement in the public health services – PNC/ANC immunization coverage, institutional delivery
3. Waste disposal management.	Segregation of organic and inorganic waste, compost pits Village Panchayat,	NGO, SHG, VHSC Environmental sanitation	production of organic manure and augmentation of Panchayat income
4. Health awareness to adolescent girls	Monthly meeting and special meeting in all habitation	Village Panchayat, SHG, Anganwadi Teachers, VHN	Attendances in the periodical meetings improves personal hygiene of adolescent girls improves
5. Construction of drainage	SGRY	Village Panchayat, Union Panchayat	Improvement in sanitation
6. Construction of soak pits	In creating awareness among the people to put up soak pits	Village Panchayat, SHG, Youth and NGO	Improvement in sanitation
7. Construction of household latrines – 691 numbers	TRSP	Village Panchayat, NGO and SHG	Improvement in health and sanitation
8. Construction of public toilets – 5 numbers	TRSP and MLA Area Development Fund	Village Panchayat, Village Health and Sanitation Committee	Improvement in heath and sanitation
9. Awareness building on toilet – usage	Individual counseling to householders in all habitations	Village Panchayat, SHG, NGO and Village Health and Sanitation Committee	Improvement in health and sanitation

(Contd...)

(Contd...)

10. Provision of smokeless chula	Central Scheme	Village Panchayat, Union NGO	Women health status improves
11. Orientation to OHT operators in chlorination	Orientation training to all OHT Operators	Village Panchayat and Union Engineers	Protected drinking water supply and prevention of water born diseases.
IV. Provision of Basic Facilities			
1. Deepening of drinking water well	SGRY, Village Panchayat Fund	Village Panchayat	Adequate provision of drinking water to public
2. Extension of pipeline 1455 metres	SGRY	Village Panchayat and TWAD	Adequate provision of drinking water to public
V. Women Development			
1. Strengthening of SHG activities	Ensuring periodical meeting	SHG, NGO and Village Panchayat	SHG members awareness increases and their socio-economic status improves. Improvement in the participation of women.
2. Arrangements for entrepreneurs training and income—generating activities	Availing orientation programme	SHG & NGO, WDC	Economic status will be improved
3. Enrolling poor women in SHGs 48 numbers	Identifying and enlisting	Village Panchayat, SHG and NGO	Social justice will be ensured
4. Provision of handpump 4 numbers	SGRY, Rural Water Supply Scheme	Village Panchayat, Union Panchayat, TWAD and NGO	Adequate provision of protected drinking water.

(Contd...)

(Contd...)

	5. New OHT – 1	SGRY, Swajaldhara	Village Panchayat, SHG and water and sanitation committee	Adequate provision of protected drinking water
	6. Construction of dhobi ghana – 1	SGRY	Village Panchayat and Union Panchayat	Improvement in the work atmosphere
	7. Street light – 32 numbers	Village Panchayat Fund, MLA Fund	Village Panchayat	Improves the facility to the public
	8. Pucca roof and platform to burial grounds – 6	SGRY	Village Panchayat	Improves the facility to the public
	9. Solar light – 7 numbers	Non-conventional energy scheme	Village Panchayat and DRDA	Adoption of non-conventional energy, reduction in electricity charge
VI.	**Road/Bridges Improvement**			
	1. Conversion of gravel roads into CC Roads – 4750 metres	SGRY, MLA Local Area Development Fund	Village Panchayat	Improves road condition
	2. Conversion of gravel roads into metal Roads – 2 km	SGRY, MLA Local Area Development Fund	Village Panchayat	Improves road condition
	3. Road to graveyard – 5 kms	SGRY, MLA Local Area Development Fund	Village Panchayat	Improves road condition
	4. Small bridges and culverts – 23	SGRY	Village Panchayat, Union Panchayat	Improves facility to the public
	5. Retaining wall – 1550 metres	SGRY	Village Panchayat, Union Panchayat	Improves facility to the public

(Contd...)

(Contd...)

6. Bunding wall – 1550 metres	SGRY	Village Panchayat, Union Panchayat	Improves facility to the public
7. Footpath bridge – 1	SGRY	Village Panchayat, Union Panchayat	Improves facility to the public
VII. Public Distribution System			
1. Permanent building for Public Distribution Shop	SGRY & Local Area Development Fund	Village Panchayat, Public Distribution Committee	Improves facility to the public
2. New family ration cards – 140 numbers	Submitting the application and follow-Union Panchayat	Village Panchayat, Public Distribution Committee	All eligible families will be provided with ration cards
VIII. Other Infrastructure Facilities			
1. Establishment of veterinary dispensary (or) dispensary sub-centre	SGRY and veterinary development scheme	Village Panchayat, Village Agriculture Committee	Improves facility for veterinary care
2. Passenger shelter – 9 numbers	SGRY	Village Panchayat	Improves the facility to the public
3. Community Hall	SGRY, MLA development fund	Village Panchayat	Improves the facility to the public
4. Threshing floor – 4 numbers	SGRY	Village Panchayat	Improves the facility to the public
5. Library building – 1	SGRY, Panchayat Fund	Village Panchayat	Improves the facility to the public

(Contd...)

(Contd...)

6. TV Room – 2 numbers	SGRY, Panchayat Fund	Village Panchayat	Improves the facility to the public
7. SHG Building – 5 numbers	SGRY, NGO Fund	Village Panchayat, SHG, NGO	Improves the facility to the public
8. Open air theatre – 3 numbers	SGRY, Village Panchayat Fund	Village Panchayat	Improves the facility to the public
9. Building for cooperative milk society	SGRY	Village Panchayat	Improves the facility to the public
IX. Common Property Resources			
1. Deepening of Oorani – 7 numbers	SGRY	Village Panchayat, Village Agricultural Committee	Storing of more rainwater, better protection and proper management of CPR, stakeholders entitlement will be ensured
2. Desilting of ponds – 21 numbers	SGRY	Village Panchayat, Village Agricultural Committee	Storing of more rainwater, better protection and proper management of CPR, stakeholders entitlement will be ensured
3. Construction of bathing ghat – 1	SGRY	Village Panchayat, Village Agricultural Committee	Augmentation of more rainwater, better protection and proper management of CPR, stakeholders entitlement will be ensured

(Contd...)

(Contd...)

X. Marginalized Sector			
1. Socio-economic development for: Physically handicapped – 19 numbers	Social welfare schemes, SSA scheme,	Village Panchayat, NGO, District disabled rehabilitation office, Union Panchayat	Social justice will be ensured
2. Widows – 131 numbers (total number of widows upto 40 years – 22 numbers)	Persons to avail, from SGRY – 22.5% allocation individual benefit	Social welfare department	Social justice will be ensured
3. Poor craftsmen – 14 numbers	Persons to avail, from SGRY – 22.5% allocation individual benefit, NABARD Scheme	Village Panchayat, NGO	Social justice will be ensured
4. Electricity to hutments – 45 numbers	AD Welfare	Village Panchayat and AD welfare	Social justice will be ensured
5. Rural housing to poor families – 40 numbers	IAY	Village Panchayat, Union Panchayat	Social justice will be ensured
6. Patta to poor families – 38 numbers	Poor welfare scheme	Village Panchayat & revenue department	Social justice will be ensured
7. Employment opportunity through food for work programme – 168 poor families	SGRY and NGO -fund	Village Panchayat, NGO	Social justice will be ensured

Note:

VP	–	Village Panchayat
UP	–	Union Panchayat
SGRY	–	Sampoorna Grameen Rozgar Yojana
NGO	–	Non-Governmental Organization
VHSC	–	Village Health and Sanitation Committee
AD Welfare	–	Adi-Dravidar Welfare
WDC	–	Women Development Corporation
DRDA	–	District Rural Development Agency
TWAD	–	Tamil Nadu Water Drainage Board
VHN	–	Village Health Nurse
EO (SW)	–	Extension Officer, Social Welfare
PTA	–	Parents Teachers Association
SHG	–	Self-Help Groups
TRSP	–	Total Rural Sanitation Programme

Village Development Plan – Activities for People's Participation

Sl.No.	*Activity*	*Responsibility*	*Methodology*
1.	School enrollment	Youth Associations, Self-Help Groups, Ward Members	Ward-wise verification and identification of school age children; contact the parents and ensure 100 percent enrollment.
2.	Conducting School Annual Day Celebration	Parent Teachers Association, Youth and SHGs, Village Panchayat	Plan to identify the hidden talents among school children, arrange for necessary orientation to improve their skills and talents; assist in conducting the Annual Day Celebration, prize distribution
3.	Establishing of garden at school; tree planting	PTA, Youth Associations	Join hands with school students, assist in establishing a garden and tree planting in school campus. Assist in availing of subsidy/free of cost tree saplings from the government.
4.	Implementing adult literacy/ Neo-literacy programme	Youth Associations, SHGs, Village Panchayat	In association with staff of literacy programme, identify the individuals who need literacy: assist in the implementation of the literacy programme.
5.	Bringing the reading centre into utility	Youth, SHGs	In consultation with the Village Panchayat, the volunteers can look after the reading centre; can collect books from donors.
6.	Enrollment of Dropouts	Youth, SHGs, Village Panchayat	Through VEC the youths and SHG volunteers can assist in counselling the parents of concerned school dropouts and help the dropouts to join the formal school or special school. The Village Panchayat can give special consideration to those families who are very poor whose dropout wards have been enrolled by extending socio-economic welfare programmes.

(Contd...)

(Contd...)

7.	Immunization Programme – Implementation	Youth Associations, SHGs, Ward Members	Through the VHN and *anganwadi* workers, children can be listed for immunization; the concerned parents can be contacted for timely attendance to receive immunization due to their ward. Any left out children can be further identified by proper follow up. In this way 100 percent immunization can be achieved.
8.	Enrollment of children in *anganwadi*	Youth Association, SHG, Ward Members	Those children who have completed two and a half years can be identified and their parents contacted. The significance of childcare through *anganwadi* can be shared with them and the eligible children enrolled in the anganwadi. In habitants at a distance can be persuaded to engage volunteers to look after children in the village itself.
9.	In *anganwadi* – maintaining the cleanliness of children - periodical trimming of nails of children	Youth Associations, SHGs	Nail cutter can be purchased by the volunteers, periodically they can visit and trim the nails of children.
10.	Establishment of garden at *anganwadi*	Youth Associations, SHGs	Garden can be formed; papaya, drumstick saplings, greens, creepers can be planted. The vegetables and fruits produced can enrich the nutritional status of children.
11.	Supervision of distribution of free noon meal, nutritional porridge powder	Youths Associations, SHGs, Village Panchayat	Ensure the distribution to all eligible children, cleanliness in the kitchen and proper intake of the food, and porridge powder by the beneficiaries. Prevention of misuse and wastage.
12.	Proper delivery of RCH services	Youth Associations, SHGs, Village Panchayat	Assist in the prompt and timely registration of all pregnancies, ensure proper check up and follow-up of referral services; assist in availing cash incentive to eligible pregnant women. Counselling on small family norm.

(Contd...)

(Contd...)

13. Utility and maintenance of women sanitary complex	SHG, Women Ward Members	Counselling of nearby families – forming of users' group – collecting of maintenance fee – maintenance of the complex - awareness building on personal hygiene and environmental sanitation, development of garden in the yard of the complex.
14. Prevention of water wastage, misuse, and proper water supply management system and its delivery	Youth Associations, SHGs, VWSC	Monitoring of pipeline burst, leakage and promptly reporting to the Village Panchayat, assisting in the repair work; monitoring the supply of water -- wastage, misuse during the time of scarcity, assist in the regularization of supply equally to all – assisting in simple maintenance by encouraging voluntary contribution construction of RWH structures near the handpumps.
15. Maintenance of streets	VWSC, Youths and SHGs	Awareness generation in sorting of bio-degradable and non-bio-degradable wastes by the householders and traders and vendors; with the guidance of NGOs; maintaining the manure yard, installation of soak pits; cleaning campaign at public places periodically through *shramdan*.
16. Greening of the village	Youth Associations, SHGs, Village Panchayat	Availing of the subsidized tree saplings from the government; encouraging householders to plant tree saplings at public places; undertaking planting of avenue trees, fruit bearing trees; assisting in social control of felling of trees in common lands.
17. Proper delivery of PDS services	Youth Associations, SHGs, Village Panchayat	Assist in providing family cards to all eligible householders; monitoring of distribution of essential commodities; prevention of pilferage and theft; if necessary, come forward to independently manage the PDS by an SHG.

(Contd...)

(Contd...)

18. Welfare service for the marginalized sector	Youth Associations, SHGs, Village Panchayat	Listing poor widows, oldage persons, and assisting to avail of welfare; identification of poor who do not possess house site, patta and bring housing scheme to them; identification of physically/mentally disabled and assist to avail of medical check up for the measurement of the percentage of the disability; assist in availing of eligible rehabitation services from government and donor agencies; identification of poor women who are not enrolled in SHGs and help them become SHG members.
19. Eradication of untouchability	Youth Associations, SHGs, Village Panchayat	Mass awareness programme, procession, cultural programmes; in case untouchability exists, undertaking counselling and peace-making initiatives; if necessary, initiate legal action against the culprits; organizing social programmes to enable all sections of the community to mingle and understand one author.
20. Promotion of SHG activities	Youth Associations, SHGs, Village Panchayat	Establishing good rapport with the concerned NGOs; assisting SHGs to get proper link with various departments and avail of welfare services from the same; assisting to get adequate skills development; assist in the maintenance of SHG building; encourage them to participate in the Gram Sabha; providing opportunity to the members in Standing Committees. Involving the SHG members in common activities related to provision of drinking water supply, environmental protection and other social development activities.

(Contd...)

(Contd...)

21. Uplift of poor traditional artisans	Youth Associations, SHGs, Village Panchayat	Assisting to an SHG; to update their skills and technology; to protect the CPR from which they get raw materials; assist to avail of welfare schemes pertaining to them; to improve their market by buying their products; to enable them to understand the market system and trend.
22. Welfare of Adolescent Girls	SHGs, Village Panchayat	Assist in awareness programme on personal hygiene anemia, AIDS awareness, prevention of child labour, availing of vocational training, counseling them to be cautious against exploitation in their workspot.
23. Management of common property resources	Youth Associations, SHGs, Village Panchayat	Identification of village commons and verification of its status; removal of encroachment through persuasion and, if necessary, through legal action; protection by natural fencing; protection of water sources from pollution through social control; undertake social forestry; plan for fuel, raw materials for village artisans, and fodder and medicinal plants.
24. Augmentation of resources of Village Panchayat and improving of people's participation in Gram Sabha	Youth Associations, SHGs, Farmers Committee, other CBOs	Mass awareness on the income and expenditure of Village Panchayats; details of fixation of various taxes; dues collection; necessary revision; promotion of remunerative social forestry; village based management system for the distribution of water supply and providing opportunity to discuss the above issues in the Gram Sabha; efforts to activate the Standing Committees; the significance of self-sufficiency and self-governance.

(Contd...)

SECTION - II

Reconstruction of Villages after Tsunami through Micro Planning

Introduction

Villages and communities affected and damaged due to tsunami on 26th December, 2004 are still in the process of reconstruction and rehabilitation of livelihoods and infrastructural facilities. Despite the huge and generous commitment by donor agencies and governments, rehabilitation and reconstruction activities have not produced the result to the level of investment. By nature, the relief and rehabilitation activities are both target and process oriented. Social dynamics are so intense and as a result the speed of the rehabilitation activities reduced.

All the coastal line Panchayats are grappling with the issues such as the division of communities which were dormant but became active as relief activities were carried out sectorally and segmentally by the donor agencies and government departments. Ironically, a number of development activists are involved in relief and rehabilitation activities, yet people are not empowered, instead they have been reduced to the position of beneficiaries and petitioners. The approach of distribution of relief is one of charity.

As a result, people are not made as part of the decision-making process of the entire relief and rehabilitation activities. Both government departments and civil society organizations due to their sectoral approach, unintentionally made the people to fight against each other to get relief and rehabilitation benefits. Politicians have started looking at the problems from the perspective of their respective party ideologies. Instead of solving the problems, the situation led to an intensification of conflict among the groups.

Even the specialized research agencies have analyzed the problems of the people sectorally, instead of doing so holistically, and have projected the damages and the losses of the groups leaving many marginalized groups unattended. There are institutions that have done great damage to the constitutionally created Panchayats.

Box-1
From pillar to post

A group of farmers went to the Assistant Director of the Department of Agriculture in order to submit a petition to seek relief and remedy for their farms that had been devastated and had incurred a huge loss to them. The department officials instructed them to meet the related Departments for the problems. Subsequently, the affected farmers went to the Department of Horticulture where the officials informed them of their sphere as limited to dealing only with issues such as loss of mangoes and other fruit yielding trees. They were directed to go to the Department of Social Forestry where the officials told them that they will deal with a few species only and for other kinds of trees you have to go to other departments. After hearing this explanation, a few farmers shouted at the officials. A sensitive, responsible officer claimed them and advised the farmers to classify the problems and sent them to various departments according to their need. The affected had to literally run from pillar to post merely to reach the government departments working in their required area. For the farmers, 'problems of agriculture related but for the officials. They are of different departments' namely, Agriculture Animal Husbandry, Agriculture Engineering, Horticulture, Public Works Department, Social Forestry, Forest Department, District Rural Development Agency.

In fact, it will not be an exaggeration to say that the constitutional Panchayats have been totally sidelined in relief and rehabilitation activities at many places excepting in a few where the constitutional Panchayats themselves took a lead role.

Having seen the conditions that destabilized the Panchayat institutions which are supposed to be strengthened to prepare themselves to respond to natural disaster, Rajiv Gandhi Chair for Panchayati Raj Studies at the Gandhigram Rural Institute started exploring the possibility of involving the communities in the preparation of the micro plan in each and every Gram Panchayat for reconstruction of the tsunami-affected areas. The key assumptions with which the work was started are that:

- People already possess energy, skill, capacity and capability to participate in the reconstruction process and by which they can establish their self-dignity.

- Communities which are torn apart by conflicts, especially the conflict between traditional Panchayats and Constitutional Panchayats, should work together to empower the community and the people.
- People have the ability to participate in decision-making as claimants and empower themselves and not remain mere affected people to be looked at with pity.
- Women and Dalits should be integrated as core groups in decision-making.
- There is a need to reverse the process of powerlessness to empowerment of the people.

The course of this task has not been an easy one as it is primarily process oriented. It must be mentioned that the action research was planned amidst a lot of debate on its relevance with many of the Panchayats. Of these Panchayats, seventeen Gram Panchayats agreed to conduct this experiment. The Rajiv Gandhi Chair has started working in seventeen Gram Panchayats with the active support of The Hunger Project, and the Swiss Agency for Development and Cooperation, New Delhi.

Methodology

The work began with the selection of the 17 Panchayats located in 3 clusters, one at the South of Nagapattinam and two clusters at the North of Nagapattinam. Subsequently, the panchayats were contacted and after receiving assurance from the panchayats to work on the preparation of the micro plan, Rajiv Gandhi Chair for Panchayati Raj Studies looked for community based non-governmental organizations who are working in these 17 Gram Panchayats.

Three NGOs—Sevalaya, SCORD and Reform Trust— work closely with the local community and have succeeded over the years in establishing a good rapport and credibility with the people were selected. With the help of these NGOs, individuals having the power to influence the community in these areas were identified. They comprise self-help group leaders, traditional Panchayat leaders, youth group leaders, farmers association leaders, ward members, caste leaders, political party unit representatives, retired employees living in the respective villages and guild leaders.

The project was decided to be undertaken in two phases, the first phase dealing with the identification of priorities by the stakeholders, and develop a plan document and the second part dealing with the implementation of the plan with active support of the government and other agencies involved in rehabilitation activities.

Phase-I: Micro-planning and Identification of the Community Priorities

- Orientation for the leaders who are influential among the community on micro-level planning,
- Constitution of the planning group in each and every Gram Panchayat,
- Constituting statutory committees in the Panchayat,
- Intermix the new initiative to the people through Gram Sabha,
- Database creation with the tool prepared by GRI,
- Benchmark survey and resource-mapping with the active participation of people,
- Village profile preparation,
- Identification of problems and needs,
- Identification of disparities among villages in Panchayats
- Prioritizing needs through Gram Sabha,
- Resource identification,
- Preparation of draft village Panchayat development plan,
- Approval of village development plan by the Gram Sabha,
- Dissemination of development plan among the officials.

Phase-II: Implementation

- Community mobilization and empowerment,
- Organising regular meetings of both the traditional and constitutional Panchayats,
- Facilitating women's participation in the Panchayats and Gram Sabha meetings,

- Working closely with the Panchayat Disaster Management Committees and imparting trainings on disaster preparedness,
- Facilitating the linking up of the needs of each community regarding shelter, compensate for the loss of lives and livelihoods with the Government,
- Organising community leadership especially with those of women,
- Establishing local communication system for disaster preparedness in collaboration with MSSRF,
- Training and skill-building for livelihoods,
- Ensuring the Government Departments working in the people's plan.

Planning Exercise at Grassroots

It would be pertinent to mention the daylong workshop organized at Nagapattinam on 9th April, 2005 to get opinion of the possible stakeholders about the micro-planning exercise to be done at the Panchayat level. The entire day was devoted to analyse the contextual powerlessness of the people and the reasons for their powerlessness. In the end, the manner in which people can be empowered were discussed. Central to the discussion was the issue of divisions and conflicts in the community that help the outsiders to control and dominate the people easily. A few observations were made by the participants in the course of the consultation. These are about:

- The need to gain confidence and self-respect and not to think of oneself in terms of charity.
- The need to be conscientised and oriented to lead a healthy, human living.
- The need to have an authentic database which can guide the relief and rehabilitation operations.
- Issues relating to natural resource management, women and children especially of the fishermen community and Dalits have to be given special emphasis.

The participants agreed to mobilize people from the community to involve in the preparation of micro-plan for the overall development of the villages. All the leaders also showed their readiness to work with the Gram Panchayat. The notion that was held by all was that Gram Panchayats should be made people-centric and not leader-centric.

First condition stipulated was that this exercise should be based on mutual consent and that the process should be based on inclusion and gender equity. In the whole process of relief, injustice was done to the disabled, widows, destitute women, labourers, and Dalits. Hence it was reiterated that the problems of all segments must be incorporated in the plan.

Subsequent to this, meetings were held with the District Administration, the District Collector and Project Officer, District Rural Development Agency whereby information regarding the exercise was given and support was sought. The effort found support from these officials as they found it very difficult to carry out development works in the midst of conflict among the groups. The officials mentioned it as especially true in the case of relief and rehabilitation activities. The District Administration seemed to have found out a new opportunity for their work. They agreed in principle, to support this endeavour of preparing the micro-plan. With the assurance of the leaders and opinion makers of the communities, the three NGOs and the District Administration, the micro-plan initiative was undertaken in seventeen Gram Panchayats in Nagapattinam District by the Rajiv Gandhi Chair.

Table 3.1 of the 17 Panchayats with the unions they belong to and the NGO coordinating the process of planning.

Since micro-planning efforts were undertaken in order to ensure people's perspective both in terms of procedure and substance in the village development plan, the following steps were used during the preparation:

- Discussions with the village panchayat and ward members.
- Discussion with the community leaders, Self-Help Group leaders.
- Collection of data by the Panchayat leaders, clerks, NGO field staff.

Table 3.1 : Gram Panchayats

Sl. No.	*Gram Panchayat*	*Coordinating NGO*	*Panchayat Union*
1	Pradhabaramapuram	Sevalaya	Keelaiyur Union
2	Kameshwaram	"	Keelaiyur Union
3	Vizhundamavadi	"	Keelaiyur Union
4	Pudupalli	"	Keelaiyur Union
5	Vettaikaraniruppu	"	Keelaiyur Union
6	Chandrapadi	SCORD	Sembanarkoil Union
7	Maruthapallam	"	Sembanarkoil Union
8	Kalamanallur	"	Sembanarkoil Union
9	Pillaiperumalanullar	"	Sembanarkoil Union
10	Manicka Pangu	"	Sembanarkoil Union
11	Vanagiri	"	Sembanarkoil Union
12	Kaveripoompattinam	Reform Trust	Sembanarkoil Union
13	Thandavankulam	"	Kollidam Union
14	Vettangudi	"	Kollidam Union
15	Perunthottam	"	Sirkali Union
16	Thenampattinam	"	Sirkali Union
17	Thirumullaivasal	"	Kollidam Union

- Damages caused by tsunami understood through social mapping.
- Consultation with village elders to know the history of the villages.
- Focused Group Discussions with various occupational groups to understand various demands and needs.
- PRA exercise carried out in every hamlet.
- Assessing the needs.
- Prioritizing the needs.
- Matching the needs with departmental resources.
- Final consultation with the District Administration especially with the District Collector and Project Officer, DRDA about its operational feasibilities.
- Getting concurrence from the District administration in the form of a letter from the District Collector.
- Planning the same plan document before the Gram Sabha for its approval.

- Printing of the plan document.
- Disseminating the document among the different stakeholders to claim ownership.
- Disseminating the document among the different department officials for ensuring their commitment for implementation.

Focused Objectives of the Project

Certain objectives were focused sharply by the facilitating institutions for the project prior to its initiation. These were integrated into the training programme through orientations on decentralization, issues relating to disaster management and considering the problems of the marginalized sections such as women, Dalits, children and the physically handicapped.

- Strengthening local governance through the constitutional Panchayat system.
- Facilitating interface between constitutional and traditional Panchayats.
- Strengthening women's participation in local governance.
- Strengthening dalit participation in local governance.
- Preparing the people to face disasters in future with minimum risks.

The Planning Process

With the help of the three local NGO partners, people had been mobilized for the task of preparing the micro-plan for the Panchayats. While mobilizing the community for active participation, the leaders of the Panchayats and communities were sensitized and conscientized on the potentials of the Panchayats, issues of social development, economic development and social justice. Further they are oriented in empowerment and right-based development. A four-day-capacity building programme was designed and carried out for which the leaders were mobilized by the district administration. For the first time the leaders of different communities stayed together and discussed the common issues of the communities in the Panchayat areas. It was a great opportunity for them to mutually discuss about their problems. The dialogue during the capacity-building exercise helped them to bring harmony among the social groups. Officials have been requested to cooperate with Panchayat leaders and the three lead NGOs in the preparation of the micro-plan. The Panchayat leaders and the community leaders and the field staff of the lead NGOs were trained to be sensitive on the issues of exclusion and marginalization. Panchayat constituted the Statutory Committees including the Planning Committee. NGO staff, Panchayat leaders, community leaders, Panchayat clerks and officials were involved in preparing the database. Following the data collection, needs of the people were assessed. For need assessment, prioritization of the works was carried out as well as PRA exercises were conducted in all the villages. Focused group discussions were also held. As a result, needs are generated and activities are identified. To carry out activities, resources were identified. Disparities among the hamlets (villagers) within the jurisdiction of Panchayats were identified, and activities and steps were evolved.

With the support of the NGOs, Panchayat Presidents prepared the documents. The contents of these documents could be divided into three parts:

1. The first part is concerned with the profile of the Panchayat describing the damages caused to the village by tsunami, basic objectives of the plan, general information about the Panchayats and the facilities available in the Panchayats.
2. Second part deals with the methodological nuances adopted to generate data and analyze the same. Details have been explained as to the manner in which the priorities were set and activities decided with a specific focus on development and social justice.
3. Third part deals with the sectors such as agriculture, water supply and sanitation, services, education, health, economic activities, farm and non-farm activities. The availability

and requirements of each sector have been explained in this part. In each document a SWOT analysis incorporated based on the responses of the communities.

The plan drafted has been submitted to the villagers during the Gram Sabha meeting scheduled on 26th January, 2006 for verification, ratification and approval.

It must be stressed here again that all the activities undertaken by the government and many of the non-governmental agencies relating to tsunami had been perceived by the people as supply driven. During the process, complaints were received about the lack of coherence in the spending of the government departments and the felt needs of the society. While the procedures are followed through convening the Gram Sabha four times every year through which people express their needs, bare minimum expectations and aspirations of the citizens are not met. Variety of activities are carried out by various departments in the villages but these are also marked by a mismatch between the people's needs and government activities. During the discussions, people demanded that government departments should not plan and spend money in the villages without getting the consent of the Gram Sabha.

Against this background the micro-level plan becomes significant as the prioritized needs are matched with the departmental activities of the government. People realized during the process of discussion that different activities need support from different sources. Certain activities can be matched with the Department of Agriculture, while a few others can be done by the horticulture department. Likewise all the activities are classified as specific departmental activities. There are certain activities which cannot be done by any of the government departments thus needing the help of the donor agencies and civil society organizations. There are certain activities which can be done by the community itself.

The village and the community fixed the responsibilities among themselves to carry out the activities. Further the plan document is legitimized with the approval of the District Administration. The plan document with the signature of the Gram Sabha members is being submitted to all sectoral departments. The entire exercise from mobilizing the people for planning exercise, constituting committees for plan preparation, training the groups in micro-level planning, conducting PRA exercise in the villages, conducting focused group discussions in the villages, preparing a plan document, getting the approval of Gram Sabha for plan document to getting the approval of district administration have raised hope among the people, and have raised confidence among the people.

In the entire process of mobilization and participation, the issues of dalits, women, widows, disabled, vulnerable families, farm labourers, children, available government services and delivery institutions have been included in the planning exercise. In this sense, it is an inclusive plan. While discussing various problems faced by the people of the Panchayats, they were repeatedly sensitized and conscientised on the above issues.

It must also be mentioned that during the process of attending to the demands of various segments, deliberate attempts were made to manage conflict among the groups. It took near about six months to bring the different groups together. There was an intense fight between Gram Panchayats and fishermen Panchayats, fishermen's fight against Dalits and *vice versa*. The issues of the physically challenged, widows, the destitute, children and labourers were not highlighted in the relief and rehabilitation process. Therefore, the process took special care to bring these issues into the planning. Even the details of the Panchayati Raj System had not percolated into the society before the tsunami hit Tamil Nadu. But during the entire process of preparing the micro-plan, people came to know the potentials of the Panchayats. They were also found to be informing the facilitators about realizing the potentials of the collectives. It was clear that many of the development issues were not known to them. For instance, after the plan everyone started discussions on health governance, people were demanding hospitals for their villages as one of the major issues. People were also found being not aware of many of the government schemes and offices which are dealing with the schemes. After this exercise they are having grip over the schemes and the government departments.

Though Panchayat provided the opportunity to the poor and the excluded to raise their voice, they could not do so as there was no conducive climate. But now all the excluded have been included and with the help of external agencies, they are raising their voices. Substantial amount of activities are identified for widows, destitute, adolescent girls, disabled, children and vulnerable families. In normal relief and rehabilitation, the above segments are neglected. It is also clear that neither the community nor the leader of the community sensitive towards governance, development and equity. But now they have realized the importance of the inclusion and equity.

About the Selected Village Panchayats

The village panchayats selected for the micro-planning exercise are all coastally located that were badly affected by the tsunami waves in 2004. In terms of destruction, more than 800 lives were lost, livelihood and assets worth crores have been reportedly destroyed. Among the villages selected for planning, the worst hit were Pradhabaramapuram, Manicka Pangu, Kaveripoompattinam, Thennampattinam, Chandrapadi, Thirumullaivasal, Vanagiri with more than 50 confirmed loss of human lives and loss of innumerable milch animals and destruction of assets such as houses, boats, nets and land. Other village panchayats that were hit badly but less than 50 deaths have been confirmed are Maruthapallam, Pudupalli, Kameshwaram, Thandavanakulam, Vizhundamavadi, Kalamanallur, Pillaiperumunallur, Perunthottam, Vettangudi and Vettaikaraniruppu.

Given the fact that the population of the above-mentioned villages have predominantly been dependent on agriculture and fishing, loss of agricultural land and boats—Wooden catamarans, FRP boats, *Vallams*—and nets are to be seen not merely in terms of immediate damages to be filled through relief efforts but as damages having a long-term impact on the livelihood of the inhabitants. Agricultural lands have been washed away by seawater leaving the lands in an unusable condition. Loss of mechanized boats have especially been damaging for the Kaveripoompattinam village that is known to be the most popular tourist place of the district. Besides these, most noteworthy are the destruction of the common property resources and public property that have a strong impact on the cultural sphere of the villages. In Pudupalli Kalahasthneswar temple, Shri Ramaayaana and Shri Mazhai Muthumariamman temples were affected badly. In Vettaikanraniruppu, a total of 2 hectares of public lands were damaged that included 1 hectare each of palm trees and cashew farm.

Certain common points about the villages could be observed :

- Irrigation channels (inlet as well as outlet) are not properly maintained in the villages resulting in the shrinking of acreage of land under cultivation.
- While a number of ponds, tanks exist, due to lack of proper maintenance, they are exposed to salination.
- Sources of livelihood such as agriculture, fishing and animal husbandry need support to be profitable.
- On the coastal side the natural vegetation have been replaced with casuarina, cashew nut, and coconut cultivation.
- Destructions of sand dunes and other sandy structures which prevent the seawater result in the water directly getting into village land/polluted the water bodies.
- Migration of farmers and labourers to other areas in search of employment has increased in the post-tsunami period.
- Prawn farms are on rise as they are a good source of income and give employment but the costs in terms of pollution of water/land are high.
- During tsunami, wherever the water structures existed seawater rolled in and washed away the men and materials and filled the salt water in the agriculture land causing a lot of damages to crop.
- Porambokku lands have been encroached, grasslands were destroyed and so cattle-rearing was also a challenging one. But given the fact that in many villages milk cooperative societies are defunct, cattle rearing is no longer a profitable business.

- The quality of inputs of agriculture, marketing arrangement, lack of transportation, lack of good roads are other problems faced by the agriculture sector.

Critical Issues Emerged

During the process of micro-planning, a number of issues critical to the lived realities of the inhabitants of the panchayats came to be discussed. The facilitators, on their part, encouraged the people to look at these issues not as personal issues but as having governance and developmental perspective. These issues relate to the education, health and livelihoods of the inhabitants. At one level, these issues could be attributed to the general underdeveloped context that we live in. While at another level, they are intricately related to the destruction caused by tsunami. Tsunami has not only meant damages in terms of lives and infrastructure but in terms of people's faith in asserting control over their own lives and those close to them. In this sense, the post-tsunami phase must be seen not only as providing relief and rehabilitation in material terms but as an opportunity to reinstate the faith of the people in their communities and in their institutions. Below discussed are the issues significant to the lives of the people as articulated by them during the process of micro-planning.

Status of Women

One of the most significant of all marginalized sections in the village communities is that of women. Both in the fishermen community and the farming community women were found to be bearing the double burden of poverty and conventional male subjugation. As the sphere of agricultural activities shrink primarily due to the desalination of land in the post-tsunami period, women agricultural labourers find it hard to get employment and are increasingly being engaged in production of thatches from coconut leaf, in milch animal rearing and other petty trades. During discussions and surveys, majority of them were found to be in poor health with many suffering from anemia.

A large number of widows were found in the target villages. It was observed that due to acute diseases resulting from alcoholism and smoking, mortality rate is high among middle-aged men. The diseases that were found common in the fishermen community are asthma, jaundice and arthritis.

There have also been cases of poor landless agricultural labourers committing suicide due to abject poverty and their inability to repay loan. The suffering of their widows who are left without any material and emotional support are heartrending. Due to societal control, their mobility is restricted that makes their situation worse. Widows of the fishermen community especially are in a bad situation as they are not allowed to switch over to choose any other vocation that makes them completely dependent on the families. In a resource scarce society, this leads to an unpleasant atmosphere as they are considered as an additional burden. Low production of agriculture and fishing in the post-tsunami period has only added to the problem.

Divorced women and those separated from their husbands also have been found to be having problems similar to those of the widows. Lack of proper education along with absence of opportunities of livelihood make the bargaining power of these women very low.

What also came to the notice of the facilitators during the course of micro-planning are the problems faced by the adolescent girls. Majority of them are not permitted to continue their studies after secondary school and are compelled to go for wage employment in agriculture/construction sectors. Due to poor literacy, lack of maturity, lack of understanding of the society and the world around them, the adolescent girls are subjected to exploitation, many of them anemic and unaware of personal health and hygiene. The educated among them have shown interest to learn new skills—tailoring, toy making, and coir production—that would help them to earn some wage of their own. During the course of discussion, it was known that the girls sought guidance to acquire computer knowledge/skill. These go on to show the keenness among the adolescent girls to be independent.

The SHG activities among women are yet to scale up to economic activities. They have been getting training in trades like coir production, candle production, hand works from palm leaves but due to various issues in the credit linkages they are in lack of production activities. Illiterate women members of SHG demand good education to their ward and vocational training to their adolescent girls.

It is learnt that the fisherwomen and women agricultural labourers have habits that are harmful to their health. It was found that they have the practice of chewing *pan* (betel leaf) with tobacco and are used to manage their hunger by having just tea and bun. This has been the main cause of the deterioration of their health. Many mothers in poor families shared that due to demand—cash and jewels—as dowry, the marriage of their daughters are getting delayed. This leads to the womenfolk of the selected villages living with stress and tension.

Status of Children

One section that has been badly affected by the tsunami is the children. Their education and development has been impaired due to the closure of the already fragile educational infrastructure for a long time after the calamity.

It is noted that there are lack of proper *balwadi* facilities in many target villages. It is only after tsunami that some NGOs have come forward to organize *balwadis*/children's centre in the tsunami-affected villages, especially in fishermen hamlets. Further among the *balwadis* run by the government, facilities with regard to safety and extra-curricular activities are completely absent. In most places, shaded trees, fencing, vessels and play materials are not available. In some *balwadis* the basic amenities like water supply and toilets are not attended.

In many cases *balwadis* are located far off (in other hamlets) from the small hamlets from where children have to come over to the place where centres are located. But due to lack of caretakers, parents do not want to send their children to other hamlets. Hence there is no service like mid-day meals, health check-up, taking weight of the children to monitor the nutritional status of the children. Many children were found not attending the *balwadis* as they belong to groups that do not understand the value of sending the children to these institutions.

Generally it is observed that the basic knowledge and practice of childcare and child-rearing is missing among the present generation of mothers due to gap between the younger and the older generation. Hence it is noted that in target villages, personal hygiene of children is below the normal. Mothers are aware of immunization but are not able to understand to correlate immunization to the disease. Mothers have to be sensitized in this regard. Though there is health assistance to work in this regard, the interface between the field/district officials and the community is not as expected. Families still prefer to have delivery of the baby at home than to go to the hospitals.

Status of Fishermen Community

Like all disasters, tsunami left a trail of destruction but it has also brought to light many a communities whose needs have not received attention till now. They usually have fewer interfaces with other sections of the village community as their socio-cultural activities are entirely different from the others. They have their own fishermen Panchayats that is seen as the community decision-making committee about social, political, cultural and economic issues relating to the fishermen community. The social control exercised by the traditional committee is very strict and strong. It regulates the indiscipline found among the members. What is noteworthy is the lack of participation by women in these committees, even during deliberation.

Lack of communication between the fishermen community and the general community has led to many a misunderstanding between the traditional fishermen Panchayats and the Constitutional Panchayats. While the fishermen blame the constitutional Panchayat for not taking into account the specific needs of the community, the Constitutional Panchayats feel exploited by the fishermen community. The fishermen community does not give real value to the elected Panchayats. This difference of opinion has led to a lot of misunderstandings during the implementation of relief and rehabilitation activities by the Panchayats. The traditional committee members had their own perspective and objectives in tsunami relief activities which failed to give attention to the problems of children, widows, dalits, disabled and mentally retarded persons in the community. This led to the rejection of their suggestion by the constitutional Panchayats. Again, when the constitutional Panchayat stepped into assist the members among the non-fishermen community especially the dalits, the members of the fishermen community explicitly expressed their unhappiness with the assertion of power and position by the elected Panchayat president. This was mainly expressed through non-cooperation in the Gram Sabha meetings. Therefore, the plan proposed to rebuild the environment, faith and self-dignity of all villages in meeting the social challenges through the constitutionally elected Panchayats.

It must be mentioned that the habitation of the fishermen is far from the main habitation in the village. In general, there is an inadequacy in fulfilling the basic felt needs of the community. Condition of the roads are very poor, sanitation is also very bad, and the place is marked by a lack of the provision in supply of protection, drinking water and streetlights.

Both the lack of infrastructure as well as poor quality of the same in the areas of marketing of the fisheries product, educational institutions such as schools and *balwadis* and disaster related to seas are the main problems that the community faces. Awareness about disaster preparedness among the community members is very poor.

While dry fish is a good source of income, there is hardly any clean and scientific management available for dry fish processing.

During the facilitation, some problems of the youth in the fishermen community were noted. They have been usually found either having completed their secondary school or to have dropped out during high schools to join the family vocation. This is mostly due to the compulsions to become breadwinners at a young age which again leads to their marriage at a young age. Given the fact that fishing as an occupation demands their full energy, they prefer to utilize their leisure time enjoying life with the peer groups. Many of them were found to be addicted to alcohol. Their knowledge and interests in other fields is less and have very less interface with the youth of other community.

During the articulation of needs of the communities, fishermen demanded facilities like refrigerator to stock fish, transportation facilities to market fish as early as possible, proper maintenance of roads that lead to coastal areas, and construction of small ports wherever feasible. Further they have also demanded to desilt the outlet-inlet channels of the local irrigation system. They have also made complaints against prawn-farming which checks the free flow of water. After tsunami, they shared the need to have village knowledge centres where they can get all information needed to ensure their safety and security.

Status of Scheduled Caste Community

Invariably in all target villages, the scheduled caste communities were found to be living along with other sections of the community implying almost no discrimination on the lines of caste. Symbols of traditional caste discrimination such as two-glass system were not found in the target villages. Majority of them are landless labourers. Many of them are marginal farmers. Most of these families live in huts and some live in tiled houses. There are a considerable number of families who are living in poramboke lands and temple lands. These people obviously do not have any patta—the valid document for ownership over the land. Some of the families were found to be owning group/colony houses. Generally in the habitations of the scheduled caste community, basic needs like water supply, streetlights, drainage, roads, culverts, and public toilets are not found.

In the post-tsunami period, with the salination of cultivable lands, many of the agricultural labourers have turned to construction work. Several of them have migrated to the nearby districts/cities seeking employment. Within the villages, a few scheduled caste youth have been oriented in fishing activities along with the fishermen youth. They are at present engaged in subsidiary tasks such as categorizing the fish according to the varieties, loading them to the auction centre, washing and loading them for transportation and even in selling the fish.

It was known from the interaction that the number of college girls among the scheduled caste youth has increased over the years. But even after getting educated in the college, these educated youth have been engaged in agriculture and allied activities due to lack of employment opportunities. There is certainly a need for counselling/guidance/skill orientation to get into government employment or employment in private concerns. Scheduled caste youth were found to have organized themselves either in their own caste organization and becoming a part of the Dalit Panthers. This implies an ongoing process whereby the scheduled castes are gradually empowering themselves politically and culturally. A number of youth of this community were found to be addicted to alcohol and tobacco.

THADCO schemes for their socio-economic development are being successfully implemented in the two charters located at the northern side of Nagapattinam.

Status of Disabled and Mentally Retarded

A sizeable number of physically and mentally challenged persons were found in the target villages. Most of them come from resource-scarce poor families that face hardship in maintaining the health and life of disabled persons. There is a lack of mindset and community sensitization with regard to welfare of the handicapped.

Due to absence of centres for the physically and mentally challenged persons in the district of Nagapattinam, most of them live lifes of helplessness and dependence. The entitlement earmarked for disabled persons by the government schemes have been not yet properly reached the right beneficiaries. Tools and equipments pertaining to them are not properly distributed to the needy one.

Issues in the Provision of Drinking Water Supply

Provision of safe drinking water adequate to all who live in target villages is a serious challenge that the Village Panchayat administration is facing. In the post-tsunami period with the salination of the water sources, potable water has become a difficult commodity. Most Panchayats complained the available water of being saline with bad odour. Even the colour of the water is muddy making it unsafe for drinking purposes.

Prawn farming, soil erosion, application of channels for agriculture, irrigation of seawater into soil are some of the major issues faced by community. Desalination plant has been established in a few villages but are not enough to resolve the problem.

The Kollidam comprehensive water supply scheme is proposed to cover as many villages as possible. Target villages especially worth of Nagapattinam will be benefited through this.

The village community does not have any sense of ownership of the sources of water supply. Even for minor repairs they expect official intervention instead of initiating on own. Structures like OHT, pipe and power pumps/motor rooms are not properly maintained due to paucity of funds in the Village Panchayats.

Many of the Village Panchayats do not have any pipe connection to the households. The cost of electricity is high as the unit cost is fixed by the State Government under commercial/ business section for public buildings, power pumps and streetlights. In many of the villages the SFC grant has been dedicated to pay to the electricity board due to overdue of electricity board charges payment.

Issues in Environmental Sanitation

Increasing usage of plastic, polythene-based products is gradually becoming an issue of serious concern. Due to the non-availability of proper system of water management in the villages, maintenance of cleanliness becomes a tough task. The villagers do not have the orientation to manage wastes from bio and non-bio sources at house level itself.

The number of staff for sweeping/scavenging in the villages is very few thus making it difficult for them to cover all the hamlets. This, in turn, creates a lot of scope for communicable diseases. There is no awareness even among the educated in this regard.

The composte pits provided by the block administration is not put into use due to want of community cooperation. Further there is no knowledge in the construction of soak pits, to drain out wastewater. Women's sanitary complexes have been provided in many villages. But majority of them remain unutilized. Further the number of household latrines are also few. In general a lot of initiative needs to be taken out by all stakeholders with regard to maintenance of sanitary complexes. In some villages, the sanitary complexes are in use by involving SHG women members. Invariably in all the 17 Village Panchayats, villagers demanded public toilet for men and women in all the hamlets. There is also a demand for household latrines. As sanitation is a way of life, without proper orientation and change in the mindset of villagers, the utility of public toilets/household latrines cannot be achieved. Due to functioning of several NGOs in all the tsunami-affected villages, it is expected that process-oriented activities focusing on human development would be the main focus. The village Panchayat proposed the activities in association with all other NGOs also in this regard.

Issues in Public Distribution System

Except in a few villages where the number of hamlet villages are many, villagers have not demanded for additional PDS shops. But invariably in all villages, there is a demand of ration cards for those families who have not obtained ration card so far. Further in the villages where the PDS shops are functioning in rented buildings, the villagers demanded their own building. With regard to both quality and quantity, the villagers felt that the monthly entitlements of all commodities and the list of the beneficiaries should be made available at the end of concerned month so as any poor family householder could get his/her eligible ration commodities when he/she has money. Further villagers preferred afternoon/evening time for part-time PDS instead of morning. In a few villages there were complaints with regard to underweight and the same had to be rectified. There is yet another proposal in the plan to add the number of ultra poor who have the eligibility to avail free rice under AAY. The list of such poor persons are referred in the plan document.

Issues in the Sector of Education

It is observed that in all the 17 target villages, the number of educational institutions, namely the primary school, the secondary school and the high school are not adequate in number. Regarding the higher secondary school, the students have to travel 5 to 6 km when there is no higher secondary school at the local level.

In some schools, the infrastructure facilities especially the classrooms, laboratories, toilets, playgrounds are not adequate. Provisions of safe drinking water supply is also yet to be ensured in a few villages to the schools. Furnitures are not adequate in all the schools.

Further in several villages the student-teacher ratio needs to be improved. In two or three Village Panchayats, the proposal to upgrade the primary school to the middle level is being considered by the government authorities.

It is observed that in many schools the Parent Teachers Association activities have to be strengthened. Moreover, no serious steps have been taken to improve the extra-curricular activities of the students.

The management of aided schools in the target villages need orientation in respect of improving the school environment so as a conducive atmosphere is created promoting learning. In general it is felt that community participation in the activities of educational institutions has to be sensitized and the role of village Panchayat institutions in this regard has to be emphasized.

About the Village Panchayat Council

One noteworthy point about the 17 target villages is their multi-cultural nature reflected through the presence of different castes. The council members are working in harmony and the relationship between the council members and the Presidents was understood to be cordial in all Panchayats except in a few. In the Chandrapadi village Panchayat, three ward members belonging to the fishermen community resigned due to difference of opinion in distributing relief materials to non-fishermen and in implementing rehabilitation activities in the non-fishermen habitation.

With regard to the performance of women Presidents of our target villages, almost all of them have real interest and commitment in their activities. They are not completely independent but have facilitation and guidance from their male family members. There are exceptional women Presidents like the President of Kaveripoompattinam, Maruthampallam, Thennampattinam and Thirumullaivasal who are effectively involved in THP-GRI-Tsunami intervention project activities.

Among the men Presidents of the target villages, almost all of them are seriously involved in the project activities. In some villages difference of opinion between the President and the representatives of fishermen community was evident that had resulted in cases of non-cooperation in the Gram Sabha meetings. Except on some issues, there exists a functional relationship between the President and the community.

Irrespective of their party affiliation, almost all Panchayat Presidents were found to be having cordial relationship with their respective communities cutting across political party and caste differences. The periodical meetings of the Panchayat Council in all the 17 Panchayats are conducted properly. With regard to the Gram Sabha meetings, participation of women in Gram Sabha meeting is slowly increasing in number.

All the 17 Village Panchayats have very cordial relationship with the collaborative agencies like NGOs and other sectoral department of the Government of Tamil Nadu through which the welfare and development activities are implemented in their respective Panchayats.

In some of the village Panchayats, difference of opinion between traditional Village Panchayat leaders and the elected Village Panchayat Presidents were found. All the Presidents spared their time in identifying the issues in Panchayati Raj and have dedicated their time/spirit to equip the village community.

Based on these issues, the plan documents of the Panchayats have included the following demands:

- Enrolling all the children who have completed five years of age in school.

- Ensuring that the enrolled children continue their studies without dropping out.
- Conducting school annual day celebration to enable the students to display their creative potential.
- Providing basic amenities like drinking water, toilet, playing ground and vegetable garden in the school.
- Creating a sanitation and toilet culture among the students.
- Establishing reading rooms to encourage the desire to learn among the villagers and putting to use the Ayyan Thiruvalluvar Library.
- Providing toilet facility and playthings for children in the *anganwadi* and trimming their nails to ensure hygiene.
- Enrolling all the children who have completed two and a half years of age in the *anganwadi* and helping them to learn the habit of attending to their personal cleanliness.
- Ensuring the age-specific weight and the general health of children by providing them with appropriate balanced nutritious meal and ensuring the proper conduct of activities such as providing nutritious flour and noon-meal under the integrated child welfare scheme.
- Preventing female infanticide by creating awareness among the villagers.
- Ensuring that all the children receive fully and properly the benefits of the immunization programme.
- Creating an environment free of child labour.
- Adopting measures to prevent child mortality.
- Creating awareness among the people about gender equality.
- Ensuring that all deliveries take place only in hospitals.
- Creating awareness among women about prenatal and postnatal care.
- Helping women to fully receive the benefits of the activities under the postnatal child welfare schemes.
- Helping pregnant women to properly receive benefits such as prenatal care, medical examination, immunization vaccines, nutritious flour and pregnancy assistance money.
- Providing the required minimum basic facilities in the sub-health centre.

- Helping the village health nurse to discharge her welfare functions well.
- Taking steps to ensure optimum utilization of the women's sanitary complexes.
- Ensuring that all the people get safe drinking water.
- Completely eradicating open air defecation.
- Arranging for common public toilets and their proper use.
- Removing waste in order to create a sanitary village.
- Creating awareness among the people about the dangers to the village from non-degradable substances like plastics and polythene and taking steps for their prohibition.
- Augmenting finances by converting public wastes into fertilizer.
- Planting, rearing and protecting saplings in public places to transform the village into a green village.
- Ensuring minimum basic amenities to all the habitations of the village.
- Installing solar lights on streets.
- Ensuring that all eligible families get ration cards.
- Arranging to issue pattas to those who own no house sites.
- Ensuring that essential commodities are properly available under the public distribution system.
- Building houses for houseless people.
- Eradicating untouchability and creating social harmony.
- Ensuring that the Adi Dravidar community gets all the benefits it is eligible for.
- Organizing poor women into self-help groups and helping them to achieve social and economic upliftment.
- Making all the arrangements required to enable the self-help groups to produce articles and to market them.
- Bringing together the village artisans into a federation, enhancing their manual skills and arranging for employment opportunities for them.
- Creating awareness to ensure that girls are married only after they complete twenty-one years of age.
- Observing the families of weak, destitute, elderly people, poor widows, poverty-stricken artisans and guaranteeing their livelihood.

- Identifying the disabled and reaching to them benefits that ought to reach them.
- Showing the way for male as well as female self-help groups to function robustly.
- Motivating and guiding self-help groups participating fully in public welfare activities and in Gram Sabha meetings.
- Repairing and maintaining water sources such as ponds, tanks, *ooranis* and *kanmois*, collecting rainwater in them and using them properly.
- Creating the right perspective among the people regarding the importance of water, water management and utilization of water.
- Developing natural resources and protecting them from damage and degradation.
- Creating awareness among the people to cultivate medicinal plans in public places in the village and in habitations and to use them.
- Creating awareness among the people to effect changes in agriculture to suit circumstances.
- Reclaiming common property resources from encroachment.
- Regulating common property resources and taking steps to augment the Panchayat income through them.
- Reorienting the Panchayat activities to a people-centred mode and carrying them out with people's participation.
- Transforming the Panchayat into an arena for people's action.
- Transforming the people into social citizens and making them participate in all Panchayat activities. Transforming the Gram Sabha into a forum for social upliftment instead of a forum for collecting grievances.
- Involving women and Dalits in a big way in all the activities of the village.
- Synergising the different organizations functioning in the village for development activities.

Certain indicators were developed by the facilitators for strengthening the local governance in the selected area. These are discussed below :

Box-2

Monitoring Indicators

Indicators for the Gram Panchayats

- Attendance in the meetings
- Presence of Dalits in meetings
- Presence of women and nature of their participation
- Presence of the traditional Panchayats and ward members
- Regularity of the conduct of the Gram Panchayat meetings
- Accountability
- Transparency (sharing of information on financial issues and funds).

Indicators for the Gram Sabha

- Regularity of conducting the meetings
- Attendance of women, Dalits, fishermen and the disabled
- Rotation of venue for Gram Sabha
- Mobilization of all sections of society.

Indicators for the Delivery System

- Meeting with the District Collector
- Meeting with the Project Officer–DRDA
- Meeting with heads of sectoral departments
- Interaction with MLAs, MPs, NGOs and others
- Linkage with block and district Panchayats
- 17 Panchayats federation link up with the district administration.

Analysis

During the course of the process, the facilitators made a few observations which have implications for furthering the planning from below both in the same areas and doing so in other areas.

A consistent use of charity approach towards development has done more harm than good to the people. This was evident in the way people looked at the issues and problems concerning them and their villages. Having gotten used to being treated as mere recipients, they had started thinking of decisions about these to be taken by the government and others while it was their destiny to suffer from the wrong policies and benefit from the right ones. During the orientation at the beginning of the process, these were explained clearly through examples. Therefore, during the micro-planning process, people started looking at the issues as their own and this facilitated the process of articulation and integration of various spheres.

The micro-planning process has not only been a discussion to come up with a document but one whereby a deliberate attempt was made to build the already existing capability among the participants. The facilitators took it upon themselves to inform the people to be their own selves while sharing the problems and not to feel intimidated by the facilitators. These efforts at creating a feeling of ownership among the people went a long way to make people realize their strength individually, and most importantly, collectively.

Prior to this exercise, the people themselves agreed of not having looked at the issue of disaster as something that can be managed. A scientific and logical understanding of disaster in general and of tsunami in specific, with an analysis of the manner in which it makes people vulnerable to damages gradually made people to feel confident of managing natural disasters. It was during the discussion that people themselves shared the absence of disaster preparedness and lack of availability of infrastructures that can help them to overcome large-scale damages.

Previously, people had looked at planning as a process that is necessarily directed from above. It was for the first time that they came to be part of a process meant for planning the development of the village. This entailed a process of collective envisioning that at one level brought the people together, and at another level, made them to look optimistically at the developmental issues.

Box-3

Joining Hands

In case of the capacity-building exercises conducted by Gandhigram Rural Institute, the fishermen community shared that it is the first time they are coming together they were sitting together, with the other communities for a common dialogue. This resulted in both the communities understand each other taking up construction of houses together. Both the communities thanked Gandhigram Rural Institute for new synergy.

The facilitators took special care to base the planning process, right from the beginning, on the principles of inclusion. The need for this was especially felt when the marginalized voices among started asking for their relevance of planning for their lives. The facilitators felt that a planning from below with exclusionary notions are not going to be any different than planning from the above primarily because the focus of the both would be more on coming out with a planning document than on touching upon the lived realities of the people living on the threshold.

Box-4

Marginalized Voices

In a small meeting in Marutha Pallam in the temple premises, the number of women and disabled were found to be more than others. In the discussion, these sections made a plea that they had been neglected in relief and rehabilitation activities by officials as men of their community could not listen to their problems. Some of the men who were present in the meeting objected as these are not their problems and suggested that the NGOs and community should work for the net, hut and boats while the government departments have to work for women and disabled. This made the facilitators take special note of the demands of the marginalized voices such as the women and the disabled.

Special care was taken to include the voices of women through providing special sessions and to integrate the issues of various sections of women with the larger issues of social development. In all the sectors, women's problems were articulated. It was found out that the dropout rate was more in case of girl students than the boys, that parents were not ready to send their daughters to schools that had no proper sanitation facilities. Many women were also found not being sent to hospitals even during the delivery as these are considered to be intricately linked to family prestige and women's honour. Poor attention to reproductive health of women was primarily due to the lack of awareness as well as lack of access to healthy sanitation provisions.

Since the beginning, the planning process was deliberately made to be a people-centric one as against a leader-centric one. This was the primary reason behind taking community leaders and giving them as much importance as the Panchayats leaders. Further, the sessions were open more to sharing and participatory discussion than mere trainings and feedback.

Box-5

Training for a Humane Living

Muthuswamy (55) of Maruthapallam, an uneducated fisherman came out from a training programme by seeing our vehicle with a perception that we are reaching village with some doles when we asked him about how to maintain toilets and use toilets. But they were not having any toilet at all. In the fifty-five years of his life, he disclosed of never having used a toilet. He used only the beach as the toilets. He was not aware of the importance of sanitation. Only after tsunami, when groups came to train the people about health and sanitation then he started thinking of using the public toilet seriously.

What must also be shared in this section is the support and cooperation extended by the government officials to the people during the process of micro planning. In fact, the support given by the district authorities, especially the District Collector, the Project Officer and the District Rural Development Agency, is no less than a partnership for development.

Box-6

Officials as Friends

On the day of plan dissemination, the Panchayat of Manickapangu shared with the Project Officer the need to construct bridges which was delayed due to paucity of funds. The Project Officer brought this to the notice of the Collector who, in turn, instructed the Block Development Officer to put up a file for sanction.

This has led to the successful implementation of a lot of government schemes. Vanagiri is one such Panchayat experimenting with the National Rural Employment Guarantee Scheme under which all agri-related activities have been carried out. This is certainly emerging as a model village in the implementation of the National Employment Guarantee Act.

Conclusion

Prior to the planning process, the facilitators had repeatedly debated about the manner in which sensitivity, people-centricity have to be maintained throughout the process. As has already been mentioned in the previous section, the idea behind facilitating this grassroots level planning was to take forward the process of decentralization started by the new Panchayati Raj Institutions system incorporated into the Constitution through the 73rd Amendment. This necessitated a methodology that would grant space to a proactive participation of the community and to an inclusive process. In many senses, this could be termed as a novel method of planning for social development. The highlights of this method are :

- The participatory nature of the entire process ensured through a clear role for the facilitating agencies and the people. As has been repeatedly mentioned in the present document, people have been the chief planners in this project while GRI-SDC-THP along with the local NGO partners have been supporters of the process.
- The two-phased process based on public-private partnership that made the government to forge new partnerships with a facilitating group of the academic institution, NGOs and INGO chiefly for the development of the community. All the programmes undertaken in both the phases have been designed with people's participation and people's learning at the centre. The first phase focused on capacity-building through orientation, focus on the Panchayats as the chief mediating agencies (for constituting planning group/statutory committee, prioritizing of needs, identification of disparities, preparation of Panchayat Development Plan, approval of the plan and dissemination of the plan). The second phase concentrated on ensuring the continuing support of the government departments,

strengthening the Panchayats through enhancing the pro-active participation by dalits/women in the meetings, resolving conflicts between the traditional and constitutional Panchayats, and partnership with agencies such as MSSRF.

It must be noted that special attention was given throughout the process to keep it as a people's plan where the agencies involved including the government played the role of guiding, supervising and facilitating the process.

The process, however, has not been one without challenges and inconveniences. The challenges came in the shape of bringing the community together, facing the attitudes regarding caste and gender, and collection of data.

While mobilising people for the planning process was not difficult given the repute of the institutes such as Gandhigram Rural Institute, the problem lays in keeping the people together. It took a great deal of energy to bring conflicting communities to one platform to discuss about the development of the village. The facilitating agencies had to make use of techniques to resolve conflicts between the communities.

Related to this has been discussing the issues of exclusion that are so much a part of the village society. Getting to talk about special needs of women is an issue that needs special mention. More difficult was integrating their needs into the planning process. Given the rigid patriarchal mindset that marks the village society, this task became even more difficult for the facilitators as it also involved creating space for the women to talk.

Difficulties confronted while collecting data and later during the confirmation of data as a follow up was an extremely difficult task given the fact that most of the agencies, both governmental and non-governmental, focused on distribution of relief and efforts towards rehabilitation of tsunami-affected villages. Political parties added to the chaos with lists based on biased collection of data. Therefore, the plan document based its analysis on the information available from the panchayats and from people through administering PRA exercises.

The process of micro planning must be seen as one that not only led to a new process of planning from the below but has set a new trend by doing so. As a Panchayat President shared during the plan dissemination workshop: "the process was one of drawing a plan for the development of the people along side the village as also one whereby we all came to know what Panchayats stand for" (A.K. Ananthan, President of Pillaiperumalanullar on dated.13.6.2006 at the Collectorate, Nagapattinam). Indeed, the process has been one of understanding the real sense of planning from the grassroots.

APPENDIX

About Nagapattinam

Nagapattinam district has a very rich historical significance owing to its cultural heritage that dates back to 2000 years ago. It has been known to be one of the constituents of *chola mandalam*, acclaimed as the most prominent among the ancient Tamil Kingdoms. The selected villages are all strongly aware of their cultural history and tradition that is reflected in the community lifestyle.

What also should be mentioned here is the fact that Sirkazhi block and Tharangampadi Sembanarkoil block, two of the three blocks covered by the present initiative used to be popular tourist spots of the district.

As a district, Nagapattinam was carved out by bifurcating the composite Thanjavur district on 18.10.1991. Traditionally referred to as East Thanjavur and Paddy granary of South India, Nagapattinam District lies on the shores of the Bay of Bengal between Northern Latitude 10.10' and 11.20' East Longtitute 79.15' and 79.50', This is peninsular delta District surrounded by Bay of Bengal on the East, Palk Strait on the South and land on the West and Northern sides. This is predominantly a Coastal District having a large coastline of 141 kilometres. At present, the district has an area of 2715.83 sq. km in its fold. With the district headquarter at Nagapattinam, it envelops 11 panchayat unions, 3 municipalities and 9 town panchayats. On the Revenue side, it houses 2 revenue divisions with 4 and 3 taluks respectively and 523 revenue villages.

Tsunami damaged 80 villages of the Nagapattinam district leaving 6065 people dead and devastating an entire coastline. Estimates by the NGO Coordination and Resource Centre point towards the destruction of around 73 habitations in 38 revenue villages and 5 taluks.

The Scale of Damage in Nagapattinam

Total Area : 2.7 lakh hectares
Total Population : 14.88 lakhs
Urban Population : 3.3 lakhs
Rural Population : 11.58 lakhs
Affected Population : 1.96 lakhs
Fishermen : 87 %
Agricultural Labourers : 5 %
Traders : 5 %
Tourists/Pilgrims : 3 %

Source: http://www.ncrc.in

MAP OF NAGAPATTINAM

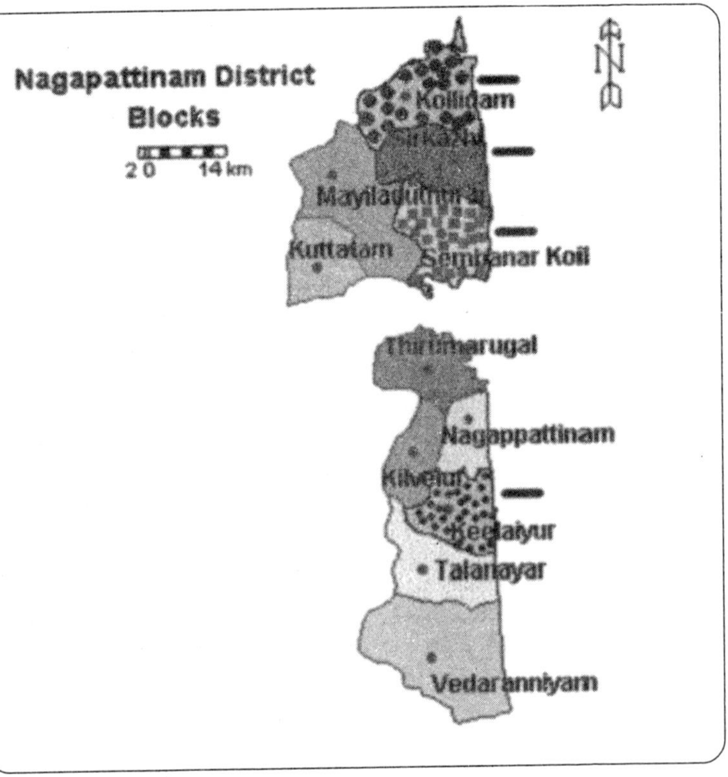

Tsunami Damages

Sl. No.	Panchayats	Damages in terms of lives and assets								
		Lives lost	Assets							
			Houses		Boats		Nets (in Kg.)		Land	Total Area
			Fully	Partially	Fully	Partially	Fully	Partially	Lost	
1	Vettaikaraniruppu	NA	75	45	1	36	10	8	10	480 ha
2	Pradhabaramapuram	153	360	37	69	78	30	27	15	432 ha
3	Vizhundamavadi	17	26	101	54	82	10	5	7	191.63 ha
4	Maruthapallam	34	52	125	52	12	593	NA	NA	117.84 ha
5	Kalamanallur	6	60	35	4	7	140	135	5	191.11 ha
6	Pillaiperumalanullar	22	150	5	40	6	25	NA	NA	216.47 ha
7	Manicka Pangu	102	779	84	6	96	428	NA	NA	162.8 ha
8	Kaveripoompattinam	110	710	223	NA	NA	NA	NA	NA	161.55 ha
9	Thandavankulam	20	NA	NA	NA	NA	NA	NA	NA	500 ha
10	Thennampattinam	97	430	195	NA	NA	NA	NA	NA	420 ha
11	Vanagiri	50	300	400	7	76	92	NA	NA	245.49 ha
12	Chandrapadi	95	180	208	35	30	200	NA	NA	225.49 ha
13	Pudupalli	1	15	7	5	1	5	10	7	160 ha
14	Vettangudi	NA	NA	NA	NA	NA	NA	NA	NA	180.06 ha
15	Perunthottam	NA	NA	NA	NA	NA	NA	NA	NA	375 ha
16	Kameshwaram	38	72	138	35	24	10	25	37	175 ha
17	Thirumullaivasal	85	NA	NA	35	24	NA	NA	NA	480 ha

Basic Information: Panchayats

Panchayats/Blocks	*Villages/ Hamlets*	*Total Population*	*Occupation (Families)*		*Marginalized Population*			
			Agri.	Fishing	BPL	Women	Chil.	PC
Vettaikaraniruppu	Natchiappankadu, Nattankadu, Kandiankaddu, North Sallikulam, Sadayankadu, Sooriavinayagar Street, South Sallikulam	4709	584	110	1162	2460	272	118
Pradhabaramapuram	Pradhabarapuram, Ramar Madum, Seruthur	12776	1799	621	1200	6012	NA	31
Vizhundamavadi	Vadapatti, Tambirankudiyiruppu, Thenpadi, Manalmedu	6800	493	552	1146	3515	519	43
Maruthapallam	Chithambarampakkam, Maurthampallam, Munthirithoppu, Perumalkoilpatthu, Chinnangudi	4081	355	2600	NA	2004	791	64
Kalamanallur	Kalamanallur, Sungenthi, Vadakattalai, Radhanallur, Thottam, Kumarakudi,	3451	628	610	NA	1706	727	46

(contd...)

Pillaiperumalanullar	Pillaipermalnallur, Veppanchery, Thirumeignanam, Jeyapuram Thazhampettai	3612	372	463	NA	1749	971	73
Manicka Pangu	Kuttiyandiyu, Vellaikoil, Perumalpettai, Pudupettai, Sinna Manickapangu, Pillai Colony, Valluvar Colony, Vadakku Colony, Manickapangu Anaikoil	5836	458	637	NA	2748	1172	85
Kaveripoompattinam	Poombukar, Mandakarai, Keezhaiyur, Niethavasai, Pudukuppam, Kunthirimedu	8267	2657	2728	1386	3868	NA	NA
Thandavankulam	Ellaisandu, Periavaguppu Main Road, Pudutheru, VOC Street, Mettu Theru, Kallar Street, Annangur, Sundarampillai Street, Karaltankuthu, Palakadu,	5338	312	626	530	2724	888	45

(contd...)

(contd...)

	Balasubramaniapuram North Street, Sithuvinayagapuram, Sinnavagappu Main Road, Navaneethakannapuram, Keelatheru, Gandhinagar, Sinnakottaimedu, Kottaimedu							
Thennampattinam	Annappanpettai, Thennampattinam, Mathampattinam, Konaiyampattinam, Melamoovarkrai, Keelamooverkarai	5092	650	35	625	2472	861	73
Vanagiri	Keelavanagiri, Melavanagiri, Naganathankoil, Palayagaram, Eramplayam, Dosaikulam	7292	1930	3948	2700	3622	1399	95
Chandrapadi	Chandrapadi, Sinnoorpettai	2256	108	1821	NA	1025	710	28
Pudupalli	Keela Pudupalli, Mela Pudupalli Mela Pudupalli	3150	800	650	660	1535	209	21
Vettangudi	Vettangudi, Kamarakottam, Jeeva Nagar, Vadi,	7448	743	NA	470	3677	1078	39

(contd...)

(contd...)

	Vembadi							
	Eravarkollai							
	Kaveroddai							
	Koozhiyar							
	Vellakulam							
Perunthottam	Peruthottam	5787	2123	229	535	2993	NA	67
	Agaraperunthottam							
	Periaperunthottam							
	Chavadikuppam							
	Naickerkuppam							
	Maduthukuppam							
	Kadaikadu							
Kameshwaram	Vairavankadu	5676	722	210	960	2858	325	57
	Vettarkadu Fishermen Colony							
	Anaiyathoppu							
	Kallarkadu							
	Melakadu Sivan Temple Street							
	Thandavamurthykadu							
	Melakadu Sivan Temple Street							
	Thandavamurthykadu							
Thirumullaivasal	42 Radhanallur	18463	NA	2274	1074	9297	2700	132
	Vazhuthalakudi							
	Thazhathondi							
	Thirumullaivasal							
	Thoduvai							

Water

Panchayats	*Available OHTs, HPs and PTs Vs. Current Needs*					
	OHTs		*HPs*		*PTs*	
	Available	*Need*	*Available*	*Need*	*Available*	*Need*
Vettaikaraniruppu	6	1	671	107	80	25
Pradhabaramapuram	9	3	137	50	184	20
Vizhundamavadi	9	1	170	36	131	30
Maruthapallam	5	1	25	15	72	17
Kalamanallur	7	2	41	15	57	35
Pillaiperumalanullar	3	3	58	10	69	10
Manicka Pangu	3	2	55	10	115	10
Kaveripoompattinam	13	–	–	66	30	87
Thandavankulam	4		17		37	37
Thennampattinam	5	2	95	81	64	5
Vanagiri	8 (2 mini OHTs)	2	30		54	50
Chandrapadi	2	–	63	–	25 (not in use)	–
Pudupalli	4	1	102	53	49	25
Vettangudi						
Perunthottam	12	2	65	14	120	35
Kameshwaram	4	2	135	70	57	10
Thirumullaivasal	9	3	129	6	152	56

Educational Facilities

Panchayats	*Facilities Available Vs. Needs*				
	Buildings	*Food and Nutrition*	*Sanitation*		*Play-ground*
			Water	*Toilet*	
Vettaikaraniruppu	Y	Y	Y	Y	Y
Pradhabaramapuram	Y	Y	Y	Y	Y
Vizhundamavadi	Y	Y	Y	Y	Y
Maruthapallam	Y (Building need to be made spacious)	Y	N	N	N
Kalamanallur	Y (2 buildings needed)	Y	N	N	N
Pillaiperumalanullar	Y	Y	N	N	N
Manicka Pangu	Y (2 additional buildings needed)	Y	Y	N	N
Kaveripoompattinam	Y	Y	N	N	N
Thandavankulam	Y	Y	N	N	N
Thennampattinam	Y	Y			
Vanagiri	Y	Y	N	N	N
Chandrapadi	Y	Y	N	N	N
Pudupalli	Y	Y	N	N	N
Vettangudi	Y	Y			
Perunthottam	Y (2 additional buildings needed)	Y	N	N	N
Kameshwaram	Y	Y	N	N	N
Thirumullaivasal	Y	Y	N	N	N

Health

Panchayats	PHCs			Sub-center		VHN	Other Needs
	Distance from the Panchayat Office	*Doctors/ Nurses*	*Medicine Availability*	*Doctors/ Nurses*	*Medicine Availability*	*Visits per Month*	
Vettaikaraniruppu		NO PHC					
	A Red Cross building is there.		No doctor is available.	VHN	Satisfactory	16	PHC needed RCS hospital should function well.
Pradhabaramapuram		1+2	Satisfactory	VHN	Satisfactory	16	Quarters for doctors and VHN needed.
Vizhundamavadi		1+2	Satisfactory	VHN	Satisfactory		Compound wall store room drinking water and an additional VHN needed
Maruthapallam	7km	1+2	Satisfactory		Satisfactory	16	1
Kalamanallur	7km	1+3	Satisfactory		Satisfactory		More doctors needed
Pillaiperumalanullar	2km	1+3	Satisfactory		Satisfactory	16	More doctors should be there.

(contd...)

(contd...)

Manicka Pangu	5km	1+3	Satisfactory		Satisfactory	16	1
Kaveripoompattinam	5km	1+2	Satisfactory				One more PHC and 2 health sub-centers needed.
Thandavankulam	—	—	—	—	—	—	PHC needed
Thennampattinam	—	1+2	Satisfactory				Only one hamlet has a health center. At least 1 PHC and 2 sub-centers needed.
Vanagiri	5km	—	—	2	Satisfactory	4	More doctors needed, sub-health center should be upgraded to a PHC.
Chandrapadi	Karaikal-10 km	1+2	Satisfactory	1	Satisfactory	Frequent	More doctors needed.
	Aakur-20km (also has a private hospital)	Satisfactory Serivce					
	Parayar-7km	2 doctors					
Pudupalli	3/4km from the village	Satisfactory Serivce	Satisfactory	VHN	Satisfactory	16	More doctors needed
Vettangudi	4km	Satisfactory Serivce	Satisfactory	—	—	—	More doctors needed

(contd...)

(contd...)

Perunthottam	—	Satisfactory Serivce	Satisfactory	—	—	—	Quarters of doctors and VHN to be upgraded.
Kameshwaram	—	Satisfactory Serivce	Satisfactory	VHN	Satisfactory	16	More doctors needed.
Thirumullaivasal	3km	Satisfactory Serivce	Satisfactory	—	—	—	More doctors needed.

Tsunami Relief: NGOs/INGOs Interventions

	NGOs	*Issue Focus*
Vettaikaraniruppu	Sevalaya	Land reclamation agriculture, horticulture, women's development
	DHAN Foundation	Land reclamation
	LISA	Rehabilitation
	Kudumbam	Land reclamation housing
	World Vision	Education
	Lasal Kadalise	Children's education
	Ekta Parishad	
	YMC	
Pradhabaramapuram	Sevalaya EKTA Parishad	Land reclamation
	Kudumbakam	
	MSSRF	Village Knowledge Center
	ASA-Vidiyal BWDC	Tsunami Relief & Rehabilitation
	SNEHA	Fishermen development
	Swami Dayananda Education	Temporary Shelters
	Trust OHFOM PDA TVS-Lucas	Education
	PDA Peace Trust Rose TMSSS	
	DMI Dhan Foundation Yushuf	
	Mehrali Centre Sevabharati	
	SOS DHAN	Children's Activity Centre
	SSDET	Shelter Community Place
Vizhundamavadi	Sevalaya	Self-Help Groups Land Reclamation, Farmer and women's welfare
	Real Plan Ekta Parishad	Land Reclamation
	Kudumbakam Dhan	
	Foundation DPG Real Plan	
	Speech	Dalit Development
	NAMCO	SHGs
Maruthapallam	SNEHA SJDT	Children Activity Centre
	OFFER SIFFS SCORD	Sanitation and temporary shelter livelihoods training
	UNICEF SAWS Hope Calcutta	Education
	Kudunmbakam	Organizing the Farmers Vermin Compose
Kalamanallur	SNEHA SJDT	Children Activity Centre
	OFFER SCORD RDT	Sanitation and Temporary Shelter livelihoods training
	CCD	Agricultural, Rehabilitation, Irrigation Channel Repair
	SEED WORD	Self-Help Groups
	SAPI RIM	Students Welfare Educational Development
Pillaiperumalanullar	SCORD, RTT, DMI, OFFER, SNEHA, GGF, RTP, DONBOSCO, St. Joseph Trust,	Relief Rehabilitation Developmental

(contd...)

(contd...)

	REK, SISU	
	ASHA GRMA VIDIYAL	
	ROJA	
Manicka Pangu	EFFICOR	Relief/ Permanent Shelter
	IAHV World Vision	Children Activities Centre
	SNEHA SJDT PEDA DON	
	BOSCO ANBU ILLAM	
	Real Plan	
	CASA	Permanent House for Dalits Fisheries, Anganwadi Community Centre
	OFFER	Sanitation temporary shelter Livelihoods Training
	RIM TMSS OXFAM ROJA	Educational Development
	SEVAI	Agriculture & Irrigation
	GGF	Sanitation
	RDT	Net and Boat
	Real Plan	
	TNVHA	Agricultural Rehabilitation Crop
	PREPARE	Production, Kitchen Garden Agro Forest
	CARE India SEED	Information Center
	SCORD SAPI	Livelihoods Training
	Red in Kind	Ice Box
	ASSIGI	Drinking Water Project
Kaveripoompattinam	SWEETS SNEHA CCD ISED	Relief and Rehabilitation
	AVVAI DHAN	
	Fish Foundation	
Thandavankulam	REFORM Avvai CARE	Relief Rehabilitation
	PLAN VDS SIRD DHAN	
	SNEHA CASA Sri Vallabai	
	RUBA St.Joseph SEVALAYA	
	Unisem	
Thennampattinam	SEVAI TVS ISED and others	Relief and Rehabilitation
Vanagiri	DHAN Foundation	Permanent housing
	WORD & DEED India	Self-Help Groups Village Development Activities
	Hope Kolkata	
	ISED Dhanam Trust	
	Divya Shanti Trust	
	PCI	
	Punthur Oli Pannathu Peravai	Balwadi Anganwadi
	Dhanam Trust	
	AVVAI	Children Welfare Activities Educational Development, Self Help Groups
	SEVAI	Health and Sanitation

(contd...)

(contd...)

Chandrapadi	SJDT SNEHA PEDA	Children activity Centre
	BEST	Agricultural Rehabilitation Children Activity Centre
	OFFER	Sanitation Temporray Shelter livelihoods training
	UNICEF	Drop-out Coaching Center
	SEED	Self-Help Groups formation
	SCORD	Livelihoods training
	The Red in Kind BUILD	Shelter
Pudupalli	Sevalaya	Land reclamation agriculture
	Kudumbakam	horticulture women's development
	BWDC	Old age care center
	Dhan Foundation	Tree Planting and Knowledge Centre
	Namco Sevalaya	Self-Help Groups
Kameshwaram	Sevalaya	Land reclamation agriculture horticulture women's development
	DHAN Foundation	Public Channel Deepening
	AID	Fishermen Area Relief Work
	International Rotary Club	
	World Vision Sevabharatthi	
	Karam	
	Rose HOSHOT Saceed	Children Activity Centre
	St.Annal Sabai SFI	
	TMSSS	
	Help Age India	Old Age Care

CASE – II

Village Reconstruction and Development Plan after Tsunami

Kameshwaram Village Panchayat - Keezhaiyur Union

Nagapattinam District

Foreword

(Translated Version)

The District Administration, Nagapattinam District, in collaboration with other Non-Governmental Organizations implemented a number of activities for the socio-economic development of the village affected by Tsunami. At this juncture, the Gandhigram Rural Institute and The Hunger Project, New Delhi suggested that the plan for reconstructing the village should be prepared with the participation of the people. When the citizens were fully involved in this activity of planning at the grassroots, I could feel the emergence of a new culture in the community for participation. Apart from that I could also see the new opportunity that is emerging for people's thinking together for the development of their village. So, all the departments of the government are instructed to help in this activity of planning.

I feel happy that a plan has been prepared for the socio-economic development of all the social groups in Thiruppoondi Panchayat of Keezhaiyur Panchayat Union. I appreciate all those involved in preparation of this plan document namely the President of the Panchayat, Ward Members, Fisher Panchayat Leaders, Members of Youth and Members of Self-Help Groups, farmer clubs, leaders of Dalits and other communities. I appreciate the help rendered by SEVALAYA (NGO) to this task.

The village community must equip itself with the capacity to translate this plan into action without depending upon the government alone. I feel happy that The Hunger Project, New Delhi and the Gandhigram Rural Institute, Gandhigram have come forward to guide continuously and facilitate the Village Panchayat for all its actions. I strongly believe that the government departments with the active involvement of the community can create a new life to the people of this village. I request all the government departments, and NGOs to help this Panchayat in implementing the plan activities.

Thanks

(Signature)
J. Radhakrishnan, I.A.S.
District Collector

ACKNOWLEDGEMENT BY THE PANCHAYAT PRESIDENT

(Translated Version)

26-01-2006

The Hunger Project, Department of Political Science and Development Administration, Gandhigram Rural Institute, Gandhigram and SEVALAYA helped Thiruppoondi-East (Kameshwaram) Panchayat in Keezhaiyur Panchayat Union in preparing a plan for reconstruction and development of the village after tsunami. This plan consists of the basic necessities for the village, status of various social groups, and the economic status of the people. We express our gratitude to Shri J. Radhakrishnan, I.A.S., District Collector, Shri G. Radha, the Project Officer, DRDA, and the Block Development Officer of the Keezhaiyur Panchayat Union for their support in preparing this plan document. We also express our deep sense of gratitude to The Hunger Project, New Delhi, the Gandhigram Rural Institute, Gandhigram and SEVALAYA.

(Signature)
G. Kanagasundaram

KAMESHWARAM—THIRUPPOONDI EAST PANCHAYAT

I. Introduction

(a) Location

Thiruppoondi East Panchayat, which is also called Kameshwaram, is located at a distance of 16 km from Nagapattinam, on the Nagapattinam-Vedaranyam highway. This Panchayat is surrounded by Pradhabaramapuram Panchayat on the north, Vizhunthamavadi Panchayat on the south, Thiruppoondi West Panchayat on the west,

Keezhaiyur Panchayat Union, Thirupoondi East (Kameshwaram)

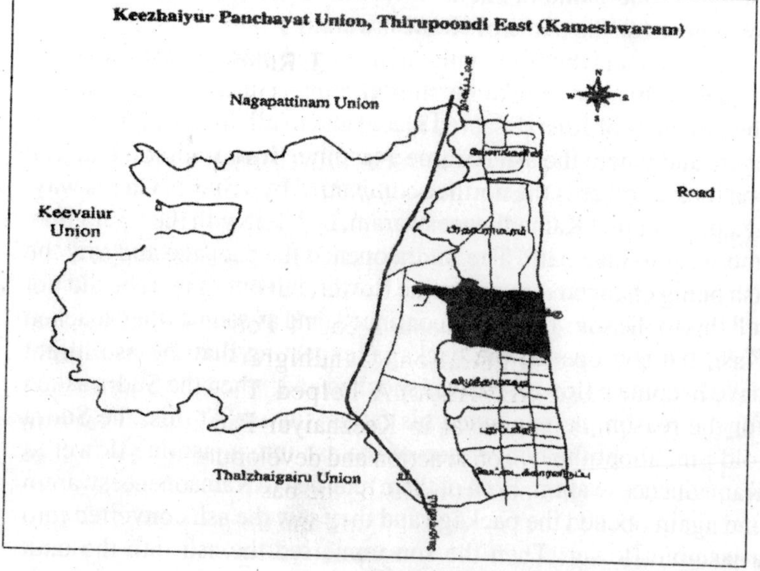

the Bay of Bengal on the east and the Keeran Lake on the north-west. The total geographical area of this Panchayat is 9,36,050.0 sq.kms.

(b) Geographical Profile

Located on the seashore, the geographical area of the village is marked by ups and downs with sand dunes to a height of 10 feet. The south-western part of this village is a low lying area whereas the central part is high. Following the sand dunes, in the western part of the village, there are agricultural lands with sandy soil, where fruit-bearing trees are cultivated. At the western end of the Panchayat there are clay soiled agricultural lands. In the southern part of the seashore, casuarina trees are grown in an area of 150 hectares and there are coconut trees in the western part of the seashore.

(c) Kameshwaram — History

Thirupoondi East Panchayat has another name also, Kameshwaram. The revenue village and the Panchayat are called Thirupoondi East but, in the other places, this village is called by its traditional as well as proud name of Kameshwaram. There are many historical evidences for the name of Kameshwaram.

A old man who was living in the sacred place of Rameswaram requested his son to take his mortal remains towards the north in the direction of Kasi (a sacred place) and to all the Siva temples *en route* and where the ash became a jasmine flower, dissolve it. The son took it towards the north accompanied by a Sudra. On his way, at a place called Kamadheneeswaram, he left it with the Sudra man and went to take bath. The Sudra opened the package and saw the ash being changed into a jasmine flower; but out of fear, he did not tell this to the son. The travel continued, and as soon as they reached Kasi, the son opened the package, expecting that the ash might have become a flower. He was shocked and, when the Sudra asked for the reason, he explained his father's wish. At this, the Sudra told him about the conversion of the ash into a jasmine flower at Kamadheneeswaram. Both of them returned to Kamadheneeswaram and again opened the package and they saw the ash converted into a jasmine flower. Then the son immersed the ash into the tank located in that village. From that day onwards, on the new moon days of January, people take a holy bath in the sea and pray god to get rid of their sins. During these days, it is believed that the god Agastheeswaran from the temple located at Thiruppondi West village pays a holy visit to the Bay of Bengal, takes bath and offers blessings to the devotees.

The Siva temple located in the traditional Kameshwaram Village was constructed during the Chola period with excellent carvings. In the meantime, Kamadheneeswaram became Kameshwaram. Because of this traditional pride, the people demand that the government use the name of Kameshwaram in the revenue records instead of Thiruppondi East.

Chronology of Events in the Panchayat Area

1954	-	Affected by Cyclone
1960	-	Commencement of Adi Dravidar Welfare School
1965	-	Commencement of Panchayat Union Primary School
1970	-	Commencement of Sub-Post Office
1975	-	First graduate of this village emerged—Mr.Veerabathirasamy (BA) of Thandava Murthi Kadu Hamlet
1975	-	Panchayat Union aided primary school was started in Melakadu Hamlet
1977	-	Cyclone — Supply of milk, clothes and bread
1980	-	St. Joseph's Primary School was started in Fisherman's Colony
1982	-	Cyclone Protection Centre was constructed in Kallar Kadu Hamlet
1985	-	First tar road was formed between Thandva-murthykadu and Pudhu Road
1986	-	Commencement of bus transport
1990	-	Overhead tanks for supply of drinking water were constructed in Kallarkadu, Vairavankadu, Fishermen's Colony, Thandavamurthykadu Hamlet
1996	-	Buildings for public television were constructed in Thandvamurthykadu and Fishermen's Colony

2002	-	Building for public distribution shop was constructed in Kallkarkadu Hamlet
2003	-	Office of the Village Administrative Officer was constructed in Kallarkadu Hamlet
2003	-	Building for women Self Help Groups was constructed in Kallarkadu
2003	-	Sub-Health Centre was constructed at Vairavankadu
2004	-	St. Sebastian's School in Kallarkadu was upgraded to a high school

II. Cultural Pattern of the People

The socio-economic condition and the life of the village people are based on the cultural aspects. So, while preparing the micro-level planning for a village, it is essential to understand the cultural pattern of the people.

(a) *Marriage*

Marriage is a mirror that reflects the culture of a community. There seems to be minor differences in the marriage ceremony of various caste groups. The marriages of people belonging to the Kallar community takes place in the house of the bride. The betrothal also takes place in the bride's house. The bridegroom has to take all his relatives along with new clothes and 'tali' to the bride's house. All the other expenses are met by the bride's family. The dowry is also included in the name of gift. Most of these men marry at the age of 30-35 years. These marriages are conducted with the help of priests following the Hindu practice. Of the total marriage expenses, 40 per cent is met by the bridegroom's family and the remaining 60 per cent by the bride's family.

Though the Scheduled Caste people do many things according to the Hindu practice, they do not engage a priest for their marriages. These marriages are conducted in the bridegroom's residences and the expenditure depends upon their economic condition. As this Panchayat is a traditional and ancient one, 80 per cent of the marriages are organized only in their residence and only, the remaining 20 per cent are organized in marriage halls, temples etc. Generally, love marriages are prohibited, especially, inter-caste marriages are strictly forbidden.

(b) *Care of the Elderly*

The aged parents are taken care of by their children. In some places, in families below poverty line, the elders are not taken care of properly.

(c) *Worshipping*

Special *poojas* are organized on Sivarathiri day during the Tamil month of *Masi* (February-March) in the ancient Kamadheneeswaram temple which was constructed during the Chola period. On every Monday during the Tamil month of *Karthigai* (November-December) special *poojas* are held. The other temple is Mazhai Muthu Mariamman temple. The annual festival is arranged in this temple during June. The first day's festival is common and from the second day onwards the celebration is caste-wise. But, during all the days, all the people, irrespective of caste, do participate. During the festival days, the deity is adorned with jewels and taken on a procession round the boundary of the village.

During the new moon day of July and January, the Lord Subramanian from the Agastheeswaran temple of Thiruppoondi is decorated and taken for a bath in the sea and the devotees are blessed. On this occasion, thousands of village people come and take bath in the sea. The other village deities like Veeran, Munian, Periachi, Ayyanar are worshipped as family deities. During such worship, people sacrifice goat/sheep/poultry and offer *pooja*. They also celebrate other festivals like Deepavali, Pongal, Pooja, Vinayagar Sathurthi etc. On Tamil New Year day, they visit the local temples of Lord Siva, Amman etc. In the hamlets of this Panchayat people belonging to 19 caste groups live together. Each caste has its own caste Panchayat. For example, it is the 'Nattar' for the fishermen group. Similarly, for the Scheduled Caste people, the 'Nattamai' is the President of the caste Panchayat. The people of each group are under the social control of this caste Panchayat. All these caste Panchayats are federated into one community

Panchayat and Shri. R.Kuppusamy is its President. He is also the Trustee of the common Mazhai Muthu Mariamman Temple. In Kameshwaram village, all the caste groups live together peacefully.

III. Basic Details about the Panchayat

Name of the Village Panchayat	:	Thiruppoondi East (Kameshwaram)
Hamlets	:	1. Vairavankadu 2. Vettarkadu Fishermen Colony 3. Anaiyathoppu 4. Kallarkadu 5. Melakadu Sivan Temple Street 6. Thandavamurthykadu
Panchayat Union	:	Keezhaiyur
Taluk	:	Keezhvelur
District	:	Nagapattinam
Total Households	:	1622

(a) Population Details

Total Population	:	5676		
Males	:	2690		
Females	:	2858		
Children	:	325		
Total Voters	:	3377		
Males	:	1669		
Females	:	1708		
Widows	:	283 (before tsunami)		
Physically Challenged	:	45		
Aged persons	:	50		
Literates:		Male	Female	Total
5th to 10th standard	:	1175	675	1850
10th to 12th standard	:	215	110	325
Above 12th	:	62	38	100

(b) Religious Groups : Hindus, Muslims, Christians

(c) Caste Groups

1. Konar	:	362
2. Scheduled Caste	:	198
3. Fishermen (Pattanathar)	:	210
4. Nadar (Christian)	:	82
5. Goundar	:	184
6. Nadar (Hindu)	:	1
7. Thevar	:	6
8. Ambalakarar	:	137
9. Dhobi	:	6

10. Muslim	:	20
11. Kuravar	:	2
12. Barber	:	3
13. Koliar	:	67
14. Mudaliar	:	3
15. Pandaram (poosari)	:	74
16. Melakarar	:	1
17. Kammalar (blacksmith)	:	8
18. Pillai	:	3
19. Karaiyar	:	2

(d) Occupation

Agriculture	:	722
Agri-labour	:	627
Animal rearing (subsidy)	:	1000
Palm tree processing (seasonal)	:	70
Fishing	:	210
Construction work	:	28
Brick kiln industry	:	10
Government service	:	25
Palm leaves products	:	10
Small industry (carbonated water)	:	2
Petty shop	:	17
Idly (tiffin) shop	:	3
Barber shop	:	2
Head load vendors	:	20
Chicken stall	:	2
Tailoring shop	:	4
Cycle rental	:	15

(e) Infrastructural Facilities Available

The following basic facilities are available in the Panchayat area:

1. Sub-health centre - 1
2. Primary school - 4
3. High school - 1
4. Anganwadi - 2
5. Fair price shop - 2 (Public Distribution Shop)
6. Natural Calamity Protection Shed - 1
7. Post Office - 1
8. Over Head Tank - 4
9. Sanitary Complex - 1
10. T.V. Room - 2
11. Building for self-help groups - 1
12. Passenger shed - 5
13. Village Administrative Office Building - 1
14. Panchayat Office Building - 1
15. Transport facilities

(a) city bus - 2
(b) mini bus - 2
(c) sub-urban bus - 1

16. Government ponds - 69

(f) Panchayat Administration

In the beginning, when the Panchayat was started for the first time, Mr. Chokkalingam from Vairavankadu hamlet was the President. Following him, Shri Pakkirisamy of Kallarkadu, G.R.Vadivel, Shri K. Munusamy of Vairavankadu and from the year 2001, Shri L.G. Kanaga Sundaram served as the President of this Panchayat. It is to be noted that the present President L.G. Kanaga Sundaram is the grandson of Shri Chokkalingam, the first President of this Panchayat.

After the present President assumed charge, the 3.33 acres of encroached tank land was desilted at a cost of Rs. 2.25 lakhs. As a result of his effort, an amount of Rs.10 lakhs was provided as building fund to the St. Sebastian's Middle School by the CPI (M). During his Presidentship, a number of roads and drinking water facilities were provided.

Panchayat Board

Sl. No.	*Name*	*Position*	*Caste*	*Sex*
1.	C.G. Kanaga Sundaram	President	BC	Male
2.	M. Subramanian	Vice-President	SC	Male
3.	V. Kirubalan	Ward Member (1)	BC	Male
4.	R. Susila	Ward Member (1)	BC	Female
5.	M. Rengasamy	Ward Member (1)	BC	Male
6.	S. Veerasekaran	Ward Member (2)	BC	Male
7.	T. Senthamaraiselvi	Ward Member (2)	SC	Female
8.	P. Lalitha	Ward Member (2)	SC	Female
9.	C. Saroja	Ward Member (3)	BC	Female
10.	K.S. Sivaganesan	Ward Member (3)	BC	Male

Address: Shri C. G. Kanaga Sundaram, Panchayat President
Thirupppoondi East Panchayat
Kameshwaram PO - 611 110, Kezhaiyur Union
Nagapattinam District, Ph. 954365-258720

In this Panchayat the Gram Sabha meetings are organized effectively every year on 26th of January, 1st May, 15th August, and 2nd October and on other days as announced by the government. The Panchayat Council meets once in a month on matters of urgency, the President convenes emergency meetings.

As soon as the President receives the communication from the Panchayat Union regarding the convening of the Gram Sabha, he informs to the Ward Councillors along with an agenda for the meeting. The people are informed through the public address system. The people assemble in the St. Sebastian's School complex where the Gram Sabha meeting is held usually. The meeting starts at the latest by 11.00 a.m. The village Administrative Officer and officials from the Panchayat Union participate in the meetings. Hundreds of Gram Sabha members and women self help group members attend the meetings. People's requirements are heard, prioritized and decided upon. Whenever the government demands a list of beneficiaries for any scheme, the Panchayat members are informed. They prepare a list for their wards and these are discussed in the Gram Sabha meeting and then finalized. In these meetings all the people participate, discuss and get benefits.

(g) Functioning of the Gram Sabha - Flow Chart

People's needs are listed, prioritized and decision taken. Eligible beneficiaries are selected only after discussion

↓

In the Gram Sabha meetings, public, Ward Councillors, Panchayat President, Village Administrative Officer and other representatives from the government departments do attend

↓

The date of the meeting will be informed to theCouncillor through the Panchayat Assistant

↓

The Gram Sabha meetings are held on January 26, May 1, August 15, October 2 and on the days announced by the government through the BDO

↓

The public will be informed through public address system

↓

The resalutions will reach the Panchayat Union

↓

The Panchayat Union will send these to the District Rural Development Agency

↓

From the District Rural Development Agency they come to the Panchayat Union

↓

The Panchayat Union will inform the Village Panchayat of its decisions

IV. Planning Process

People's participation in development planning is essential for its success. To rejuvenate the livelihood sources of the people affected by the tsunami and to rehabilitate them, this micro-level plan has been prepared with the involvement of the people. The plan which has been prepared on the basis of the people's problems, issues and demands, aims at the development of the village as a whole. The following steps have been followed in preparing this plan :

(1) Discussion with the Village Panchayat President and the Ward Members.
(2) The damage caused by the tsunami and the condition of the village before the tsunami were understood with the help of a social map.
(3) The demographic details of the village were collected.
(4) The village elders were consulted to know the history of the village and focus group discussions with members of various occupations were held to understand the various types of demands and needs.

V. Drinking Water

Drinking water is one of the important issues that stimulate the total development of a community. Even today, several people have to spend most of their time and energy in fetching drinking water. Providing drinking water is an important function of the Village Panchayat. Since ground water is available within 10 to 25 feet, most of the people use hand pumps. In some places the water is saltish. In those places, water is supplied through overhead tanks. This water is transported to places where the population is dense.

Sl. No.	*Hamlet*	*No. of Over-head tanks*	*Capacity (litres)*	*Public Taps*	*Hand Pumps*
1.	Vairavankadu	1	30,000	13	25
2.	Vettarkadu (Fishermen Colony)	1	30,000	10	28
3.	Kallarkadu	1	30,000	19	19
4.	Thandavamurthykadu	1	30,000	15	18
5.	Melakadu Sivan Temple Street	-	-	-	21
6.	Anaiyan Thoppu	-	-	-	-

Since the people do not follow sanitary practices with regard to drinking water, they suffer from jaundice, dysentery, fever, etc. After the tsunami, the water from the handpumps located upto a distance of 1000 metres from the sea shore has become salitsh.

Needs

- Water should be taken to the tsunami affected areas.
- The number of Panchayat hand pumps to be increased:
  1. Vairavankadu : 15
  2. Vettarkadu (fishermen colony) : 15
  3. Anaiyan Thoppu : 10
  4. Thandavamurthykadu : 8
  5. Melakadu Sivan Temple Street : 12
  6. Kallarkadu : 10

★ Water is supplied only once for two hours through public taps. This should be supplied two times, i.e., both morning and evening.

★ Pipeline for a distance of 2 kms with 5 taps are needed in Vettarkadu.

★ For a distance of 300 metres from St. Sebastian School to Srirangam Road, four pipe connections are needed.

★ From Vairavankadu to Thiruppoondi Azath Nagar, pipe connection for a distance of 2 kms with 4 taps is required.

VI. Education

There are one high school and four primary schools in Kameshwaram Village. A total of 1087 students (539 + 548) are studying in these schools. Apart from this, another 125 students are studying in schools that are located at Thiruppoondi and Vizhundamavadi (3 kms) and Velankanni (5 kms). 50 students from this Panchayat are also studying in colleges at Thiruvarur and Nagapattinam. In this Panchayat, 60 per cent of the people are literate.

Issues

1. Since there is no higher secondary school in this Panchayat, the girls have to go to other places for studying beyond 10th standard.
2. As many as 960 families live below poverty line. So, they cannot send their children to study in colleges that are located at Thiruvarur and Nagapattinam. Moreover, they cannot pay any donations to the colleges.

Needs

1. Higher Secondary School
2. Library
3. Reduction in the educational fees and provision of education loan
4. Basic amenities in schools

Play Materials to be supplied to

1. Adi Dravidar Welfare School (Vairavankadu)
2. Panchayat Union Girls Middle School, Melakadu
3. St. Sebastian High School, Kallarkadu
4. Panchayat Union Primary School, Thandavamurthy Kadu
5. St. Josephs Primary School.

Sanitation Facilities to be provided in

1. Adi Dravidar Welfare (ADW) School, Vairavankadu
2. Panchayat Union Middle School, Melakadu
3. St. Sebastian High School, Kallarkadu
4. Panchayat Union Primary School, Thandavamurthy Kadu
5. St. Joseph's Primary School.

Drinking Water Facilities to be provided in

1. Adi Dravidar Welfare (ADW) School, Vairavankadu
2. Panchayat Union Middle School, Melakadu
3. St.Joseph's Primary Schools.

VII. Sanitation

In sanitary conditions, this Panchayat lags behind. Lack of awareness and the prevalence of illiteracy are the major reasons for this.

Diseases that affect the people mostly

1. As this is a sea shore village, the air is cool and so the people are affected by fever, cold, etc.
2. Due to lack of awareness, leprosy is seen there.
3. Due to poor drinking water, they suffer from jaundice (especially the Dalits).
4. During the months of June and July they are affected by cholera to a small extent.
5. Occasionally viral fever affects them.

Toilets

Due to lack of awareness and as the village is full of open fields, most of the people opt for open defecation.

Dustbins

1. There are no common dustbins in the village.
2. The families have dug pits near their houses (15-20 mts distance) and dump domestic wastes and animal wastes).

Sub Health Centre	:	1 (Vairavankadu)
Village Health Nurse	:	1 (P. Chandra)
Total pregnant women	:	32
Lactating mothers	:	83
Adolescent girls	:	420
Children	:	525
Public Latrine	:	1 (Thandavamurthy Kadu)
Individual household latrines	:	339
Primary Health Centre	:	Pradhabaramapuram (2 kms)

Sanitary Needs

1. The Sub-Health Centre has to be upgraded into a Primary Health Centre.
2. All the houses should be provided with household latrines.
3. Women sanitary complexes have to be constructed in crowded areas like Sivan Temple Street, Vairavankadu, Fishermen Street.
4. Dustbins have to be placed in

   (a) Sivan Temple Street (under the banyan tree)
   (b) (Near the school in) Thandavamurthykadu
   (c) Fishermen Colony area
   (d) (Near the school in) Vairavankadu
   (e) (Near the Matha Temple in) Anaiyanthoppu.

5. Immunization for typhoid, jaundice, etc.
6. Creating awareness among the people on the methods of using toilets, use of safe drinking water, etc.

VIII. Animal Husbandry

In this Panchayat there is a large area for animal grazing and animal feeds like grass are abundant. Even then animals are reared only to a limited extent. There was a mobile veterinary centre functioning in this area where the veterinary doctor used to visit just for two days in a week for treatment. But last year, this mobile unit was upgraded and shifted to Vhizhundamavadi Village. This has affected this Panchayat very much.

Hamlets	*Cows*	*Bullocks*	*Buffaloes*	*Sheep*	*Goats*
Vairavankadu	220	34	90	140	360
Vettarkadu Fishermen Colony	145	6	15	-	280
Anaiyanthoppu	130	12	5	-	290
Thandavamurthykadu	115	16	10	160	450
Melakadu Sivan Temple Street	240	22	65	-	380
Kallarkadu	85	8	15	180	420

There are a 150 hectares of agricultural land where paddy is cultivated once a year and, after that, the land is used for animal grazing. Apart from this, another 100 hectares of forest area is used for grazing. The causuarina trees available on the sea shore also give good fodder to the goats. Though the people are interested in rearing more livestock, because of the lack of a veterinary hospital and a proper dairy farm to collect and transport milk, this occupation does not attract good profit. If these facilities are provided, about 800 families will have a good income.

Note: Under the DANIDA scheme a contact couple has been selected and trained in livestock rearing. Of these two, Mr. M. Ambikapathi has been trained in artificial insemination and a centre for this purpose has been planned to be opened. To store the equipments for this centre, a building is urgently needed.

IX. Agriculture

There are a total of 722 farmers (22 large-scale farmers and 700 small-scale farmers) in this Panchayat. These land owners also work on their lands as labourers. Due to continuous monsoon failure, increase in the cost of agricultural inputs and low market value, these farmers suffer a lot.

Coconut, mango, paddy, casuarina, cashew, tamarind, flower, vegetable and greens are cultivated. Of the total 581. 48.5 hectares of cultivable lands, paddy is grown on 175. 00.0 hectares. Paddy cultivation starts during September and October and ends in January every year. Paddy is sown directly on the lands. Weeding and manuring are done using the north-east monsoon during November and December. Harvesting is done during December and January. About 500 tonnes of paddy is cultivated. After domestic consumption, about 300 tonnes of paddy is marketed. The major part of the harvest is procured by TNCSC and a small portion is sold to local small businessmen.

Groundnut

Groundnut is cultivated in an area of 50 hectares. They start sowing the seeds during December and January. They get the seeds from Pradhabaramapuram and Vedaranyam. The major portion of the seeds are received from a person named G. Arumugam of Pradharamapuram on credit basis. The harvest starts during March and April. The approximate total yie!d is 120 tonnes.

Mango

The total annual harvest of mango is 700 tonnes from cultivation in an area of 50 hectares. These are sent to juice extracting units in Salem, Dharmapuri Districts of Tamil Nadu and to some other mills in Andhra and Kerala.

Casuarina

Casuarina is grown in an area of 135 hectares. These are used as fuel wood and for construction purposes. These are sold to private individuals locally as well as sent to other parts of the district.

Coconut

Coconut trees are cultivated in an area of 125 hectares. The coconuts are sold in two varieties, namely tender coconut and mature coconut. The tender coconuts are sold in Velankanni and Thiruppoondi. The coconut fronds are sold as thatches for houses in the nearby villages, namely Thiruppoondi, Melapidagai, Keelapidagai, Sinthamani, Karapidagai, and Keezhaiyur.

Vegetables

Brinjal, ladies finger, cluster-beans, snake-gourd, bitter-gourd and greens are cultivated in an area of 10 hectares. Generally these are sold in the daily market located at a village called Paravai.

Seasonal Chart for Agricultural Produces

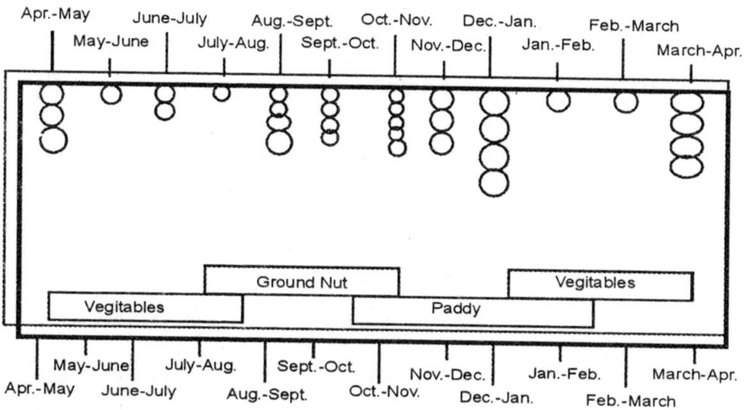

Cashew

Cashew is cultivated in an area of about 20 hectares and about 30 tonnes per year is harvested and sold. The cashew fruits are not used by anybody. About 30 per cent of the cashew fruits are used for animal feeding and the rest are destroyed.

Rain

The wetland cultivation of Thiruppoondi East Panchayat depends mainly on rain water. During the last year the north-east monsoon brought 454 mm of rain during September and 116 m of rain during October, which was the highest rainfall in Tamil Nadu. During November, the Panchayat received 967 mm of rain. These rains resulted in heavy floods and the farmers were affected.

Thus the farmers suffer in many ways because of both drought for many years and heavy flood during other times.

Soil Condition

As Thiruppoondi East Panchayat (Kameshwaram) is a coastal village, 70 per cent of its lands are sandy in nature. The eastern part of this Panchayat is a sea-shore area suitable for tree crops. Adjacent to this is the western part which is suitable for cultivating mango, coconut, casuarina, chashew, etc. Next is the clay soil, suitable for paddy cultivation.

Irrigation Sources

1. In this Panchayat ground water is available at a depth of 10 feet to 26 feet.
2. There are 69 tanks belonging to this Panchayat. Of these, 20 are used for storing rainwater and the remaining 49 tanks have water that comes from underground.
3. To the north-west of this Panchayat there is a big tank with an area of 1000 acres called Keeran Tank. The rainwater stored in this tank can be used for irrigating agricultural lands.
4. The water from the river Cauvery has been canalled to the tank in the Thiruppoondi West Panchayat and this is being brought here through small channels.

Irrigation Method

1. Though rain serves as the major source, during times of lack of rain, the water from the lakes/tanks are brought through small channels.
2. The water in the tanks is lifted using diesel/kerosene motors.
3. If there is water in the Cauvery river, it is lifted through lifting system and brought by small channels to the fields.
4. The tree crops are irrigated with the help of tank water using oil or electric motors. Some farmers use drip irrigation system also.
5. For irrigating the groundnut-cultivated lands, they follow the sprinkler irrigation system.
6. For the casuarina seedlings, they fetch water in pots and irrigate them. From the second year onwards they make small canals and irrigate them.

Cultivation Method

As the sources of river irrigation is limited, paddy is cultivated in rainfed lands and also depending upon seasonal rains.

In earlier days, ploughing was done with the help of bullocks whereas at present, tractors are used for this purpose. As they depend on rain, they mostly sow the seeds directly on the lands.

Horticultural Crops and Vegetables

Horticultural crops like mango, cashew, coconut, tamarind, lemon and vegetables are cultivated here and these crops yield them a good income.

Technology

In agriculture, people have started adopting the latest technology. Instead of using bullocks, they use tractors for ploughing their lands. There are four tractors in this village. For irrigating the groundnut crops, a few farmers follow the sprinkler method. Though the use of natural manure is in practice, fertilizers also used in large quantities. At present they are experimenting with the natural method of farming.

Natural Resources

There are 69 government tanks/ponds with a total extent of 17 hectares in this Panchayat. To the north-west of this Panchayat, there is the Keeran Tank with an extent of 1000 acres.

In the 40 hectares of land that belongs to the Thiruppoondi East Agastheeswaran temple, there are a large number of trees like naval, Alexandrian tree, etc.

1. All the 69 tanks should be recovered from the encroachers and they should be deepened.
2. Since the wetlands depend on the Keeran Lake, it should be deepened to a large extent.
3. The water canals should be cleared to enable easy and undisturbed flow of water.

To protect the farmers from floods during rainy season, the water canal from Kameshwaram to Pudupalli has to be broadened and deepened. The other canals in the village have also to be desilted.

Needs of the Farmers

Agriculture

There are a total of 722 farmers (700 small and 22 big) in this Panchayat area. Tree products like coconut, mango, casuarina, cashew, tamarind and greens, paddy, groundnut etc. are cultivated on the lands of this Panchayat. Most of the lands are rainfed. Water from tanks is used for irrigating the lands.

Needs/Demands

1. The Keeran Tank, with an extent of 1000 acres, has to be deepened up to 6 feet since about 100 hectres of land could be irrigated through this tank.
2. Water for this Keeran Tank can be diverted from the Vennaru by constructing a check dam.
3. The water canal from the tank up to Pudupalli canal can be deepened for a distance of four kilometres.
4. Marketing facilities have been provided for some agricultural products like groundnut, cashew, mango, coconut and vegetables.
5. Small-scale industries can also be started using these agricultural products as raw materials.
6. Subsidy for agricultural inputs is needed.
7. 161 hectares of sand area may be reclaimed.
8. The sand dunes created by the tsunami may be removed.
9. Loans with subsidy to purchase agricultural implements are needed.
10. As a result of the tsunami, the sea water has converted the ground water into saline water and so the farmers should be helped to put up drip irrigation/sprinkler irrigation system. For this they should be provided with the instruments needed free of cost.
11. The government has not paid compensation to the farmers whose casuarinas and coconut trees were damaged by the tsunami. This should be given.
12. Marketing facilities (avoiding intermediaries) have to be created for the agricultural products.

Keeran Lake

The Keeran Lake, located in the north-west of this Panchayat, covers an area of 500 acres of three Panchayats, namely Thiruppoondi-East, Pradhabaramapuram and Thiruppoondi West. But its uses are more to the farmers of Thiruppoondi East Panchayat. The farmers of Vizhundamavadi, Thiruppoondi West, Pradhabaramapuram and Cholapuram Panchayats also take water from this lake.

The farmers of this area depend on this lake for irrigating their lands. If it is deepened and water is stored,

(1) 500 acres of land will be used for summer cultivation of groundnut, vegetables and millets;
(2) the ground water level can be raised; and
(3) a picnic centre can be created.

Steps to be taken

1. A check dam may be constructed in the catchment area of Cholavidhyapuram canal, and this can prevent wasteful flow of water into the sea by diverting the water to the lake.
2. Deepening the lake up to 2-4 feet.
3. Heightening the tank bund and also strengthening it.
4. The outlet area of the lake should be repaired.

Agricultural Labourers

There are 627 agricultural labourers living in this Panchayat. All these live below poverty line. Due to heavy rain or severe drought conditions they are severely affected. So, their economic standard has come down. The present condition is that they have to leave the village for want of food. Both male and female workers have lost their employment opportunities. So, the entire family gets affected. This also affects the education of the children in the family. Also the adolescent girls migrate to places like Tiruppur, Erode and Coimbatore in search of employment. Due to acute unemployment, these agricultural labourers have to borrow money from others and suffer a lot.

Lakshmi is an agricultural labour. She was living in a place that belonged to her relative. The tsunami damaged her dwelling place. She lost all her belongings purchased through her hard work and she also lost her sheep. Now she is living in the temporary shelter offered by an NGO named DHAN. She said that the tsunami washed away her hut which was her only asset. Before the tsunami, she was earning Rs.40 per day as a labourer. That amount was useful to lead her life for a day. After the tsunami, as sea water had entered the lands, the farmers could not cultivate them. So, she could not get any employment. She leads her life with the money provided by the government.

She says that she has got training in rope making, palm leaf basket making, pickle making, mango juice extraction. She needs loans with subsidy to start self-employment in any of these trades.

Details of Wages of a Woman Labourer

Month	*Nature of Work*	*Duration of Employment (per month)*	*Daily Income*	*Total Monthly Income (in Rs.)*
April - May	Harvest	20	35	700
May - June	Groundnut sowing	20	35	700
June - July	Weeding	10	35	350
July - August	Weeding and harvesting	10	35	350
August - September	Land levelling	5	35	175
September - October	Paddy sowing	20	35	700
October - November	Weeding	25	35	875
November - December	Groundnut sowing, weeding	20	40	800
December - January	Weeding	15	40	600
January - February	Harvesting	15	35	525
February - March	Harvesting	20	35	700
March - April	Harvesting, processing paddy	20	35	700
	Total Income			7175

Agricultural Labourers

All the 627 agricultural labourers of this Panchayat live below poverty line. After the tsunami, their economic condition has deteriorated and they have started migrating to the other towns in search of employment.

Now, their needs are:

(1) The government has to create a food for work scheme for them.
(2) Compensation has to be provided to families which are not able to engage in agricultural labour.
(3) Loans with subsidy has to be given to them for animal rearing.
(4) Providing alternate employment to the agricultural labourers.

Tree Planting

As Thiruppoondi East Panchayat is a sea-shore area, it is suitable for cultivation of tree species. Trees like mango, coconut, cashew, casuarina etc. have grown up in the major portion of this Panchayat. There is a vast area of poramboke lands where fruit bearing trees can be planted and social forestry can be pursued this will enable them to get a good income and create a good environment. Also by planting trees on the sea-shore, they can protect the people from the dangers of cyclone and tsunami. Places where trees can be planted:

- Government poramboke lands - 8.00.0 hectares
- Sea shore area - 10.00.0 hectares (this does not come under the Revenue Department)
- Poramboke tank bunds - 64
- Keeran Lake bund - 30 feet wide and 2.5 km long
- Road sides - 10 kms

Palm-Tree Workers

There are 82 Christian Nadar families living in this Panchayat.

Among these, 15 are engaged in agriculture and two families run petty shops. The remaining 65 families were engaged in palm-trees work-climbing the palm tree, collecting palm juice, etc. Among these 65 families, 30 had licence to extract palm juice. But there were no marketing facilities for the juice they prepared. Further, there were no industries to prepare palm gur from the palm juice. These factors forced the workers into unemployment and they had no income opportunities. Also, these members have no skills for alternate employment and necessary finance. Further as this palm tree climbing is a dangerous occupation, they want to leave this profession. To improve their economic standards, they have offered the following suggestions:

Needs

(1) Training in improved techniques of palm gur preparation.
(2) Since the majority of these workers want to get relief from the work, they need loan facilities with subsidy to start small business like petty shop, tea shop and animal rearing.
(3) In case of loss of life when they engage in their profession, compensation has to be provided to these workers.
(4) Entrepreneurial training to educated youth.
(5) Entrepreneurial training to the women and help in marketing the palm leaf products.

Youths

In the overall development of a village, the youths of that village play an important role. There are 445 youths living in this Kameshwaram Panchayat. Among them, 89 are graduates. Among these graduates, 15 are in government service and 40 in private sector. Among the remaining 390 youths, barring 23, all the rest are engaged as agricultural labourers.

Needs

(1) The youths may be provided with technical training in various trades.

(2) They need an information centre to disseminate information regarding employment opportunities.
(3) Playground and gym.
(4) Loan facilities with subsidy to start various trades like two wheeler workshops, welding centre, carpentry, and to start small industries like cool drinks and packaged drinking water.

X. Kameshwaram Fishermen

All the 210 families living in the eastern part of Kameshwaram Panchayat depend only on fishing. All these families belong to the Pattinavar community. Since they could earn only by fishing, they doubt whether they could earn such an income from other occupations. So, the fishing community does not like any other occupation.

Livelihood and Occupation

(a) Details of Fishing

There are 59 Maruthi boats and 90 Kattumarams. All the remaining families are engaged in other activities related to fishing.

The major reason for their using the Kattumaram in large numbers is to fish within a short distance of 2-4 kms. But, in the present situation they have started using the latest technology and use Maruthi boats to fish at long distances of up to 40 kms.

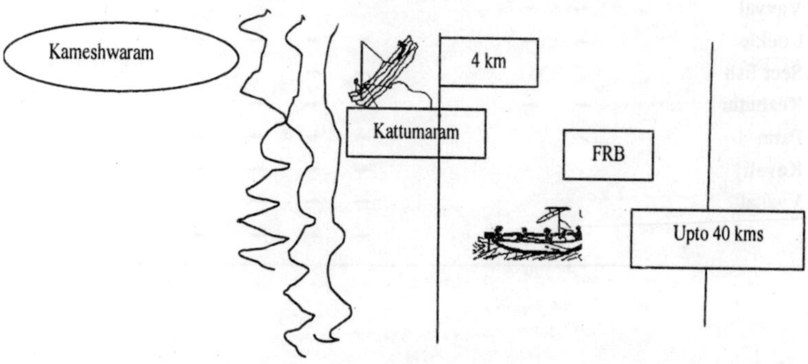

Their income depends upon the quantum of the fish they catch.

Generally, they earn a good income during the months between June and September. The income they earn during these months becomes their savings for the year. They make use of this savings amount during the period when they earn a meagre income.

There is a good demand for a type of fish named *cockle matti* (in Tamil) which is also available in large quantities during these months.

Also, these farmers used to migrate to other places during the rainy season. Those families engaged as labourers in fishing related activities, manage their family expenditure either by borrowing or by pledging their jewels.

Comparison of fishing by Maruthi Boat with fishing by Kattumaram

Kattmaram

During fertile seasons they catch fish from 40 to 50 kgs, during off season only a maximum of 10 kgs.

Maruthi Boat

During fertile seasons they catch fish from 100 kgs to 120 kgs, and during off season from 50 kgs to 60 kgs.

Fish;	*Jan.*	*Feb.*	*Mar.*	*Apr.*	*May.*	*Jun.*	*July*	*Aug.*	*Sep.*	*Oct.*	*Nov.*	*Dec.*
Gar fish		–	–									
Vavval		–	–									
Cockle		–	–			–	–	–	–			
Seer fish						–	–	–	–			
Kezhuthi		–	–			–	–	–	–			
Parai						–	–	–	–			
Kavali						–	–	–	–			
Vazhai						–	–	–	–			
						–	–	–	–			

Sharing Methods

Kattumaram

Generally, two to three members go for fishing in the Kattumaram. They travel only to a limited distance for fishing. The sharing method of their catch is that, in case three members go for fishing, the entire catch will be sold. First, they will keep for the cost of fuel for the boat. The remaining amount will be divided into five shares, of which one share will be for the fishing net, another share for the fishing instruments and the remaining three shares will be taken by the three members.

Maruthi Boat

Six to eight members join together for fishing in the Maruthi Boat. These Maruthi Boats are used for fishing at long distances with a high quantum of catch. Suppose, four members join together and go for fishing, from the total income, they will deduct the fuel cost. The remaining amount will be divided into seven parts. One part will be allotted to the boat, another to the fishing instruments and one more part will be for the fishing net. The remaining four parts will be shared by these four members.

Marketing Process

These fishermen take all the fish to the auctioning centre in the village and auction them and get the money then and there daily. The big fish merchants send the fish (purchased in the auction) to other states. The small merchants and head load vendors process the purchased fish and take them to the nearby towns and villages for sale.

Traditional Fishermen Panchayat

Nattar

The fishermen community selects one of their members as their leader. He is also called their Nattar. At present, Shri Subbiah is functioning as the Nattar of this community in this village. He is assisted by eight members. This group works for the welfare of the village with some rules. If this group commands on anything after a discussion among themselves, the people accept it. If any dispute arises among the people, they do not approach the police. Instead, they discuss among themselves and take a fair decision and justice is offered.

Details of the Members of the traditional Nattar Panchayat

1. Subbiah	-	Nattar (leader)
2. Singaravel	-	Accountant
3. Palanivel	-	Member
4. Tamil Selvam	-	Member
5. Murthy	-	Member
6. Jeyapal	-	Member
7. Vadivel	-	Member
8. Kannimuthu	-	Member
9. Soundararajan	-	Member

Sources: of Income to the Fishermen Panchayat (Traditional Panchayat)

- Lease amount from prawn auction.
- The collected fish are auctioned by the fishermen in a common auction centre and four persons used to take the auction and pay Rs. 4000 at the end of every month.
- During festivals, each family will contribute Rs.60 and this amount will be spent for the village festival.
- During disputes, the offenders will be fined a sum of Rs.1000 to Rs.10,000 and this amount will be added to the income of this fishermen Panchayat.

Fisher Women

In the Kameshwaram fishermen colony, there are 175 women engaged as head load vendors of fish. They purchase fish for Rs.1000 to Rs.1500. They carry the fish to places like Thiruppoondi

(3.5 kms), Melapidagai (6 kms), Ettikudi (20 kms), Karapidagai (8 kms), Karunkanni (10 kms) and to Nagapattinam (22 kms) and sell them.

They spend Rs.40 to Rs.100 for their transport, tea, etc., and this expenditure depends upon the places and distances they travel to sell the fish. They go both on foot and by bus. They save a margin for their future use. They lead a luxurious life and they do not know to lead a simple life.

Self Help Groups

There are a total of 16 Self Help Groups in this village, including 6 men Self Help Groups and 10 women Self-Help Groups. They have not yet been trained in any trades.

There is one Mariamman temple, one Idumban temple and one Andavar temple in this village. Festivals are celebrated during April and July. The women of this community and the children have not yet been relieved from the effect of tsunami. They have been affected much.

The fishermen of this area find it difficult to bring the diesel from the Nagapattinam Fishermen Cooperative Diesel Bunk because they have to carry it for a distance of 18 kms. So, a few persons of this village bring diesel and sell it here.

If the fish is good, they will purchase for Rs.1000 and if it is not good, they will purchase only for Rs.500. If they cannot sell the entire fish, they dry it and take the dry fish to places like Thiruvarur, Thiruthuraipoondi for sales.

There are 30 women who are not involved in fish vending. They need the machine to dry the fish. After the tsunami, they are unemployed and have no source of income. They maintain their family with the amount of Rs.1000 along with the rice and groceries provided by the government every month.

The General Needs of this fishermen and women are:

(1) Health Centre
(2) Road facilities from Kameshwaram Fishermen Colony to Thanneerpandal

(3) Fishing boats with engine and net
(4) Household as well as public latrines
(5) Dustbins (20 numbers)
(6) Street lights.

XI. Women

There are 2580 women, including 420 adolescent girls in a total population of 5676. It is to be noted that the women are more (168) than men. More than 50 per cent of the women go for coolie work. The income of the women is an important part in those families which are below poverty line. In this village, the women are improving. They have started understanding the economic activities through the women Self-Help Groups.

Women Self–Help Groups

In this Panchayat, there are 54 women Self–Help Groups and 19 men Self–Help Groups. A total of 783 persons have been enrolled as members. Of these, 26 groups have got revolving funds. These groups, without engaging in any trade, lend the money among themselves. Of late, one group, namely, Udayam, has started vermiculture with financial assistance from DRDA and with technical assistance from DMI, an NGO.

After the tsunami, the Sarvodaya organisation is providing training in palm leaf products, extracting fruit juice, pickle making, etc.

NGO : SEVALAYA, Thirukkuavalai

Sl. No.	*Name of the Group*	*Bank*	*Loan Amount*	*Animator*
1.	Roja, Fisherman Street	IOB, VLK	R.F. 25000	Anjammal
2.	Poonthalir, Fisherman Street	IOB, VLK	R.F. 25000	Dravidaselvi
3.	Anbu, Anaiyan Thoppu	PACB TPI	R.F. 50000	Gokila

(Contd...)

(Contd...)

4.	Amarthyasen, Sivan Kovil Street Poonkodi		IOB, VLK	R.F. 25000
5.	Valamburi, Dhanvamoorthy Kadu	IOB, VLK	R.F. 25000	Pappathi
6.	Marudham, Melakadu	IOB, VLK	–	Gandhimathi
7.	Malaithuli, Sivankovil Street	IOB, VLK	–	Ambihgapathi
8.	Thiruvundhuvar, Vairavan Kadu	IOB, VLK	–	Gunasekar
9.	Valamburi, Fisherman Kadu	IOB, VLK	–	Paramasivam
10.	Mahatma Gandhi, Fishermen Colony	IOB, VLK	–	Subramanian

NGO: NAMCO, Thiruthuraipoondi, Vairavankadu

Sl. No.	*Name of the Group*	*Bank*	*Loan Amount*
1.	Kundu Malligai	PACB, TPI	R.F. 25000
2.	Kamadenu	PACB, TPI	R.F. 25000
3.	Udhayam	PACB, TPI	R.F. 25000
4.	Vasantham	PACB, TPI	–
5.	Porkovil	IOB, VLK	–
6.	Daivamsam	IOB, VLK	–
7.	Etukudi Murugan	IOB, VLK	–
8.	Kayal Ilamparuvam	IOB, VLK	–
9.	Kilinjal	IOB, VLK	–
10.	Pothigai Kalanjiyam	IOB, VLK	–
11.	Uthiripookkal	IOB, VLK	–
12.	Kaleeswari	IOB, VLK	–
13.	Annai Sivasakthi	IOB, VLK	–

Vettarkadu Fishermen Colony

Sl. No.	*Name of the Group*	*Bank*	*Loan Amount*	*Animator*
1.	Jathimalli	PACB, TPI	R.F. 25000	Gokila
2.	Porkalam	IOB, VLK	–	Chandira
3.	Salangai Mullai	IOB, VLK	CL 40000	Bagavathi
4.	Kurinji Malar	PACB, TPI	RF 25000	Gandhi

(Contd...)

(Contd...)

5. Vidimalar	PACB, TPI	RF 25000	Jayalakshmi
6. Annai Indira Gandhi	PACB, TPI	RF 25000	Pushpavalli
7. Bharathadesam	IOB, VLK		Maheswari
8. Vangakadal	IOB, VLK		Poonkodi
9. Devamatha	IOB, VLK		Arokiamary
10. Sahayamatha	IOB, VLK		Stella Rani

Anaiyanthoppu

Sl. No.	*Name of the Group*	*Bank*	*Loan Amount*	*Animator*
1.	Thamarai	IOB, VLK	RF 20000	Sulakshana
2.	Suriyakanthi	PACB, TPI	RF 25000	Vasantha
3.	Gopuram	PACB, TPI	RF 25000	Chellamani
4.	Puratchikadal	IOB, VLK		Chitra
5.	Minmini	IOB, VLK		Padmavathi
6.	Adhisivan	IOB, VLK		Sakunthala
7.	Yogam	IOB, VLK	RF 25000	Kamalavalli

Kallar Kadu

Sl. No.	*Name of the Group*	*Bank*	*Loan Amount*	*Animator*
1.	Jansi	IOB, VLK	R.F. 25000	Sumathi
2.	Muthumariamman	PACB, TPI	RF 25000	Thamilarsi
3.	Semparuthi	PACB, TPI	RF 25000	
4.	Novel	PACB, TPI	RF 25000	Indira

(a) *Issues*

The agricultural lands have been damaged. Hence the womenfolk cannot get employment opportunities and so face economic constraints. Before the tsunami, the males could get employment. But, after the tsunami, their employment chances have dwindled. In villages with more number of adolescent girls and in those with more families under poverty line, the men spend 50 per cent of their income on alcohol.

There are sanitary problems for women. The members of below poverty line families are affected by a number of health problems as they cannot afford nutritious food.

(b) *Needs*

1. Earlier, there were large stretches of non-agricultural waste lands and these were used for open defecation. But, now, as the situation has changed, they need individual household latrines and women's sanitary complexes.
2. Adequate loan facilities to the women Self-Help Groups.
3. Postnatal care facilities.
4. Training in pickle making, tailoring, rope making, etc.
5. In order to earn a good income, the women should be provided with subsidy linked loan to rear poultry.

(c) *Adolescent Girls*

There are 420 adolescent girls in this Panchayat. They face the following problems:

- The colleges are in far-off places.
- There is difference of opinion about going to far-off places for education.
- Pre-occupation with household work.
- Not interested in education.

They have listed the following needs:

1. Adequate number of computer systems for training.
2. Regular medical check up at least once a month.
3. Financial assistance for higher education.
4. Loans to launch some small business.

Widows

Problems

- There are a total of 277 widows in this Panchayat, 37 per cent of them young widows. This is because, a large number of men are drug addicts and so die at an early stage of their life. This number includes the new widows whose husbands died because of the tsunami.

- In their young age itself they are not cared for both by their parents and the parents in law.
- Having no source of income to bring up their children, they have to work by themselves.
- As employment in the local village is scarce, they have to migrate to other towns for employment. Even in other towns, as the income is meagre, they cannot care for their children.
- As they are widows, they are not able to participate in auspicious functions.

Mariammal, 47 years old, lost her father at the age of 8 due to alcoholism and because of the same reason, she lost her husband when she was 38. She has three female and one male children. Her first daughter was given in marriage to her relative locally. But, due to illness, her husband also died at an early age. Her only son lost a finger of his hand in an accident. At present she lives with her children facing a lot of economic difficulties. She leads her life by engaging herself as agricultural labourer.

Needs

1. Training in alternate employment like tailoring, basket making, etc.
2. As they are not aware of the welfare schemes, they do not get their pension, etc. So, awareness generation has to be given.
3. Loans to start small business/industries.

Poverty Level

In Thiruppoondi East Panchayat there are 960 families living below poverty line. Among them the following 150 families are leading a miserable life.

Sivan Kovil Street Melakadu

Sl. No.	*Name*
1.	Thirunavukkarasu
2.	Ammakannu
3.	Murugan
4.	Rajendran
5.	Natarajan
6.	Sulochana
7.	Alagarsamy
8.	Natesan
9.	Duraisamy
10.	Rajendran

Kallar Kadu

Sl. No.	*Name*
1.	Keerammal
2.	Sebasthiyammal
3.	Kamatchi
4.	Vaduvammal
5.	Devika
6.	Nagarathinam
7.	Seppunadar
8.	Mariappan
9.	Dharmalingam
10.	Kunjammal
11.	Nagappan

Sivankovil Street

Sl. No.	*Name and address*	
1.	Balakrishnan	S/o Murugaian
2.	Murugaian	S/o Natesan
3.	Kathamuthu	S/o Saminathan
4.	Anusuya	S/o Thangavel
5.	Mariappan	S/o Subramanian
6.	Subramanian	S/o Veerappan
7.	Murugaian	S/o Subramanian
8.	Murugaian	S/o Saminathan
9.	Kaliappan	S/o Chinnasamy
10.	Murugaian	S/o Nagappan
11.	Kaliappan,	S/o Chinnsamy
12.	Athmanaban	S/o Govindasamy
13.	Anjammal	S/o Rajagopal
14.	Dharmalingam	S/o Saminathan
15.	Ramasamy	S/o Murugaian
16.	Muthammal	S/o Ramasamy
17.	Anjammal	S/o Ramsamy
18.	Vasantha	S/o Ramalingam
19.	Jayalaksmi	S/o Rathinasamy

Vettarkadu

Sl. No.	*Name and address*	
1.	Veerappan	S/o Sreerangam
2.	Marimuthu	S/o Dharmalingam
3.	Seenivasan	S/o Krishnan
4.	Bakkirisamy	S/o Subramani
5.	Thangarasu	S/o Sadaiyan
6.	Arockiyasamy	S/o Anthonysamy
7.	Rajalakshmi	S/o Ganesan
8.	Tharaisamy	S/o Perumal

Vairavankadu

Sl. No.	*Name and address*	
1.	Murugaian	S/o Dharmalingam
2.	Selvamari	S/o Perianayakisamy
3.	Veerappan	S/o Vairappan
4.	Ganesan	S/o Subbaiah
5.	Dhanalakshmi	S/o Krishnasamy
6.	Indirani	S/o Jagatheesan
7.	Perumal	
8.	Thangam	S/o Arumugam
9.	Karthikeyan	S/o Soundarrajan
10.	Vijayakumaran	S/o Murugaian
11.	Vijayakumari	S/o Velumani
12.	Thuvasantham	S/o Krishnan

Thandavamoorthykadu

Sl. No.	*Name and address*		
1.	Lakshmi	S/o	Murugaiahpillai
2.	Vedhanayagam	S/o	Kunjithabatham
3.	Karoja	S/o	Veerappan
4.	Nagavalli	S/o	Veerappan
5.	Murugaian	S/o	Pakkirisami
6.	Gnanasambantham	S/o	Murugaiahpandaram
7.	Selvi	S/o	Muthukrishnan
8.	Subramanian	S/o	Murugaian
9.	Rathinasamy	S/o	Mariyendra Nadar

Dalits

In the north eastern part of this Panchayat the hamlet named Vairavankadu is located. Sambavans—a sub-group of the Scheduled Caste—live here and that is why that place is called Sambankadu. 84 Dalit families live here. This includes four government servant families and two retired government servant's families.

There are 17 colony (group) houses (1967), one pucca house with upstairs, and 62 thatched houses. The total population is 290, with 141 males and 149 females. The population includes 10 graduate families, six government servant's families, 3 farmer's families, and 75 agricultural labourers, families. These families were fully dependent upon agriculture labour upto 10 years back. But, due to continuous monsoon failure, they had to opt for alternative employment.

The graduate Mr. Velumayil says, "We must accept whatever job is available to get our food. That is what we are doing". At present 10 families have learnt the skill of brick kiln industry and are engaged in it; 20 women have started mat weaving, basket making and palm leaf products manufacture; a few youths due to unemployment, have migrated to far-off- towns like Thiruppur and Coimbatore and are engaged as temporary labourers in knitting and other factories. Still other men and women go to distant places like Ettikudi, Valivalam, Thirukuvalai, etc., which are located at a distance of 15 km and are engaged as agricultural labourers in transplanting, weeding, planting, harvesting, etc. In such activities which last for 30 to 40 days, the male labourer gets Rs.70-80 and the woman gets Rs. 35-40 per day as their wages. During other seasons, they work in the Food for Work Scheme operated by the local Panchayat and engage in manual labour work like deepening tanks, road formation, digging canal etc. But the income from these activities is meagre.

Shri Thangavelu, a labourer says, "We do not have the habit of savings", which means that they work for a short periods on meagre wages.

XII. Needs

Bus shelter to their colony. This is because a large number of children go to school in the nearby hamlets and labourers go to other towns for employment daily.

Public Latrine

As the people defecate only in the open area, the sanitary condition is poor. Further, to construct their own household latrines, they do not have the place or the money. So, they need public latrines.

Road Facility

To catch a bus to Nagapattinam or Vedaranyam, they have to go over the bunds of the lake which is very narrow. During night, they have the fear of snake bite. So, a road has to be built up.

Renovation of Colony (Group) Houses

The existing colony houses in which they are living are too old, with a lot of damage. Being under the clutches of poverty, they are financially unable to renovate the houses, which may need Rs.15,000 per house.

New Colony Houses or Housing Loans to Homeless People

There are 62 below poverty line families living in huts. They cannot construct new houses. So, new colony houses are needed by them.

Construction of a Shed in the Graveyard

The graveyard is 1.5 km away from the residential area. During summer and rainy season, the people are not able to protect themselves from the sun or the rain. So, a shed has to be put up in the graveyard.

Sivan Temple Street

This area is located in the western part of the Panchayat. As per the revenue records, it is called *Samabankadu*, because the *Sambans*, a sub-group of the Scheduled Caste, live here. In course of time, the people did not like their area to be called by their caste and so they renamed it in the name of a deity as Sivan Temple Street. There are seven graduates and postgraduates. Baring ten small farmers, all the remaining 100 families are agricultural labourers. It is to be noted that in Kameshwaram Panchayat, this area is the most backward. The majority of the families live on the temple lands.

But the situation was different 60 years back. About seventy-five per cent of the lands of this Panchayat were in the hands of these people. But now they do not have lands even to live on. The reasons are:

(1) They have cultivated the habit of less work and more spending.
(2) This necessitated borrowing. To repay the borrowed money, they had to pledge or sell their lands.
(3) They bought items like milk and grocery in large quantities on loan and when this loan accumulated they had to sell their lands.
(4) Their cultural pattern also made them poor. During festivals like Deepavali, Pongal and other village festivals, they used to spend a large amount even by borrowing.
(5) In this way their expenditure increased whereas there was no source of increased income.
(6) The others made use of these people's ignorance.

Street Lights

It is very difficult to walk during nights in the streets as there are no street lights in this area. So, street lights are essential.

Their other needs include:

- building for SHG,
- community hall,
- training in various trades and loans,
- colony houses or housing loans,
- patta to the houses that have been constructed on temple lands,
- financial assistance to children for higher studies,
- one *balwadi.*

Tsunami

This Panchayat, along with its hamlets, was also one of the victims of the damage caused by the tsunami on the 26th of December 2004. The fishermen colony of this Panchayat was one of the most affected areas; people were plugged in misery due to the loss of life and property. The tsunami caused direct damage to a few villages and indirect damage to many. The entire livelihood sources were affected and the future of the people is under question. Entire fishing communities could not continue their work and the Dalit people who were individually depending upon these fishermen by providing bamboo baskets were also to lose their livelihood sources. The agricultural labourers have started looking for the money-lenders, as they have been left unemployed during the past four months. Many have migrated to other places to work for meagre wages.

To the families which were affected directly the government provided Rs. 4,000 during the first month and Rs.1,000 per month during the next three months. Added to this, 30 kg of rice per month and inventory compensation for the damage were also provided. But, the life of families which were indirectly affected still stands in question.

Sea-shore and Tsunami

Kameshwaram Panchayat stretches to a length of 3.2 km. The fishermen community lives in the northern part of this Panchayat. Naturally, the entire seashore was full of sand dunes to a height of 20 to 25 feet for the past 15 years. But the people started transporting this sand to form house sites and to fill up the deep parts of the lands and so now, the heights of these sand dunes have come down to 5 to 10 feet.

Apart from this, these sand dunes were removed to form coastal roads and because of all these, the sea water entered the village easily. If these sand dunes were at the same height as they were 15 years back, the damage could have been reduced. As for the fishermen's houses, if they had been in the same places as earlier, only a few (5 or 6 houses) would have been damaged. But, the reason for this much of heavy damage was that these fishermen houses were constructed on the sea-shore. After the tsunami, the sea water, when it returned to the sea, caused heavy soil erosion and this resulted in diluting the small sand dunes further. So, if even a small level tsunami hits, the effect will be very serious. So, this condition should be changed immediately.

Pressures

- Sand dunes have to be formed to the height to which they were before 20 years and they should be formed to a length of 1 km.
- Forests should be formed on the sand dunes.
- The forests thus formed should be properly maintained.
- Check dams may be constructed in places of soil erosion.

(a) *Temporary Shelter*

- A total of 72 temporary shelters have been constructed by the government in Kameshwaram.
- Six toilets have also been constructed.

(b) *Issues*

- Those living in the temporary shelters face difficulties due to abnormal heat.
- Due to heavy sunshine, the children living in the temporary shelters are affected by dysentery, headache and chicken pox.
- Since these shelters are constructed in narrow rows, they cannot lead a free life.
- In the toilets that were constructed along with these shelters, there are no water facilities and so the people hesitate to them.
- Further as the people were used open defecation till now, they hesitate to use the toilets.
- Moreover these toilet have been constructed on the road sides and in places where people use to assemble in large number. This is one of the main reasons for their not using the toilet.

Needs

- To face the problem of scorching sunshine, they need electricity facilities.
- They need to be shifted to permanent shelters at the earliest.

- Under the present circumstances, they demand medical check up once in four days.

NGO Activities

Sevalaya - Thirukkuvalai

- It has supplied rice, groceries and bread and biscuits to the children.
- It has deepened 100 tanks which had been affected by the sea water at a cost of Rs.1,50,000, using 1200 man days.
- In the case of fishermen, it has supplied fishing nets worth Rs.1,20,000 to the members of two SHGs, namely Valampuri and Mahatma.
- The fisher women Self-Help Group members (35 members) were provided with life insurance at the rate of Rs. 2500 per head totalling Rs. 87,500.

DHAN Foundation

- Water canals were desilted and widened by it.
- It provided gypsum to the farmers to reclaim the agricultural lands.
- A Farmers Club was organized for men and provided it with Rs.25,000.
- It started computer training

CARAM

- It purchased 15 fibre and 25 diesel engine boats, 40 fishing nets and 2 kgs of 'sulangai' nets for 56 persons.
- It accepted the responsibility of constructing houses at a cost of Rs.1 lakh for the families which have lost their houses.

PDA

- It supplied milk daily to 210 families at the rate of 1/2 litre per family.

- It is running evening classes in Dideer Kuppam area.

TMSS

- It supplied fibre boats and nets to 20 fishermen

ASHA VIDIAL

- It constructed temporary shelters for 12 non-fishing community members.
- It supplied box, wall clock and electric fan and books to students.

REAL Plan

- It provided food for four days.
- It is running a *balwadi* in the non-fishermen village.

DPG

- It supplied 10 fish nets.
- It has imparted tailoring training for women.

Damaged Items

Houses

Fishermen colony

Fully damaged	-	72
Partly damaged	-	130
Motor boats (total)	-	59
Motor boats fully damaged	-	24
Motor boats fully damaged	-	35
Kattumarams	-	90
Maruthi boat with engine	-	25
Vettarkadu	-	32 houses partly
Anaiyanthoppu	-	29 houses partly
Thandavamurthy Kadu	-	16 houses partly

Apart from these houses, the agricultural lands were also eroded by a sea water. The extent of area affected by sea water is 160.30.0 hectares.

Area covered by sand	-	14.64.0 hectares
Total	-	175.57.0 hectares
No. of farmers affected	-	10
No. of small farmers affected	-	101

The family of Santhi, aged 35, was directly affected by the tsunami. Her house was destroyed fully and her 13 goats perished; her two acres of land, which was her only source of livelihood, was fully covered by sea water and has become saltish. The agricultural crops like groundnut and paddy were damaged. At present her life has become a question mark.

The reasons for such a condition are:

(1) The government has not provided any compensation for the damaged items.
(2) Her husband is unemployed.
(3) She has no skill in any other occupation except agriculture.
(4) No loan facility is available for land reclamation.
(5) No agency has come forward to provide technical knowhow on land reclamation.

Kameshwaram areas affected by Tsunami

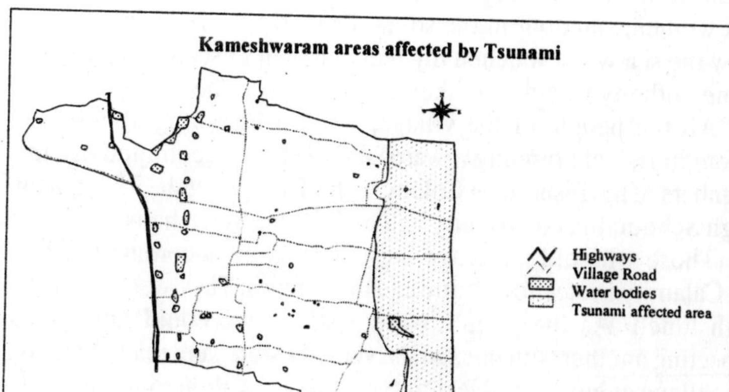

Panchayat President Shri G. Kanaga Sundaram's Experience of Tsunami Relief

It was 8.15 a.m. on 26th December, 2004. My friends from the Fishermen Colony and myself were standing at the bus stop. Chetty, the son of Thadikunju Gounder, came with utmost speed on his two wheeler and told, "Brother, high waves are coming; ask everyone to run away" by saying this, he flew away. Then, using my two-wheeler, I drove to the sea-shore. People came running from the sea-shore area and prevented me from going there. Ignoring their advice, I proceeded, approached the house of the teacher named Vaithialingam, informed about the tsunami to the police and the Thiruppoondi public telephone exchange and requested to bring all the available vehicles to Kameshwaram. Then I proceeded to the Fishermen Colony. The scene I witnessed there cannot easily be narrated.

Both men and women, were crying and weeping on the sands. I could realize the extent of damage when I saw the sea-shore. Nearly 30 houses were completely washed away. The vehicles from Thiruppoondi arrived. With the help of my friend Veerakumar, we loaded the injured persons onto the vehicles and, by this time, other friends like Vijayakumar, Udayakumar, etc., started helping us. At that time, we could find out the dead bodies of only six children. When we brought these bodies to the school, the sea waves once again started coming high. There were only 16 persons, both men and women, standing in the street. I sent them safely from there. Now the sea water touched my feet and then I escaped from there along with my friend Veerakumar on his two-wheeler.

All the people of the village, without bothering about their belongings, were running towards the west; we accommodated the members of the Fishermen Colony in the Thiruppoondi Government High School, the community hall and the marriage halls.

Those who did not leave the village were accommodated in the Calamity Protection Centre and the temples. They were provided with lunch. As the people were restless, we could not sleep, expecting another tsunami and the vehicles were kept ready to leave the village at any time. Next day, works were allotted to different individuals and they started working. The works were carried out by different groups under the leadership of specified persons. T.T.

immunization work was given to the volunteers and, after taking photos and identifying, the dead bodies were buried. To prevent the spread of communicable diseases, chlorine powder was sprayed.

Since all the people in the village were scared of the tsunami, they were accommodated in camps. Also, there was the fear of theft from the anti-social elements. To prevent this, we started working in groups. All the groups used to go round the village at nights.

On the 28th a J.C.B. arrived and the working of burying the dead bodies was started in groups. The people were immunized. The volunteers, along with the local people, sprinkled bleaching powder in the village.

Rehabilitation items started coming. We started to regulate them and arranged to reach them to the needy persons. Thus our relief work continue.

During the first 15 days alone, the six two wheelers that we used have consumed 15 litres of petrol per day. We met the expenses from our own pockets.

Role of Panchayat in Tsunami Relief Work

- Within 30 minutes of the tsunami, Ward Councillors met the President; in another 30 minutes, the injured were taken to hospitals;
- Those persons who stayed in the camps were provided with food by obtaining rice from the cooperative society.
- Dead bodies were counted and the details were given to the government.
- The dead bodies were buried properly.
- The details of the damages to the fishermen was sent to the government.
- The water in the tank in the Fishermen Colony was removed immediately and it was desilted at a cost of Rs.5,000.
- Drinking water was purified and supplied.
- The disconnected power supply was restored immediately and 100 tubelights were put up.
- Arrangements were made to construct temporary sheds.
- Since the tsunami fear continued, vehicles were kept ready.
- The assistance from the government was received and transferred to the people then and there.

- The assistance of NGOs was received and given to the people.
- Protection wall, at a cost of Rs.1 lakh, was constructed on the road.
- The soil erosion caused by the tsunami on the road was repaired at a cost of Rs.1 lakh.
- The graveyard in Thandavamurthy Kadu was reconstructed at a cost of Rs.1 lakh. The road connecting the fishermen colony to the beach road has been converted into a metal road at a cost of Rs.89,000.
- The road from Thanneerlpandal to the Fishermen Colony has been repaired at a cost of Rs.80,000.
- The link road from Vizhundamavadi to Pradhabarama-puram has been repaired at a total cost of Rs.80,000.

SWOT

Strength

Weakness	• Though people belong to 18 castes
and all the three major religions, they live in harmony • 52 women and 19 men Self Help Groups. • Participation of people in Gram Sabha meeting with interest. • Welfare programmes reached the right persons. • Transport and communication facilities. • Majority of the people are	agricultural labourers and below poverty line. • Only 30 percent of them are literates. • Absence of awareness to create employment chances using the natural resources available in the area. • Less contact between the traditional Panchayat and the constitutional Panchayat. • Absence of awareness to make use of the communication channels and disaster management system. • Marketing facilities are inadequate.

Threats	*Opportunities*
• The horticultural products like mango, coconuts, guava, tamarind, cashew etc., are grown in large quantities and cottage industries can be started using these fruits as raw materials. • Since the land is suitable for horticulture crops, a horticultural nursery can be started • Labourers of farm-based activities are more.	• The youths and addicted to alcoholism. • Due to encroachments, the water storage points may disappear. • The tsunami has eroded the sand dunes and large tidal waves may batter once again.

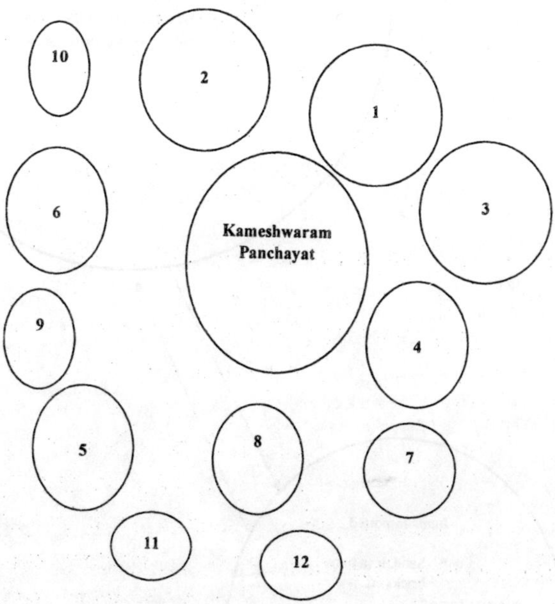

Note: The size of the circle determines the importance of the department

1. Public Distribution Shop
2. Office of the Village Administrative Officer
3. School
4. Hospital

5. Road Facility
6. Gram Panchayat
7. Electricity Department
8. Police Station
9. Transport
10. Balwadi
11. Veterinary Dispensary
12. Agriculture office
13. Panchayat union

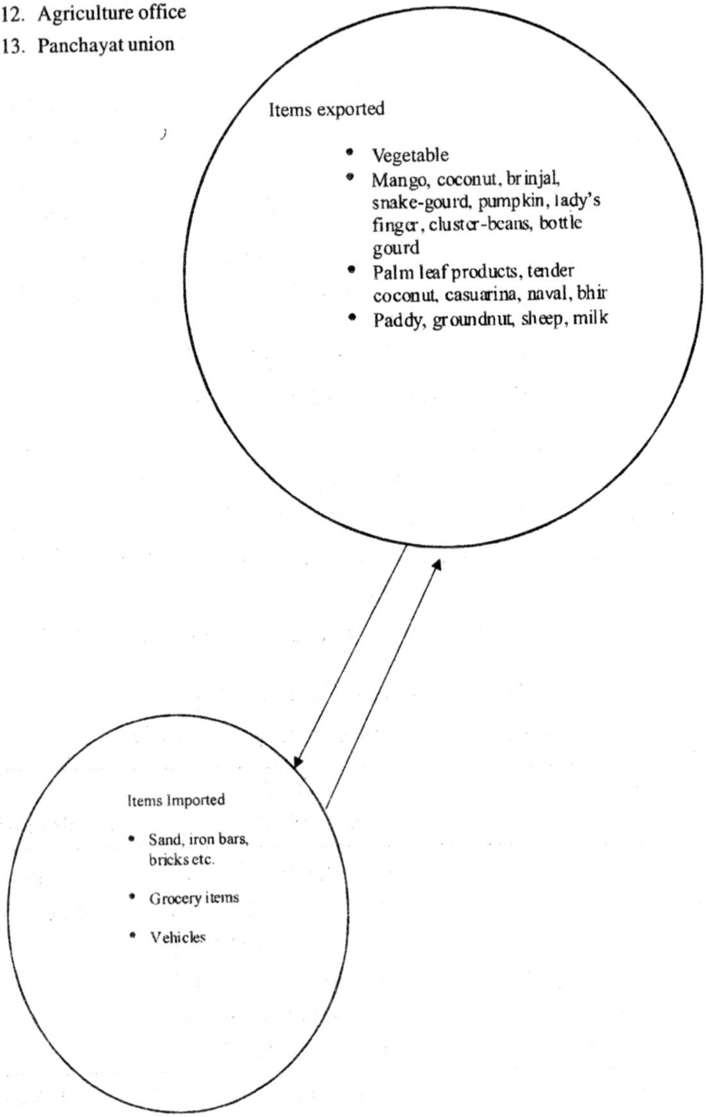

XIV. Kameshwaram

General Requirement

(a) *Infrastructure*

1. Library building
2. Threshing floors (Near Puduroad and Thennampillai Salai)
3. Shed for the graveyard (Sivan Temple Street)
4. Building for SHGs (Thandavamurthy Kadu, Anaiyanthoppu)
5. Community Hall (Vettarkadu, Vairavankadu, Melakadu)
6. Bus Shelter (Kalakadu, Vairavankadu)
7. Balwadi (Vettarkadu)
8. Post Office Building
9. Building for Fair Price Shop (Anayanthoppu)
10. Building for Veterinary Dispensary

(b) *Road Facilities*

1. Conversion of mud road into tar road from Srirangan plot-11 km.
2. Conversion of mud road into tar toad from Dideerkuppam Kamarajar Salai - 1 km.
3. Conversion of mud road into tar road from Karungulam to Adidravidar graveyard - 700 mts.
4. Conversion of mud road into tar road from Kalyani shop to Pandaram graveyard - 550 mts.
5. Conversion of mud road into tar road from St. Mary's Church to Vettankulam -350 mts.
6. Conversion of mud road into tar road from Dideerkuppam Colony.
7. Conversion of mud road into tar road from Anaiyanthoppy Rathnavel Colony - 300 mts.
8. Conversion of mud road into tar road from Gunasekaran Colony - 300 mts.
9. Conversion of the Vettarkadu to Pradhabaramapuram road into tar road.

10. Conversion of mud road opposite the Sivan Kovil Naval Thopu into tar road - 114 mts.
11. Conversion of mud road into tar road from Thandavamuthukadu to Sivan Temple Street.
12. Conversion of mud road into tar road from Vairavankadu to Manalmedu Road - 1 km.
13. Conversion of mud road into tar road from Thandavamurthykadu to Pillayarkoil Road - 500 mts.

(d) *Small Bridges*

1. Culvert - Near Anaiyanthoppu Thathakudyan house
2. Culvert - Near Kallakadu Muruganandhan house
3. Culvert - Opposite to Enago's house in Anaiyanthoppu
4. Culvert - In the link road between Kalyani shop and Pradhabaramapuram
5. Culvert - Near the house of Thangaraj in Anaiyanthoppu
6. Culvert - Near the Manmadhan Temple of Sivan Temple Street
7. Culvert in the link road connecting Sivan Temple between Melakadu and Nadukadu.

(f) *Culverts to be Converted into Concrete Bridges*

During rainy seasons, rain water does not cross the culvert and so the house as well as the agricultural crops are submerged in the rain water. So, the following culverts have to be converted into concrete bridges:

(1) The double pitted culvert
(2) The culvert in the Vzhakariyanconal
(3) The culvert in the Veerakumar house plot
(4) The drainage near the Vettarkadu

(g) *Retaining Wall*

– At the curves of Thandvamurthykadu road - 25 mts

- The drainage burn in Thandavamurthykady
- Sithaikulam - 50 mts
- Thandavamurthy beach road - 50 mts
- Near the soda company in Kalakadu - 25 mts
- Both sides of the Erattakudi tank
- From Thanneerpandal road to Andichi tank - 75 mts

(h) Street Light

- From Dideeerkuppam road to residential area - Electric post and lights
- From North Colony Street to Graveyard- posts with 10 lights
- Sozhia Pandaram graveyard road - posts and lights
- In the Ratnavel residential area - posts and lights (10)
- In the link road from Vettarkadu to Pradhabaramapuram - posts with street lights (10)
- Thandavamurthykadu - 8 lights
- Sivan Temple Street - 5 lights
- Vairavankadu - 10 lights

Village Development Plan
Thirupoondi East Panchayat
Needs

	Plan Needs	Financial Sources	Responsibility
I. Agricultural Development			
1.	Formation of milk producers, cooperative society Arranging milch animal loan to the poorest among the poor families from - Backward community - Most Backward community	SGSY Scheme, Women Development Department, Welfare of Backward and Most Backward Community Department and NGOs	Gram Panchayat, Panchayat Union, Federation of Women SHGs, Men SHGs
2.	Reclamation of 161 hectares of tsunami affected lands Agriculture and	Agricultural Engineering Departments, SGSY, National Rural Employment Guarantee Scheme - 2005	Gram Panchayat, Panchayat Union, Federation of Women SHGs, Men SHGs
3.	Desilting of 50 private tanks and - eight Panchayat tanks - forming of farm tanks	Agriculture and Agricultural Engineering Departments, National Rural Employment Guarantee Scheme (2005), SGRY	Gram Panchayat, Panchayat Union, Federation of Women SHGs, Men SHGs
4.	Formation of agricultural marketing centres	Tamil Nadu Civil Supplies Corporation, District Supply and Marketing Society	Gram Panchayat, Federation of Women SHGs, men SHGs
5.	Starting of industries using agricultural products	Tamil Nadu Civil Supplies Corporation, District Supply & Marketing Society	Gram Panchayat, Panchayat Union, Federation of Women SHGs, Men SHGs and DRDA, DIC.

(Contd...)

(Contd...)

6.	Subsidy linked loan to purchase agricultural implement	District regulated marketing authority, Tamil Nadu Civil Supplies Corporation	Gram Panchayat, Panchayat Union, Federation of Women SHGs, Men SHGs
7.	Drip irrigation and other irrigation implements	Agri and Agricultural Engineering Department, Horticulture Department, DRDA, NABARD	Gram Panchayat, Farmers Committee, Farmers Association, NGOs
8.	Compensation to the damaged coconut and casuarina groves	Agri and Agricultural Engineering Department, Horticulture Department, DRDA, NABARD	Gram Panchayat and horticulture Crop Farmers
9.	Supply of hybrid horticultural seedlings to the farmers at subsidised cost	Horticultural department, Agri Department, Krishi Vigyan Kendras (KVKs)	Gram Panchayat and Horticulture Crop Farmers
10.	Information centre for farmers and fishermen	Village Panchayat, NGOs, KVKs	Village Panchayats, NGOs, KVKs, Agri Department, Fisheries Department, Animal Husbandry Department, Horticultural Department
II.	**Palm Tree Workers Development**		
	Total No.of families - 83		
1.	Training in palm gur, palm juice processing and entrepreneurial department	Village Panchayat, Labour Welfare Department, Social Welfare Department, DIC, DRDA	Village Panchayat, NGOs, Palm Tree Workers Cooperative Society
2.	A loan to start small trades for 13 families	Village Panchayat, Labour Welfare Department, Social Welfare Department, DIC, DRDA	Village Panchayat, NGOs, Palm Tree Workers Cooperative Society

(Contd...)

(Contd...)

III. Fishermen Development			
1.	Creating awareness among the fisher women about personal hygiene, public health etc	Public Health Department, Social Welfare Department, Village Panchayat, NGOs	Village Panchayat, federation of women SHGs, fishermen associations
2.	Adolescent girls - suggestions to continue their education and guidance	Village Panchayat, Labour Welfare Department, Social Welfare Department, DIC, DRDA	Village Panchayat, NGOs, Palm Tree Workers, Cooperative Society
3.	Fish wastes - technical guidance to remove them hygienically and to convert them into manure	Fisheries Development Corporation, Village Panchayat, NGOs, DRDAs	Village Panchayat and Fishermen Associations
4.	Steps to create awareness on health and hygienic habits	Public Health Department, Department of Nutritious Meals, Village Panchayat and NGOs	Village Panchayat, Federation of Women SHGs, Fishermen Associations
5.	Drinking water facilities in temporary shelter	Village Panchayat and Panchayat Union	Village Panchayat and Panchayat Union
6.	Medical checkup in temporary shelter	Public Health Department, Village Panchayat and NGOs	Village Panchayat, Federation of Women SHGs, Fishermen Associations
7.	Fisher women - widows - self employment for 30 widows - financial assistance	Village Panchayat, DRDA, NGOs, Peoples contribution, Social Welfare Department	Village Panchayat, Federation of Women SHGs, Fishermen associations, NGOs
8.	Guidance and assistance to the children of widows to continue their education	Village Panchayat, DRDA, NGOs, people's contribution, Social Welfare Department	Village Panchayat, federation of Women SHGs, Fishermen Associations, NGOs

(Contd...)

(Contd...)

9.	Provision of fishing implements to the sons of widows	Village Panchayat, DRDA, NGOs, people's contribution, Social Welfare Department	Village Panchayat, Federation of Women SHGs, Fishermen Associations, NGOs
IV. Other Requirements of the Fishermen Area			
1.	Ice Plant	DRDA, Fisheries Department, Village Panchayat, NGOs	Village Panchayat, Fishermen Associations, NGOs, Panchayat Union
2.	Diesel Bunk	DRDA, Fisheries Department, Village Panchayat, NGOs	Village Panchayat, Fishermen Associations, NGOs, Panchayat Union
3.	Solar fish curing floor	DRDA, Fisheries Department, Village Panchayat, NGOs	Village Panchayat, Fishermen Associations, NGOs, Panchayat Union
4.	Public telephone booth	Village Panchayat, Fisheries department, Women Development Corporation, Department of Telecommunication, NGOs	Village Panchayat, Fishermen Associations, NGOs, Panchayat Union
5.	Construction of cyclone protection centre	DRDA, Fisheries Department, Village Panchayat, NGOs Village	Panchayat, Fishermen Associations, NGOs, Panchayat Union
6.	CPS fishing instrument	DRDA, Fisheries Department, Village Panchayat, NGOs Village	Panchayat, Fishermen Associations, NGOs, Panchayat Union
7.	Centre for Management of Tsunami and other natural calamities	DRDA, Fisheries Department, Village Panchayat, NGOs	Village Panchayat, Fishermen Associations, NGOs, Panchayat Union

(Contd...)

(Contd...)

8.	Deepening of the drainage in the sea area and forming a boat house	SGRY, National Rural Employment Guarantee Act, 2005	Village Panchayat, Fishermen Associations, NGOs, Panchayat Union
9.	New building for the library	Village Panchayat, MLA Area Development Fund, District Library Authority, NGOs	Village Panchayat, NGOs, Fishermen Associations
V.	**Welfare of the Physically Challenged (There are 37 such people)**		
1.	Guidance to receive the benefits of government schemes	Village Panchayat, Department for Rehabilitation of the Handicapped, NGOs, Social Welfare Department, People's Contribution, DIC	Village Panchayat and Panchayat Union
2.	Arrangement for Entrepreneurial Development Training for Self-Employment	Village Panchayat, Department for Rehabilitation of the Handicapped, NGOs, Social Welfare Department, People's Contribution, DIC	Village Panchayat and Panchayat Union
3.	Loan to start self-employment	Village Panchayat, Department for Rehabilitation of the handicapped, NGOs, Social Welfare Department, People's Contribution, DIC	Village Panchayat and Panchayat Union
4.	Awareness to create interest among the people about then welfare of the physically challenged	Village Panchayat, Department for Rehabilitation of the Handicapped, NGOs, Social Welfare Department, People's Contribution, DIC	Village Panchayat and Panchayat Union

(Contd...)

(Contd...)

VI. Widows	*There are 267 widows and 5 destitutes*		
1.	Financial help to start self-employment	Village Panchayat, DRDA, NGOs, people's contribution, social welfare department	Village Panchayat, Federation of Women SHGs, NGOs
2.	Guidance and help to the education of their children	Village Panchayat, DRDA, NGOs, people's contribution, social welfare department	Village Panchayat, Federation of Women SHGs, NGOs
3.	Help and implements to start self-employment by their sons	Village Panchayat, DRDA, NGOs, people's contribution, social welfare department	Village Panchayat, Federation of Women SHGs, NGOs
VII.	**Aged Persons** *There are 113 aged persons*		
1.	Listing out of eligible aged persons and guide them to get OAP	Village Panchayat, Social Welfare and Revenue Departments, NGOs, peoples contribution	Village Panchayat and Panchayat Union
2.	Steps for medical checkup	Village Panchayat, DRDA, NGOs, people's contribution, social welfare department	Village Panchayat, Federation of Women SHGs, NGOs
3.	Help to participate in Eye-camps	Village Panchayat, DRDA, NGOs, people's contribution, Social Welfare Department, District Blind Control Society	Village Panchayat, Federation of Women SHGs, NGOs
4.	Help to get the benefits of free meals	Village Panchayat, DRDA, NGOs, people's contribution, social welfare department and Hindu Religious Endowment Department	Village Panchayat, Federation of Women SHGs, NGOs

(Contd...)

(Contd...)

5.	Steps to start old age homes	Village Panchayat, Social Welfare and Revenue Departments, NGOs and people's contribution	Village Panchayat, Federation of Women SHGs, NGOs
6.	Awareness on the need to take care of aged persons	Village Panchayat, Social Welfare and Revenue Departments, NGOs and people's involvement	Village Panchayat, Federation of Women SHGs, NGOs
VIII.	**Development of Dalits**		
1.	Guidance and steps to train the educated youth in self employment SGSY,	DIC, DRDA, NGOs	Village Panchayat, DRDA, Panchayat Union, People's involvement
2.	Loan and other facilities to youth with skill for self employment	SGSY, DIC, DRDA, NGOs	Village Panchayat, Federation of Women SHGs, NGOs
3.	Training and Guidance to Dalit adolescent girls for self employment	SGSY, DIC, DRDA, NGOs	Village Panchayat, Federation of Women SHGs, NGOs
4.	Steps to strengthen the men SHGs	SGSY, DIC, DRDA, NGOs	Village Panchayat, Federation of Women SHGs, NGOs
5.	Steps to strengthen women SHGs	SGSY, DIC, DRDA, NGOs	Village Panchayat, Federation of Women SHGs, NGOs

General Needs

A. Drinking Water Requirements

1.	Water supply through pipeline to Tsunami affected areas	Village Panchayat, Panchayat Union and TWAD Board	Village Panchayat, Panchayat Union, NGOs, Federation of Women SHGs, the Drinking Water Committee of Namadhu Gramam Scheme

(Contd...)

(Contd...)

2.	Increasing the Panchayat handpumps to 70	Village Panchayat, TWAD Board, NGOs, SGSY	Village Panchayat and Panchayat Union
3.	Pipeline for 2 kms with 5 taps in Vettarkadu	Village Panchayat and Panchayat Union	Village Panchayat and Panchayat Union
4.	Drinking water facilities in Panchayat Union primary school and St.Joseph's School	Village Panchayat, TWAD Board, NGOs, SGSY	Village Panchayat
B.	**Panchayat Handpumps**		
5.	Pipeline from Vairavankadu to Thirupoondi Azath Nagar - 2 kms with 4 taps	Village Panchayat, TWAD Board, NGOs, SGSY	Village Panchayat
6.	Pipeline - 2 kms in Vettarkadu	Village Panchayat, TWAD Board, NGOs, SGSY	Village Panchayat
7.	Pipeline - St.Joseph's High School to Srirangam Road	Village Panchayat, TWAD Board, NGOs, SGSY	Village Panchayat
C.	**Anganwadi Centres or Child Welfare Activities**		
1.	Provision of nutritious meals to children	Tamil Nadu Nutritious Meal Department	Village Panchayat and Panchayat Union
2.	*Anganwadi* Centre in Vairavankadu area	ICDS, Federation of Women SHGs, NGOs, Village Health Nurse	Village Panchayat and Panchayat Union
3.	Children's Park and Play Materials	ICDS, Federation of Women SHGs, NGOs, Village Health Nurse	Village Panchayat and Panchayat Union

(Contd...)

(Contd...)

4.	Toilet facilities and awareness on its use	ICDS, Federation of Women SHGs, NGOs, Village Health Nurse	Gram Panchayat
5.	Awareness to mothers about child rearing	ICDS, Federation of Women SHGs, NGOs, Village Health Nurse	Village Panchayat and NGOs
D. Care of Pregnant Women			
1.	Provision of nutritious meals and create awareness about immunization	Public Health Department and Village Panchayat	Village Panchayat, Federation of Women SHGs, Women and Child Welfare Committee
2.	Prevention of anemia	VHN, NGOs, Public Health Department	Village Panchayat, Federation of Women SHGs, Women and Child Welfare Committee
3.	Awareness about sanitation	DRDA, NGOs	Village Panchayat, Federation of Women SHGs, Women and Child Welfare Committee
4.	Awareness on a immunization to prevent Typhoid, Jaundice etc.	Department of Public Health, VHN, NGOs	Village Panchayat, Federation of Women SHGs, Women and Child Welfare Committee
5.	Improving the role of VHN in ANC, PNC 100 percent immunization	VHN, Village Panchayat, Women and Child Welfare Committee, Namadhu Gramam Scheme and NGOs	Village Panchayat, PHC, Federation of Women SHGs, NGOs
6.	Awareness meeting for adolescents girls	VHN, Village Panchayat, Women and Child Welfare Committee, Namadhu Gramam Scheme and NGOs	Village Panchayat, PHC, Federation of Women SHGs, NGOs

(Contd...)

(Contd...)

E.	**Rural Playground**		
1.	Gym and playground	Village Panchayat, District Sports Authority	Village Panchayat, Men and Women SHGs
2.	Rural play ground in the southern part and Thambiran Colony	SGSY, Union Councillor Fund	Village Panchayat, Public, Panchayat Union
F.	**Educational Development**		
1.	Steps to increase the weight of those children who are below average weight and motivate the mothers to bring their children for weighing	Village Panchayats, peoples involvement	Anganwadi Teachers, Federation of Women SHGs, Social Welfare Department, VHN, Women and Child Welfare Committee
2.	Steps to create awareness on child rearing	Village Panchayat and peoples involvement	Federation of Women SHGs, Social Welfare Department, VHN, Women and Child Welfare Committee
G.	**Public Health**		
1.	Hamlet-wise monthly meeting of adolescent girls to educate on their health	Village Panchayat, Federation of Women SHGs, NGOs	Village Panchayat, Women and Child Welfare Committee, Anganwadi Teachers, VHN, NGOs
2.	Create awareness in all the hamlets on the use of toilets	Village Panchayat Village	Panchayat, women and child welfare committee, anganwadi teachers, VHN, NGOs
3.	Awareness creation on solid waste management	Village Panchayat, peoples involvement	Village Panchayat, NGOs, SHG Federation, Village Health Committee

(Contd...)

(Contd...)

4.	Grading of wastes and preparing manure	Village Panchayat, peoples involvement	Village Panchayat, NGOs, SHG Federation, Village Health Committee
H. Link Roads			
1.	Conversion of mud road to black topped road in Srirangam House Plot - 1 kms	National Rural Employment Guarantee Act 2005, MLA Area Development Scheme	Village Panchayat, Panchayat Union
2.	Dideerkuppam, Kamarajar Salai - to be upgraded into BT road - 1km	National Rural Employment Guarantee Act 2005, MLA Area Development Scheme	Village Panchayat, Panchayat Union
3.	The Dideer Colony - 500 metres sandy road into mud metal road	National Rural Employment Guarantee Act 2005, MLA Area Development Scheme	Village Panchayat
4.	From Karungulam to AD graveyard to 700 metres - Formation of mud road	National Rural Employment Guarantee Act 2005, MLA Area Development Scheme	Village Panchayat, Panchayat Union
5.	Anianthoppu - 300 mts, mud road into BT road	National Rural Employment Guarantee Act 2005, MLA Area Development Scheme	Village Panchayat
6.	Gunasekaran house area - mud road to BT road	National Rural Employment Guarantee Act 2005, MLA Area Development Scheme	Village Panchayat
7.	The link road from Vettarkadu to Pradhabaramapuram to be converted into BT road	National Rural Employment Guarantee Act 2005, MLA Area Development Scheme	Village Panchayat and Panchayat Union
8.	Thandavamurthy Kaadu border road - 1.9 kms, the mud road to be converted as bitumen road	National Rural Employment Guarantee Act 2005, MLA Area Development Scheme	Village Panchayat and Panchayat Union

(Contd...)

(Contd...)

9.	The metal road from Thandavamoorthy Kaadu to Vizhunthamavadi - 1 km to be converted to Pitumen road National	Rural Employment Guarantee Act 2005, MLA Area Development Scheme	Village Panchayat and Panchayat Union
10.	Kalyani shop - graveyard - sandy road to metal road - 550 mts National	Rural Employment Guarantee Act 2005, MLA Area Development Scheme	Village Panchayat and Panchayat Union
11.	Church - Vettarkadu - mud road to BT road - 350 mts	National Rural Employment Guarantee Act 2005, MLA Area Development Scheme	Village Panchayat and Panchayat Union
12.	Sivan Temple Street - Thandavamurthy-kadu link road - 1.5 km from sandy road to BT road	National Rural Employment Guarantee Act 2005, MLA Area Development Scheme	Village Panchayat and Panchayat Union
13.	Vairavankadu - Manalmedu - 1 km - sandy soil to metal road National	Rural Employment Guarantee Act 2005, MLA Area Development Scheme	Village Panchayat and Panchayat Union
14.	Vairavankadu Kathaiyan housing area - 400 mts sandy road to metal road	National Rural Employment Guarantee Act 2005, MLA Area Development Scheme	Village Panchayat and Panchayat Union
15.	Thandavamurthykadu - Pillayarkoil mud road to cement road	National Rural Employment Guarantee Act 2005, MLA Area Development Scheme	Village Panchayat and Panchayat Union
16.	Poomalai teacher - 500 mts - sandy road to metal road	National Rural Employment Guarantee Act 2005, MLA Area Development Scheme	Village Panchayat and Panchayat Union
17.	Thandavamurthykadu Beach Road - 1 km - BT Road	National Rural Employment Guarantee Act 2005, MLA Area Development Scheme	Village Panchayat and Panchayat Union
18.	Thandavamurthykadu South - 1 km sandy road to cement road	Namadhu Gramam Village	Village Panchayat and Panchayat Union
19.	Munusamy house area - 600 mts mud road to metal road	National Rural Employment Guarantee Act 2005, MLA Area Development Scheme	Village Panchayat and Panchayat Union

(Contd...)

(Contd...)

20.	Hospital road - 200 mts to be converted to metal road	National Rural Employment Guarantee Act 2005, MLA Area Development Scheme	Village Panchayat and Panchayat Union
21.	Formation of BT road from Thanneerpandal to Kameshwaram fishermen colony	National Rural Employment Guarantee Act 2005, MLA Area Development Scheme	Village Panchayat and Panchayat Union
22.	Formation of cement road in Kameshwaram fishermen colony	National Rural Employment Guarantee Act 2005, MLA Area Development Scheme	Village Panchayat and Panchayat Union
I. Small Bridges			
Conversion of Pipe bridges into concrete bridges			
1.	Double pipe bridge	MLA Area Development Scheme, Union Councillors Fund, District Panchayat Ward Members Fund, SGSY	Village Panchayat and Panchayat Union
2.	Vazhakaraiyan Canal Bridge	MLA Area Development Scheme, Union Councillors Fund, District Panchayat Ward Members Fund, SGSY	Village Panchayat and Panchayat Union
3.	Vettarkadu drainage canal bridge	MLA Area Development Scheme, Union Councillors Fund, District Panchayat Ward Members Fund, SGSY	Village Panchayat and Panchayat Union
4.	New bridge in the link road between Thandavamurthykadu and Sivan Temple	MLA Area Development Scheme, Union Councillors Fund, District Panchayat Ward Members Fund, SGSY	Village Panchayat and Panchayat Union
5.	Forming link outlets in Kalyani shop and Pradhabaramapuram	MLA Area Development Scheme, Union Councillors Fund, District Panchayat Ward Members Fund, SGSY	Village Panchayat and Panchayat Union

(Contd...)

(Contd...)

6.	New bridge in the link road between Melakadu and Nadukadu	MLA Area Development Scheme, Union Councillors fund, District Panchayat Ward Members Fund, SGSY	Village Panchayat and Panchayat Union
7.	Pipe bridge in Veerakumar house area	MLA Area Development Scheme, Union Councillors Fund, District Panchayat Ward Members Fund, SGSY	Village Panchayat and Panchayat Union
J.	**Small Bridges**		
1.	Near the house of Thathakudian Anayanthoppu	MLA Area Development Scheme, Union Councillors Fund, District Panchayat Ward Members Fund, SGSY	Village Panchayat and Panchayat Union
2.	Near Muruganandham house in Keevarkadu	MLA Area Development Scheme, Union Councillors Fund, District Panchayat Ward Members Fund, SGSY	Village Panchayat and Panchayat Union
3.	Near Elango house site in Anayan-thoppu	MLA Area Development Scheme, Union Councillors Fund, District Panchayat Ward Members Fund, SGSY	Village Panchayat and Panchayat Union
4.	Near Thangaraj house site in Anayan-thoppu	MLA Area Development Scheme, Union Councillors Fund, District Panchayat Ward Members Fund, SGSY	Village Panchayat and Panchayat Union
K.	**Street Lights**		
1.	Thidirkuppam street to colony - 10	MLA Area Development Fund, Panchayat Fund	Village Panchayat, DRDA

(Contd...)

(Contd...)

2.	North colony street to graveyard	MLA Area Development Fund, Panchayat Fund, Namadhu Gramam	Village Panchayat, DRDA
3.	Kozhiga Pandaram graveyard street	MLA Area Development Fund, Panchayat Fund	Village Panchayat, DRDA
4.	From Vettarkadu to Pradhabaramapuram	MLA Area Development Fund, Panchayat Fund	Village Panchayat, DRDA
5.	South of Thandavamoorthykadu	MLA Area Development Fund, Panchayat Fund	Village Panchayat, DRDA
6.	North of Thandavamoorthykadu	MLA Area Development Fund, Panchayat Fund	Village Panchayat, DRDA
7.	Manalmedu Road	MLA Area Development Fund, Panchayat Fund	Village Panchayat, DRDA
8.	Roads in house sites	MLA Area Development Fund, Panchayat Fund	Village Panchayat, DRDA
9.	Sivan Temple Street	MLA Area Development Fund, Panchayat Fund	Village Panchayat, DRDA
10.	Vairavankadu	MLA Area Development Fund, Panchayat Fund	Village Panchayat, DRDA
L. Solar Lamps			
1.	For the four hamlets	Panchayat Fund, MLA, MP Fund, Non-Conventional Energy Sources	Village Panchayat, Panchayat Union, DRDA

(Contd...)

(Contd...)

M. Retaining Walls to Prevent Sea Water entry into Villages			
1.	Thandavamoorthy kadu - 50 mts	SGRY, MLA Fund	Village Panchayat, Panchayat Union
2.	Sidherikulam - 50 mts	SGRY, MLA Fund	Village Panchayat, Panchayat Union
3.	Thandavmoorthykadu - beech road	SGRY, MLA Fund	Village Panchayat, Panchayat Union
4.	Both sides of Rettakudi tank bund - 80 mts	SGRY, MLA Fund	Village Panchayat, Panchayat Union
5.	Vellaiyaru	SGRY, Union Councilor Fund, District Councilor Ward Fund. National Rural Employment Guarantee Scheme	Village Panchayat, Panchayat Union
6.	Thandavamoorthykadu road corner - 25 mts	SGRY, Union Councilor Fund, District Councilor Ward Fund. National Rural Employment Guarantee Scheme	Village Panchayat, Panchayat Union
7.	Thandavamoorthykadu school tank bund - 50 kms	SGRY, Union Councilor Fund, District Councilor Ward Fund. National Rural Employment Guarantee Scheme	Village Panchayat, Panchayat Union
8.	Kallarkadu - near four road junction	SGRY, Union Councilor Fund, District Councilor Ward Fund. National Rural Employment Guarantee Scheme	Village Panchayat, Panchayat Union
9.	Thanneerpandal road - Vellanthangi tank bund	SGRY, Union Councilor Fund, District Councilor Ward Fund. National Rural Employment Guarantee Scheme	Village Panchayat, Panchayat Union

(Contd...)

(Contd...)

N. Handpumps			
1.	Thambiran Colony - 10	Panchayat Fund, Panchayat Union	Village Panchayat. Drinking Water Committee
2.	Manalmedu - 10	Panchayat Fund, Panchayat Union	Village Panchayat, Drinking Water Committee
3.	Perumalkoil Street - 5	Panchayat Fund, Panchayat Union	Village Panchayat, Drinking Water Committee
4.	North AD Street - 5	Panchayat Fund, Panchayat Union	Village Panchayat, Drinking Water Committee
5.	South AD Street - 5	Panchayat Fund, Panchayat Union	Village Panchayat, Drinking Water Committee
6.	South Fishermen Colony - 5	Panchayat Fund, Panchayat Union	Village Panchayat, Drinking Water Committee
7.	North Fishermen Colony	Panchayat Fund, Panchayat Union	Village Panchayat, Drinking Water Committee
8.	Kannithoppu - 5	Panchayat Fund, Panchayat Union	Village Panchayat, Drinking Water Committee
9.	North Part - 5	Panchayat Fund, Panchayat Union	Village Panchayat, Drinking Water Committee
10.	South Part - 5	Panchayat Fund, Panchayat Union	Village Panchayat, Drinking Water Committee

(Contd...)

(Contd...)

O. Formation of New Tanks/Ponds			
1.	Deepening of Keeran Lake and raising of bunds upto 4 - 6 feet	SGRY, Village Panchayat, National Rural Employment Guarantee Scheme 2005	Village Panchayat, Panchayat Union, NGOs, Peoples Contribution
2.	Checkdam in Vennaar and taking water to Keeran Lake by canal	Panchayat Fund, Panchayat Union	Village Panchayat, Drinking Water Committee
3.	Desilting of 61 ponds/tanks of the Panchayat (for inland fishing)	Panchayat Fund, Panchayat Union	Village Panchayat, Drinking Water Committee
P. Toilets			
1.	Household latrines for 800 families	Panchayat Fund, Panchayat Union	Village Panchayat, Drinking Water Committee
2.	Women Sanitary complexes in Sivan Temple Street, Vairavankadu and Fishermen Colony	SGRY, MLA Fund, Panchayat Fund, NGOs, TRSP	Village Panchayat, NGO and DRDA
3.	Dustbins for Thandavamoorthykadu Fishermen Colony, Vairavan Colony and Anaianthoppu	SGRY, MLA Fund, Panchayat Fund, NGOs, TRSP	Village Panchayat, NGO and DRDA
4.	Awareness on safe drinking water and use of toilets	SGRY, MLA Fund, Panchayat Fund, NGOs, TRSP	Village Panchayat and DRDAs
Q. Educational Facilities			
1.	Basic Education to all the children	SGRY, MLA Fund, SSA	Village Panchayat and District Panchayat

(Contd...)

(Contd...)

2.	Extension of libraries	SGRY, MLA Fund, SSA	Village Panchayat and District Panchayat
3.	Upgradation of high school into higher secondary school	Parent Teachers Association, people's contribution	Head Master
4.	Play materials for 5 schools	Village Panchayat, PTA, NGO	Village Panchayat and Head Master
5.	Concessional Educational Fees	Village Panchayat, PTA, NGO	Village Panchayat and Head Master
R.	**Public Distribution System**		
1.	Establishing of fair price shop in Vettarkadu	Public Distribution Committee and SGRY, MLA Fund	Village Panchayat and People's Contribution
2.	Extension of Kameshwaram Market	SGRY, MLA Fund, Village Panchayat	Village Panchayat and People's Contribution
S.	**Infrastructural Facilities**		
1.	Public Telephone Booth	NGO	NGO
2.	Time table showing bus schedule	Panchayat Fund	Panchayat
3.	Formation of park in all the houses	NGO, Public Contribution	NGO
4.	Planting of road side trees	Village Panchayat SHGs	Village Panchayats, NGOs
5.	Land deed to those living in temple lands	Revenue department, Hindu religions Endowment Department, Government of Tamil Nadu	SHGs, Village Panchayats, NGOs
6.	Entrepreneurial Development Training to Youths	DRDA, NGOs, Department of Youth Development, District Industrial Centres	NGOs

(Contd...)

(Contd...)

7.	Information Centre to Disseminate Information regarding Employment chances, agricultural and fishing activities and for understanding disaster management techniques	District Disaster Management Committees, NGOs, Fisheries Department	NGOs & Gram Panchayat
8.	Formation of threshing floors	SGRY	Panchayats
9.	Shed for the graveyard	Panchayat Fund, MLA Fund	Gram Panchayat
10.	Self-Help Groups buildings	SGRY, MLA Fund, MP Fund	Gram Panchayat & Mahalir Thittam, DRDA, NGO, SHGs
11.	Community Hall	SGRY, MLA Fund, MP Fund	DRDAs, Gram Panchayat
12.	Bus Shelter	SGRY, MLA Fund, MP Fund	Gram Panchayat
13.	Anganwadi	SGRY, MLA Fund, MP Fund	Educational Committee, Gram Panchayat
14.	Post Office Building	Gram Panchayat & Indian Postal Department	Village Panchayat
15.	Group houses for 100 families	IAY	Village Panchayat, DRDA
16.	Repair work of 70 groups of houses	Housing Scheme	Village Panchayat, Panchayat Union
17.	Building for veterinary hospital	Animal Husbandry Department, MLA Fund	Village Panchayat, Panchayat Union

4

EVALUATION OF THE PLAN IMPLEMENTATION

It is a well known fact that resource available at the Gram Panchayat level is very limited and they are starving for funds to manage the essential services. Moreover, there is no unassigned funds for Panchayats. Against this background, plan is developed with an objective of making the government departments work in the plan prepared by the Panchayats and approved by the people. To what extent Panchayats have succeeded in getting the works carried out by the government departments are assessed.

After the dissemination workshop it was agreed that the plan follow-up activities had to be carried out by the communities under the leadership of the Gram Panchayat Presidents. Further the officials have been instructed by the District Collector in the respective districts that they have to attend to the activities prioritized by the people through this plan. It has been declared that this plan document has got legal validity as it is approved by the Gram Sabha. Moreover any work done in any village can be supervised, monitored and evaluated by the people and the Panchayats. All beneficiaries for government schemes have to be approved by the Gram Sabha. In this context the officials have to work on the plan of the people. Against this background it was decided to evaluate how far the planned activities had been carried out by the Panchayats through its committees and how far the government officials have helped in the implementation of the plan. It is desirable to find out the strengths and weakness in the process and to decide how this process can be strengthened. With the above framework an evaluation is undertaken.

I. Objectives of the Evaluation

- To analyse the efforts taken by the village Panchayat in implementing the village development plan.
- To understand the activities focused by the village Panchayat administration.
- To list out the agencies and institutions and their level of participation in the implementation process.
- To understand the factors which contributed to the success or otherwise in the implementation of the plan activities.
- To draw lessons from this exercise for the improvement of the planning and implementation exercise.

II. Planning Methodology and Process

1. Preliminary discussion with the district administration involving project officer, DRDA, Assistant Director (Panchayat) and the District Collector to identify and finalise the potential village Panchayats where exist between the community and Panchayat administration.
2. Panchayat leader should have commitment and sincerity and they should overcome political identities.
3. Panchayats are selected union-wise and cluster-wise based on the opinion given by officials and District Collectors.
4. An orientation workshop was conducted in the respective collectorates to explain the proposed village development plan exercise and to share details about the earlier experiments.
5. BDOs and EOPs represented the union administration and the President, Panchayat clerk represented the village Panchayats.
6. The format designed for the collection of different types of data needed for the drafting of village development plan was explained and clarifications were provided.
7. At the village level data collection process was facilitated by the THP staff. Village level meeting was organized in this regard and involvement of CBOs and field staff of various departments was ensured.

8. To speed up the data collection and of the village development plan, advice of the higher level officials was availed.
9. Helped the Village Panchayat to conduct the PRA and focus group discussions in the respective Village Panchayats.
10. Assisted the Village Panchayat clerk to consolidate the data and finalize the drafting of the village development plan.
11. Facilitate the target Village Panchayats administration to discuss the draft plan in the Gram Sabha and get the approval of the Gram Sabha members.
12. Facilitated the Village Panchayat administration to brief the activities of the drafting plan with the district collector and obtained the commitment of the district administration in the implementation.
13. Organized a district level workshop on the popularization of village development plans for the wider dissemination of the experiment and the plan documentations were distributed to all village Panchayat Presidents in the respective District.
14. Distributed sufficient number of development plan copies to each concerned village and district councillors, MLA, MPs and the heads of line departments besides field staff like VHN, VAO, the school Headmaster etc.
15. Undertaken field visits to facilitate presidents in the implementation process.

III. Framework for Evaluation

1. In consultation with the Presidents of target Village Panchayats, schedule for evaluation visits were finalized.
2. The components of evaluation are as follows:
   - (a) Plan activities accomplished during the period of one year,
   - (b) Process of accomplishment,
   - (c) Experience of the Village Panchayat Council,
   - (d) Suggestions put forward by the Village Panchayat.

IV. Evaluation Methodology

(a) Focused group discussion with the Presidents and Ward Members at the Village Panchayat office,

(b) Interview with the Panchayat Clerk,
(c) Verification of registers and reports,
(d) Informal sharing of experiences with the villagers,
(e) Visit to the *Balwadi*, School, Health Sub-Centre etc.,
(f) Discussion with line department officials and Panchayat officials at the block level.

PUDUKKOTTAI DISTRICT

Village Panchayat Development Plan–Follow up
Name of the Village Panchayats Targetted

Sl. No.	*Union & Village Panchayat*	*Name of the President*	*Sex*	*Category*			
				G	*SC G*	*SC Women*	*G Women*
1.	Arimalam–K.Rayavaram	Rani Sathappan	F	–	–	–	P
2.	Avudayarkoil–Poovalur	Saravanaperumal	M	P	-	P	–
3.	Aranthangi–Merpanaikadu	Bhavani Ilango	F	–	–	–	P
4.	Ponnamaravathy–Nerinjikudi	Ramu	F	–	–	P	–
5.	Thirumayam–Virachilai	Devi	F	–	–	–	P
6.	Viralimalai–Meenaveli	Azhagar	M	P	–	–	–
7.	Pudukkottai–Mookampatti	Mangalam	F	–	–	P	–
8.	Thiruvarankulam–Melathur	Saravanan	M	P	–	–	–
9.	Karambakudi–Elaikadaividuthi	Manjula	F	–	–	–	P
10.	Manamelkudi–Edaiyathimangalam	Arumugam	M	–	P	–	–
11.	Annavasal–Parambur	Abdul Vahid	M	P	–	–	–
12.	Kunnandarkoil–Melapuduvayal	Dhanalakshmi	F	–	–	–	P

PLANNING PROCESS DOCUMENTATION

Parambur Gram Panchayat–Annavasal Panchayat Union–Pudukkottai District

In Parambur, Gram Panchayat has done a lot of improvements in the basic amenities as well as there is an attitudinal change in the mind of the Panchayat President.

Gram Panchayat President himself admitted that planning exercise with the help of The Hunger Project, Gandhigram Rural Institute, enabled him to be sensitive on social development issues. Now he is aware of the issues to be concentrated. He distributed copies of planning document to all members of Gram Panchayat, educated people in his Panchayat, farmers, Village Administrative Officer, Post-Master, Block Development Officer. He realized about the left out works only when he read planning document every month. He keeps three copies of the book with him always. Parambur Panchayat is one of the biggest Panchayats in Annavasal Union. Its population is 7860 according to 2001 census. It has 23 hamlets. It has 2 Public Works Department which maintained tanks and many small tanks around Parambur Panchayat. Planning exercise and document helped him to identify handicapped persons. He showed planning document to the Officials of Rural Development, Revenue Officer, Block Development Officer of Annavasal Block and allotted works mentioned in the planning document.

Infrastructure

Gram Panchayat of Parambur concentrated with children's health as the most important one. The Panchayat has constructed permanent buildings for Parapatti *anganwadi.* They also put temporary shelter to cook food (kitchen) for Parambur *anganwadi.* They procured vessels for all *anganwadis* in Parambur Panchayat through people's contribution.

They also purchased vessels and glasses for *anganwadis* through people's contribution. The villages have also people contributed for putting up roof in Parambur *balwadi.*

Government has appointed additional teachers for Parambur middle school and Anaipatti, Panampatti, Kadambarayampatti, Karasuranpatti, primary schools due to the efforts taken by the Panchayats.

Development of Women and Adolescent Girls

AIMSS a non-governmental organization regularly conducts

meeting for women. Gram Panchayat also regularly collaborates with NGOs and conducts meeting like eye camp (with the help of Aravind Eye Hospital) and the revision of electoral roles. They also conduct separate meetings for women. The wife of the Gram Panchayat President joined with few SHG groups and they regularly organize meetings for adolescent girls and pregnant women. Health worker are also invited. They discussed issues affected for adolescent girls and pregnant women. The Gram Panchayat has arranged and calves revolving fund for 204 individuals.

Development of Livestock

The Panchayat in collaboration with Animal Husbandry Department has distributed milch animals, poultry birds and calves. It has also helped livestock rearers to form an association. Apart from these activities, it has installed 26 handpumps, 2 OHTs (Swajaldhara Scheme), 5 taps, 15 lights and 2 solar lamps. It has converted 1¾ kms metal road into BT road, 3 km soil road into metal road through SGRY scheme fund. It has converted 1 km graveyard mud road to gravel road. It has also converted street 0.5 km mud road to cement road through SGRY scheme. It has constructed 7 small culverts, 10 pathways, 3 retaining walls under the SGRY scheme.

Public Health

People made contributions to the Panchayat to improve the basic amenities in Primary Health Centre like installation of ceiling fans. It sensitized the public on the usefulness of toilets and they targeted constructing 425 individual toilets while planning. But they have constructed 900 toilets so far under the Total Sanitation Programme. They also constructed 1 women sanitary complex.

Other infrastructural facilities in Parambur Panchayat are: 2 community halls, one library, 2 television rooms.

Common Property Resources Management

Parambur Panchayat has 62 tanks (49 big tanks, 10 medium tanks, 9 small tanks). It created awareness during planning exercise on the maintenance of common property resources management. Parambur Panchayat has a user committee which is now strengthened. They are regularly organizing meetings with the help of Panchayats. It contacted the Agriculture Department, Public Works Department Officials from these departments participated the user committee meetings. It also desilted 59 tanks with the help of SGRY scheme fund. It planted 100 saplings on the banks of tanks. It desilted 9 ooranis apart from the above works. People's contribution of Rs.2 lakh helped Panchayat to upgrade the high school to a higher secondary school. Its President proudly said that they have completely abolished the traditional Panchayat from their Panchayats. 204 households got loan-cum-subsidy. It could identify handloom weavers, powerloom weavers, handicraft makers, pottery makers, blacksmiths, tannery workers, *khadi* and rural industries workers, washermen, quarry workers, service industry persons and gem cutters during the planning exercise. But they are not able to form associations and they are not effective at present. So their livelihood is a big problem at present. This is the major concern for them.

204 families got loan from the Indian Overseas Bank for constructing houses. Each family got Rs.7,500 as loan amount. This includes Rs.2,000 as subsidy, Rs.500 as beneficiary contribution and remaining amount Rs.5,000 as loan. The Hunger Project in Gandhigram Rural Institute in collaboration with M.S. Swaminathan Research Foundation and District Administration conducted one-day orientation programme for Gram Panchayat Presidents, SHGs, community leaders on ICT and Rural Development. M.S. Swaminathan Research Foundation had decided to start ICT centres in 12 Gram Panchayats of Pudukottai where The Hunger Project is working and it has started ICT centres are in 12 Panchayats. ICT centres giving computer training to youths, children and SHGs which is very useful for farmers.

Nerinjikudi Panchayat – Ponnamaravathy Union

Nerinjikudi Panchayat is one of the underdeveloped Panchayats in the Ponnamaravathy Union. The President of Nerinjikudi Panchayat belongs to Scheduled Caste. Nerinjikudi Panchayat consists of Backward, Most Backward, Scheduled Caste and Muslim communities. The Panchayat President Ms. Ramu still depends on her husband even though she has attended so many training programmes given by The Hunger Project. She cited following reasons for her underperformance:

- Low educational qualification
- Economic condition is very poor
- Mobility is restricted
- More dependence on Union Chairman
- Scared to approach higher officials
- Lack of people's participation
- Ill-health

The Panchayat Union Chairperson of the Ponnamaravathy Block belongs to Nerinjikudi Panchayat. So, the Panchayat President fully depended on the Union Chairman. But the Chairperson could not even meet the demands of the Nerinjikudi Panchayat's basic amenities. The Panchayat Assistant is very active. But he could accomplish much due to lack of support from the Gram Panchayat President.

Children's Health

The Panchayat could provide necessary vessels, mat, toys for *anganwadi* through public contribution.

Government filled vacancies of *anganwadi* teachers in the Nerinjikudi *anganwadi* because of the constant pressure from the Gram Panchayat. It created awareness among women on the importance of maintaining proper weight in their children, women were taught how to prepare supplementary nutritious food. Apart from the children's health, it was able to construct 60 individual toilets and one women sanitary complex. It regularly celebrates school Annual Day, conducts competitions for children and distributes prizes. It provided 5 handpumps from Panchayat fund. It also installed 4 new tubelights, 5 solar bulbs. It converted 2.6 km mud road into metal road, 1 km mud road into gravel road and it repaired 4 km BT road under SGRY scheme and MLA Local Area Development Fund. It also constructed 7 culverts, 1 bus shelter using SGRY scheme funds. The Public Works Department desilted one tank. The Panchayat itself desilted 10 small tanks. It strengthened the bunds of 2 tanks and created 5 irrigation check dams.

The Gram Panchayat arranged welfare scheme for 5 poor widows. There are only 2 SHG groups in this Panchayat. They engaged in mat weaving. Basically Nerinjikudi Panchayat is very poor, and its President could not acquire required skill to run Panchayat even though she has undergone many training programmes provided by The Hunger Project, Gandhigram Rural Institute. She rarely meets the Project Officer, District Rural Development Agency and The Hunger Project Interface.

Mookampatti Gram Panchayat - Pudukottai Panchayat Union

Mookampatti Panchayat is very small, having 2 hamlets with a population of 1297. There has been a lot of improvement in the social sector after the planning process.

Child Welfare Activities

The Panchayat is able to identify the children who are below the age of 5 and made them join *balwadi.* With the help of SHGs, it ensured the attendance in the *balwadi*. SHG members' contribution enabled the Panchayat to provide mat, teaching aids and toys. It is able to provide clean space in front of *balwadi* with the help of SHGs to be used as ground. SHG also helped Panchayats to put barbed wire around *balwadi*; It has constructed 2 toilets in the *balwadi* with the help of Total Sanitation Scheme fund.

Education

There was a shortage of teachers in the Panchayat Union Middle School. The Panchayat has been sending requisition letter to the Education Department. 2 teachers have been appointed immediately. It was able to identify school-dropout children and put them again in schools. The Panchayat President proudly says they have 100 per cent school enrolments.

Apart from the above said activities, the Educational Committee had in consultation with the community has tried to improve the infrastructural facilities in the school with the active support from the people and their contribution. The old school buildings were renovated. Along with the people's contribution, SGRY Scheme Fund was also utilized in this regard.

Sanitation

Panchayat targeted to construct 227 individual toilets in the planning exercise. It has constructed 100 individual toilets so far under the Total Sanitation Scheme.

Women Empowerment

There are 15 SHG groups in Mookampatti Panchayat. The SHG groups in collaboration with Panchayat have been regularly organizing meetings for adolescent girls regarding health. Health workers and doctors are regularly invited for this meeting. They converted the SHG building into a centre for information. SHGs complained that the health workers are not staying in the Panchayat premises itself. Tamarai SHG group is maintaining the women sanitary complex properly. The Gram Panchayat has created awareness among women on forming SHGs. 7 newly formed groups have registered themselves under Mahalir Thittam with the help of Panchayats. Apart from the above said social development activities, 6 new handpumps, 9 taps, 15 tubelights were installed with the help of people's contribution and Swajaldhara Scheme. A Mud road in Mookampatti village has been converted into cement road. 2 kms metal road has been converted into BT road. This is from Mookampatti to Sevukampatti under SGRY Scheme. 100m retaining wall has been constructed with SGRY scheme fund from Sevukampatti to Mookampatti.

Apart from the above said work a tank has been desilted regularly. The Panchayat is able to provide electricity with single bulbs to 9 BPL families under the One Hut One Light Scheme. There are 83 families in need of houses. The Panchayat has built only 11 houses under IAY scheme. 20 individuals have received OAP and 3 families have upgraded their *kutcha* houses into *pucca* houses.

Meenaveli Panchayat – Viralimalai Panchayat Union

In 2001 Panchayat elections, a Retired B.D.O. contested and won the election. He attended the training programme conducted by Rajiv Gandhi Chair for Panchayati Raj Studies, Gandhigram Rural Institute. He actively participated in the training programme, and he became part of the Panchayat Presidents group, which started the planning exercise with the help of The Hunger Project, Gandhigram Rural Institute. He suddenly expired due to heart attack, and the Vice-President of the Meenaveli Panchayat became the Gram Panchayat President. He assisted in providing mats to *balwadis*, creating awareness among pregnant women about iron deficiency, upgradation of middle school, noon meal centre and the construction of toilets in the middle school.

The Panchayat has been organizing annual school day for the past 2 years, and conducting competitions among children and distributing prizes to them. The Panchayat is also running a tuition centre with the help of PTA for weaker students. It has installed one handpump, 4 street lights (2 from MLA Area Development Scheme, 2 from Namadhu Gramam Scheme). It converted a gravel road into metal road for 100 m. In SC colony, 50 m cement road was laid under Namadhu Gramam Scheme. It constructed one culvert in Namadhu Gramam Scheme. 90 per cent of households have family ration cards. It has also provided soakpits for 50 houses, drainage for 200mts, 200 individual toilets.

OHT operators of the Meenaveli Panchayat have undergone training on water management. 8 SHGs have received revolving funds. The Panchayat sensitized women on the formation of SHGs in the SC colony and 12 groups have been formed so far. 200 families have got Farmers Card.

K. Rayawaram Village Panchayat

It was proposed in the plan to make arrangements for a separate building for the branch post office. Now as there is adequate space available at the rural library, the branch post-office is functioning in one of the rooms in the library. As referred to in the plan, an increase in the frequency of public transportation service, the transport corporation authorities were contacted and they positively conceded the request. The plan of construction of a marriage hall was realized thanks to the grant given by the DRDA. About Rs.1.25 lakh was mobilized as the public contribution and Rs.3.75 lakh was the government grant.

The kitchen shed in the primary school was repaired from the village Panchayat fund as proposed in the plan. SHG members came forward to plant trees around the sanitation complex. With regard to solid waste management, as proposed in the plan, 25 dustbins were distributed to families. A separate manure yard was constructed by the union administration. 16 eligible persons among widows and aged were identified to receive the government pension and other services. 2 disabled persons were given pension.

One new SHG was organized; loan for rearing of milch animal was arranged by the Panchayat leader. With regard to the improvement in the provision of water supply, handpumps have been installed at Bharati Nagar and middle street; and the pipeline extension was completed. Rs.30,000 was spent in this regard. It was a special fund which was availed by showing the plan initiative from the district authorities.

Out of 15 street lights proposed in the plan, 11 street lights were provided from the Eleventh Financial Commission and Tamil Nadu Scheme of Namathu Gramam incentive. Rs.4 lakh was spent in the improvement of road as per the plan. Four works were completed according to the plan, i.e., the earthen road was converted to metal and three repair works have been attended. One small bridge was constructed in the middle street of Rayawaram, the main hamlet. 306 household latrines were provided apart from providing community toilets and school toilets. One auditorium/open air theatre was constructed with the people's contribution. The desiltation of irrigation kanmoi was proposed from the incentive fund awarded to the village Panchayat's efforts in keeping the Panchayat clean and tidy. Efforts to get poramboke lands for the poor, for the construction of houses to them which is yet to be materialized due to want of adequate land. From the public contribution the thorny bushes in the kanmoi were removed. The SHG members met the refreshment expenditure for the volunteers under Navapra scheme, training was received by SHG members at Kudimiyanmalai in the production of vermicompost. 25 poor families have been enlisted for to avail free noon meal scheme (AAY).

Melathur Village Panchayat

With regard to the improvement in sanitation, 400 household latrines were constructed under TRSP. In the union primary school, as per plan, construction of a new kitchen shed has been undertaken. Teaching materials and equipments were procured from the grant given under SSA scheme. To improve water supply, extension of pipeline was carried out. Under road improvement works, earthen road was converted into grave yard. The Department of Rural Highways appreciated the efforts. CC road, construction repair to bitumen road, construction of new earthen road were done from the village Panchayat fund. Four threshing floors were provided to the farmers. As per plan, the library was built from the contribution of the public. Out of nine poor, four were provided with free house sites. *Pucca* house would be given to them in the next year's allocation of IAY. This village is selected for model planning under Poverty Reduction Programme of Pudhu Vazhvu Scheme.

Veerachilai Village Panchayat

It was proposed in the plan to establish a separate *balwadi* for the children in the hamlet Piravayal. But due to lack of required number of children, it was not accomplished. The nutritional status of children are properly monitored by the SHG members and in consultation with the VHN, the mothers got sensitized on child rearing. The needed additional building in the middle school was constructed. Now the village committee in association with the village Panchayat took steps to upgrade the school into a high school. A toilet in the school was constructed. And in the Veeranampatti primary school, filling up of teachers vacancy was successfully done. Now efforts are taken to upgrade the school into a middle school.

The SHG members are not fully involved in the economic activities as they would get daily wages in farms. Disabled persons were mobilized for a national camp at block level. And doctors checked and issued certificates with regard to the percentage of disability and distributed identity cards to the eligible disabled person. Poor SC families and widows who were left out were enlisted in SHG activities, so that they could get opportunity for economic activities. To augment income to the village Panchayats, 300 trees were planted and proper arrangement was made to protect them. Community volunteers have came forward to irrigate the plants properly. To improve water supply, a special fund was received for digging one filter point and as there is adequate water supply, conversion of the filter point's into a mini power pump was successfully carried out. 3 OHT and 20 public taps were provided from the TWAD funds.

15 poor (10 SC and 5 BC) families have been provided houses under IAY scheme. With regard to road improvement, CC road and retaining wall works were completed. Step was taken to orient youths in the craft of pottery. But there was no good response from the youths as they preferred wage employment in the nearby towns and even abroad, i.e., in gulf countries, according to the president. In three kanmois, desilting work was done from the allocation under basic improvement activities. Proposal was submitted to the government to establish a veterinary hospital. A mini godown was constructed for the storage of PDS commodities.

Merpanaikadu Village Panchayat

There are four primary schools and one higher secondary school in this village Panchayat. After the preparation of plan document, a lot of activities have been carried out for the betterment of educational institutions and their service delivery. Under NABARD their assistance, at a cost of 56 lakh rupees, 13 classrooms were constructed. From the MLA allocation and TWAD assistance, over-head tank facility was provided to ensure adequate water supply to all students in the higher secondary school. The Social Welfare Department has come forward to construct a hostel for the SC and

MBC students and allotted Rs.36 lakh. Under SSA scheme toilets were provided in all schools. From the public contribution, fencing was done in one of the primary schools. Water supply is provided to schools.

At *Anganwadis*, to ensure learning atmosphere, drawing/ painting of birds, animals, national leaders were done. The VHN has properly monitored the weighing of children and their nutritional status. At PHC, a mini power pump was provided from the allocation made to Village Panchayat under Minimum Basic Amenities Improvement Scheme. The proposal in the plan in this regard was by the district administration and immediately it was looked into. Health awareness and special awareness on Leprosy was conducted to the adult and adolescence girls who engaged in coir production activities. All eligible families were given new ration cards. As per the request in the plan, the Government has taken steps to pay the heavy dues to the department of electricity. It was about 11.50 lakh rupees. Now the Government of Tamil Nadu and the union council proposed to contribute in this regard.

The encroachment problem in the Kuthirankudi lake was taken up and the revenue department has not yet initiated any action. But another encroachment process at the site of OHT was successfully solved. Now a new borewell is functioning to augment the provision of water supply. Road improvement works were carried out in four hamlets utilizing SGRY scheme fund, Namathu Gramam inclusive fund and MLA fund. As most of the roads are earthen roads, they were converted into gravel roads. The local MLA also allocated one lakh rupees to improve the approach road leading to the burial ground as proposed in the plan. 645 household latrines were constructed and members of SHG are properly utilizing the same.

The SHG members have orientation in the production of composite manure from coconut fibre through the guidance of MSSRF. This technology is very much fruitful as there is a threat to the environment from the coir pith/wastage which was lying untreated. Now the SHG members make use of the coir waste in their compost manufacturing. Further the SHG members were involved in planting of trees and they protect and water the plants. The Member of Parliament of the area supported the desilting of tank near Mariamman temple. From the allocation, the union council desilted the Koothirenkdui lake.

Due to involvement of the THP-GRI plan process, the village Panchayat was able to build alliances with the MSSRF and availed their technical guidances for the agriculture activities. Further, when the procurement of paddy was started by the government, the village Panchayat administration successfully got the procurement centre at the Merpanaikadu Panchayat jurisdiction. As there were many patients suffering from tuberculosis, suitable steps were taken by the health authorities as per plan proposal. Now, through VHN, tablets are distributed and the patients are effectively monitored.

250 poor families were identified to avail one hut one light scheme benefit. 19 aged persons are receiving pension and step was taken to avail free bus passes to 12 disabled persons. 66 members of SHG have availed housing loan of Rs.10,000 with a subsidy of Rs.2500 from the Indian Bank. The President informed that it was accomplished only through planning and guidance of THP-GRI.

Melapuduvayal Village Panchayat

The Panchayat President informed that she had the orientation in the effective management of village Panchayat. And so she was able to get in touch with the management of the engineering college, functioning near the village. She informed that the students' camp organized at her village by the engineering college was very useful. They created awareness on sanitation and public health. They helped in planting of trees. They conducted cultural programme for the school students. They helped in the construction of kitchen shed at the Anganwadi located in the hamlet, Melapuduvayal. With regard to the plan implementation, toilets in schools were provided. And it was planned to organize school annual day and parents meeting was held in this regard.

The PDS is a part time one. Step was taken to make it as a full time shop. With regard to the improvement in the water supply, 2 hand pumps and 2 mini tanks were provided. 2 OHTs were constructed and 14 new taps were provided to ensure adequate water in two hamlets, namely south Thuvaravayal and North Thuvaravayal. Funds from Namathu Gramam, Union Council Fund and District Council Funds have been utilized apart from TWAD allocation to implement the above referred works. With regard to road improvement works, two metal roads and one ground work for another road have been executed as planned. Proposal of improving of the Keeranur to South Thuvaravayal road was sanctioned. But due to problem in the auctioning of tender it was delayed. 6 culverts were proposed in the plan of which one small bridge work was executed. A proposal has been sent to sanction a sub-health centre at this village Panchayat. The Village Panchayat maintains good rapport with the NGO and their SHG activities by which the economic activity of milch animal rearing has become a success, the President told.

In three water bodies, desilting was done. The district councillor contributed for the desilting and erection of sink in one tank. Four ooranis have been taken for maintenance work like construction of a ghat. 400 eligible persons were chosen under Uzhavar Protection Scheme. Twenty poor were selected for free rice scheme.

Poovalur Village Panchayat

With regard to road improvement, five works have been completed as proposed in the plan. Fund was mobilized from the MLA of the area apart from special fund received from the district administration. Waste land development programme was implemented in this village Panchayat. Desilting of 400 of tanks, tree planting and kitchen gardening have been executed which were proposed in the planned activities. 300 household latrines were constructed. Community toilet is kept clean and SHG members are advised to undertake its upkeep. 32 SC and 5 BC families have benefited under IAY scheme. Further, under *katcha* house scheme 17 SC and 9 BC families were benefited. Selection of eligible families was properly done from the list available in the plan document. 4 disabled persons have been provided with cycle, hearing aid and monthly pension. Seven poor families have been given credit with subsidy to carry out their economic activities.

Funds for SHG was received from the union council. 17 poor families have been given household patta.

Pudukkottai District Plan Implementation Process Observation made by the Presidents

1. It enabled the people to participate and frankly express their needs.
2. Helped to understand the status/interest of the general public.
3. Served as the data bank readily available to furnish whenever and wherever there were requests.
4. Facilitated to strengthen the rapport with various sectoral department officials.
5. Equipped to mobilize resources for the fulfilment of needs projected in the plan.
6. Helped to mobilize special funds when the allocation from the routine sources was not available.
7. Helped to motivate ward members' participation.
8. Helped to identify volunteers who came forward to extend their cooperation in the process of plan implementation.
9. Encouraged to become model to other neighbouring village Panchayats.
10. Helped to take priorities projected in the plan when the fund is allocated from the other departments, without delay or deliberations.

The Status of the Nearby Village Panchayats as observed by the Clerks of The Hunger Project Plan Villages

1. No planned works were taken up. Only works which were at once demanded/or as per the institution of officials, have been taken up.
2. Lengthy/unnecessary deliberations on the selection of the works delayed the implementation process in non-plan villages.
3. For want of data/details, finalization of selection of work/ beneficiaries was delayed.

4. Improving the people's understanding was a challenging task.

Suggestions to Strengthen the Plan Exercise and its Follow-up Process

1. Ensure compulsory officials participation of field officials from line departments.
2. Ensure the participation of union councillors in the implementation process.
3. There should be more number of village Panchayats targeted in the plan drafting so as a critical mass would influence the course of action during the implementing process.
4. Periodical meetings of plan committee are very much needed to orient them in respect of their commitment/involvement in the plan implementation process.
5. There should be periodical interface between the village Panchayat and The Hunger Project—Gandhigram Rural Institute Team.
6. Interface with the higher representatives like MLA/MP/District Panchayat/Ward Members should be officially arranged by The Hunger Project—Gandhigram Rural Institute.
7. There should be a core fund allocated by the facilitator The Hunger Project-Gandhigram Rural Institute to meet the incidental/other needed expenditure during the plan implementation process. Further there should be incentive money whenever the village Panchayats make a stride in accomplishing plan activities.
8. Orient local NGOs, CBO in the process, to ensure local involvement.
9. Orient the mindset of officials in the process.
10. Orient general public as they show interest only in the provision of basic amenities like water supply, street lights, CC road etc. Development vision/interest has to be created in the public/sections concerned.

11. The absence of legal power to the Panchayati Raj Institutions in respect of the other departmental programmes is a big handicap. Generally what could be done through the department of RD and Panchayati Raj in the plan needs is somewhat accomplished; whereas the needs of other sectoral department is a hampered.
12. Political interference, the existing system of allocation funds by MP, MLA under Local Area Development should be done away to ensure planned development.

Observation made by Officials

1. The plan initiative itself in the right direction in the midst of tied up allocation situation existed in Panchayati Raj Institutions.
2. Resources are available at various points. Plan initiative motivates the Village Panchayats to pool maximum resources.
3. It mobilizes the villagers and educates them about the significance of development through Panchayati Raj.
4. Political interference/influence would make a difference on the plan implementation process. Hence public interest/ involvement in the plan implementation has to be ensured. Special efforts are needed to educate them, otherwise the Village Panchayat President is left alone in this process.
5. There should be block level-line department officials meeting to make them understand the plan-experiment undertaken by The Hunger Project-Gandhigram Rural Institute. Further, there should be a review at the district level to instill the commitment to the various officials who are involved in the experiment.
6. Mass-media have to be involved in the experiment.
7. Training to volunteers at the village level in the collection of data/details for drafting of a plan must be provided.
8. There are several volunteers/field staff at the Village Panchayat level working in the activities under programmes like neo-literacy, Namathu Gramam, Total Rural Sanitation,

Women Development. These field workers have to be grouped together, to be oriented in the concept of Panchayati Raj Institutions/Decentralization and grassroots planning - data collection exercise.

PLAN IMPACT

Success Stories

1. At the Village Panchayat ***Merpanaikkadu***, there is a planned activity of formation of new road to Kuyilan colony. When the Village Panchayat administration has taken up the work as planned, there was an objection from a local individual. He claimed that there was no public passage to Kuyilan colony and the site proposed to form the road was his personal property enjoyed over a period of time. He made a complaint to the police official and tried to prevent at any cost the efforts of the Village Panchayat. The Village Panchayat President took the issue with the police as well as revenue officials. She showed the plan document – the proof that it was the felt need, discussed openly at the Gram Sabha and approved by the Gram Sabha, and at last the acknowledgement of the Collector — by his official letter appended in the plan document. The police official got the printed copy of the plan and advised the complainant not to unnecessarily interfere in the legitimate activity of the Village Panchayat. The formation of the earthern road was successfully carried out as per the plan. The plan document served as an official document of the Gram Sabha.

2. K. Rayavaram

Desilting the village ooranis and kanmois was Rani Sathappan's (President, K.Rayavaram Panchayat, Arimalai Union, Pudukkottai District) first step after the micro-level planning exercise with the help of his people and their commitment to actively participate Rani Sathappan first removed all encroachments and over grown trees around the water bodies.

Training programme given by The Hunger Project, Gandhigram Rural Institute intensified her awareness on the importance of collaborating with the district administration. She created rapport with District Collector, Project Officer, DRDA and all other officials.

With continuous struggle for 3 years and District Collector's help she was able to mobilize funds from the Government to desilt tanks.

Evaluation Report on the Process of Implementation of the Village Development Plan in Pudukkottai District

Sl. No.	Name of the Panchayat	Activities undertaken by the Panchayat								
		Housing	*Drinking Water*	*Street lights*	*Road*	*Sanitation*	*PDS*	*Education System*	*Others*	*Observation*
1.	Parambur	204 households – loan-cum subsidy	26 handpumps, 20 OHTs, (Swajaldhara) 5 taps	15 street lights, 2 solar lamps	1¾ kms BT road, 3 km metal road	900 individual toilets, 1 women sanitary complex	—	Appointment of additional teachers	*Anganwadi* building, procurement of vessels, health camps, desilting of tanks, ICT centre	Improvement in basic amenities, concentration development on social issues.
2.	Nerinjikudi	—	5 handpumps	4 tube lights, 5 solar lamps	6 km metal road, 1 km gravel road, repairing 4 km BT road	60 individual toilets and women sanitary complex	—	Filling up of vacancies, Annual Day	7 culverts, 1 bus shelter, Desilting of tanks, 5 irrigation check dams	Low performance of Panchayat President, dependence on the Chairperson of the Panchayat Union.
3.	Mookampatti	11 houses	6 new hand pumps, 9 taps, 15 tube lights	—	2 km BT road	women Sanitary complex	—	Appointment of teachers, 100percent school enrolment, active involvement of Education Committee, renovation of old building	Active formation of SHG groups, formation of women information centre, retaining wall	Improvements in social sector.
4.	Meenaveli	—	1 hand pump, 4 street lights	—	50 m cement road	Drainage for 200 mts, 200 individual toilets	90percent family cards		Tuition centre 50 houses	Soakpits for
5.	K.Rayavaram	—	—	11	4 work, 1 small bridge	306 household latrines	25 AAY	Kitchen shed in primary school	Marriage hall, solid waste management, government pension-16 members, loan for SHGs, desilting of tanks	—

(Condt...)

6.	Melathur	—	Extension of pipe line	—	Earthen road	400 household latrines	—	Teaching materials, kitchen shed	—	Model village, Puduhu Vazhvu scheme will be implemented.
7.	Virachilai	—	Filter point, mini power pump, 3 OHT, 20 public tap	—	CC road, retaining wall	—	—	Additional building, upgradation of high school, filling up of vacancies	—	—
8.	Merpanaikadu	—	OHT	—	Road improvement	—	Ration card for all families	Water supply to higher secondary hostel for SC school, and MBC	Compost manure, encroachment removal	THP-GRI MSSRF collaboration for ICT and agriculture development
9.	Melapudu-vayal	—	2 handpumps, 2 mini tanks, 2 OHT, 4 new taps	—	3 metal road work	Awareness creation	Part time to full time shop	—	Ulavar production scheme card	—
10.	Poovalur	37 new houses, latrines 26 *kutcha* houses	-	—	—	300 households	—	—	4 disabled provided cycle, hearing aid and monthly pension	—

only 231 cards are in the RMTC Nagar and the balance is under the nearby Village Panchayat, namely Alamarathupatti. He contacted the President of that Panchayat and proposed a joint appeal for the establishment of a separate Public Distribution System shop for RMTC Nagar.

Educational Development Activities

Toilets for students in both primary schools located at Kalikkampatti and Kottaipatti were proposed in the plan. The same was completed from the allocation of union fund. Kitchen shed facilities were demanded and for providing furniture, donors were contacted, the President added.

The activities of the village Health nurse is very much useful to the community, the President informed. The nurse is staying at Kottaipatti in Munnilakottai Panchayat. She mobilises adolescent girls especially in the evening and creates awareness among them about RCH activities, the President told. It is learnt that from the Village Panchayat of Kalikkampatti several young women are working in the spinning and textile mills functioning in and around the area. It was emphasized that all working women should understand the issues of AIDS, gender discrimination and exploitation. The Village Panchayat must utilize the services of NGO and health officals in this regard.

There are two *balwadies* of which one is run by the Management of the Gandhigram Trust. Toilet for children is not available in this *balwadi*, whereas toilet has been provided in the government run *balwadi*. The President informed that he discussed the matter with the SHG members who are facilitated by the NGO, Gandhigram Trust. The Government balwadi building earlier was in a dilapidated condition and it was reported to the district administration. Now a new building has been constructed and the balwadi is functioning in the new building.

SHG activities — Earlier there were 14 SHGs and now there are 17 SHGs, the President informed. By the able guidance of Gandhigram Trust, the SHG members are engaged in milch animals rearing, spinning, petty trades, production of sambar powders and other cooking powders, cultivation of herbal plants and preparation of herbal medicine and trading of herbal medicinal plants. They meet periodically at the SHG building. The building is very much useful as they keep all their records and registers in the SHG building, the President informed. He further told that he also assisted in the formation of a few new groups and helped to get financial assistance when the central ministers organised the SHG mela at Dindigul.

Regarding the agricultural activities, the President told that the current monsoon rains was adequate. So farmers proposed to take cultivation of paddy and other crops like onion, flowers and tomato. The Assistant Agricultural Officer is visiting the farmers periodically and offers proper guidance in their farm activities, the President explained.

Welfare of the Marginalised Section – The President informed that though he made attempts to avail eligible pension and other entitlements to widows and leprosy affected persons, they paid little attention to get medical certificate. He was advised to make use of the educated volunteers in this respect instead of blaming them. He assisted four aged persons to get their pension.

Under CPR management, a tank at RMTC Nagar was desilted from the Disaster Management Assistance, the President told.

Observation

It is told that the plan document is very useful for the verification and quick selection of works and beneficiaries. TWAD Officials appreciated the Panchayat for the preparation of the document. For the knowledge and understanding of the public some more steps have to be taken, the President suggested.

N. Panchampatti Village Panchayat – Athoor Union

N. Panchampatti Village Panchayat is moderate in size with a population of 6463. The SC population is numerically very less.

Activities Undertaken after Micro-Level Planning

Provision of Water Supply

There are two pipeline extension works proposed in the plan of which one work was executed with the financial allocation from the 11th Finance Commission. Further the water distribution system in all the 12 sections are regulated to ensure equal and equitable distribution of water to all.

(i) Two street lights were provided from the incentive fund allocated for the implementation of Namathu Gramam Scheme.

(ii) Eight road works have been executed. Expenditure for these works was met from various sources like union council general fund, Namathu Gramam incentives and SGRY fund. Expect one, the remaining seven road works were the CC road.

(iii) Two small bridges in the street were constructed. Environmental sanitation was improved in this area.

(iv) The Union Administration constructed manure yard with an arrangement for separate disposal of organic and inorganic wastes. SHG members are asked to make use of the provision properly. A *pucca* drainage about 50 metre length was constructed in the area of Ward No.1. There are about fifty shops in the bazar. Notice was issued to keep plastic wastes separately.

About 325 household latrines were provided to poor families of which in 25 latrines, hollow blocks were used for construction and in the remaining toilets, improvised super structure with coconut thatches were raised.

One Women Sanitary Complex available in the Village Panchayat. It is in proper utility. There was a demand for one more complex and it has been included in the plan. The Village Panchayat Council approached the local MLA in this regard.

(v) Under educational development activities, in the Panchayat union primary school a toilet for students was constructed. With regard to the infrastructure facilities in the higher secondary school, a compound wall was constructed from the allocation of MLA and MP local area development fund. Under SSA two additional buildings were also constructed. With NABARD assistance a building complex of laboratory, library and additional classrooms were also constructed. The Village Panchayat administration provided a water tap to the school. The union administration constructed toilets for students.

The management of the government aided private school proposed to construct new classrooms. The Village Panchayat administration met the correspondent of the said school and asked him to take steps for the improvement of the school. The PTAs of primary schools and high school are functioning well.

(vi) The burial ground meant for SC needed facilities like approach road, shelter and street light. The Village Panchayat Administration have approached the officials of the Adi Dravidar welfare department in this regard.

(vii) There are six children's centres of which, three are functioning in their own building, other two in one building and the remaining one in a rented building. Hence the Village Panchayat Administration approached the union councellor to allocate funds for the construction of a building for *Balwadi*. But the councellor preferred the cement concrete road in spite of the demand in the proposal. The President suggested that in the drafting of village development plan, orientation is needed to all elected representatives and officials so that a proper perspective would emerge. Otherwise they fail to play their role when the Village Panchayat takes genuine efforts to fulfil the proposed activities earmarked in the plan.

The Village Panchayat Administration constructed toilets in three *balwadis*, utilizing its own financial resources.

(viii) SHG Activities – There are 13 SHG functioning in the Village Panchayat. There is mutual understanding and sharing between the group members and the Village Panchayat Council members. The SHG members actively participate in the affairs of the Village Panchayat.

(ix) Rural Housing: Seven houses were allotted to the Village Panchayat of N.Panchampatti under IAY. As many of the poor families belonged to the BC community, housing was allocated to them. Out of seven houses five were allotted to widows and they have a simple and good housing.

The President and the clerk whenever needed, made use of the data collected and compiled for the activities like Namathu Gramam. Further the plan document gave an opportunity to look into the real felt need of the public.

Athoor Village Panchayat—Athoor Union

Athoor Panchayat is small in size having only one hamlet village apart from the main village Athoor.

Housing

Under IAY scheme five houses were provided to five Dalit families. Among the hamlet beneficiaries five poor families were identified for the next year's IAY programme.

Drinking Water Facilities

The Panchayat Council approached the collector to have a borewell exclusively for Athoor Panchayat, as the existing arrangement of supply by the Dindigul municipality of water involves heavy expenditure. For the proper supply of water to the high level area, a system of gate valve is fitted for the distribution of water to different streets in the high level area.

To improve the water supply, a new borewell was erected and a sintex tank was provided at the Athoor middle street from the 11th finance fund allocation. From the union fund another sintex and pipeline from a new borewell was provided to the North Street of Athoor and a pipeline extension was undertaken to provide water supply to Agraharam of Athoor and Savariyar Street separately.

Street Light

Three street lights have been provided utilizing the incentive fund of Namathu Gramam.

Road Facilities

A double layered metal road at a distance of 500 metre was formed from SGRY allocation. There is only 300 metre of earthen road between Pallivasal to Kaliamman temple. A CC road of 90 metre distance was also formed from the SGRY allocation. There are other road improvement works yet to be taken. MLA has been contacted in this regard.

Two small bridges are there. One in Athoor and another in Sempatti.

Sanitation

A manure yard is constructed at IIIrd area. The President felt that as only one sanitary worker is available, it is very hard to maintain public sanitation.

Even though community toilet is available, the utility is not as expected. The SHGs are oriented about the importance of personal hygiene and safe disposal of human excreta. The ANM is staying in the hamlet and properly guiding the Panchayat in the provision of protected water supply.

PDS

The Village Panchayat helped to avail 400 new ration cards.

Education Activities

Students' toilets were provided under TRSP at the union primary school Sempatti and under SSA toilet was provided at the union primary school at Athoor. Further in Athoor school additional classroom building was constructed under SSA. In the Athoor Government High School, under SSA, three classrooms were constructed and from the MLA fund, a computer room was provided.

The President told that with the help of the ward members, she worked to ensure no dropouts in schools.

Child Welfare

The Village Panchayat was engaged in organizing a special medical camp and an eye camp by Coconut Farmers Association along with mobilizing *balwadi* and school children to attend this camp. The *balwadi* building in Athoor is not in good condition. New building is needed. MLA has been contacted in this regard.

SHG Activities

The SHGs have shown interest in activities like animal husbandry, weaving, cloth merchandise, petty shop and sericulture.

Agricultural Activities

The President informed that there is no proper communication from the agriculture department and further the AAO's extension activities are not up to the expected level.

Welfare of the Marginalized

Panchayat administration helped old age persons and widows to get pension from the government. The handicapped have been mobilized to attend forthcoming camp to be scheduled in the month of December.

Classification

The plan document is very much useful in the selection of works, submission of statistics to various line departments, selection of beneficiaries and to get attention of the officials for the sanction of fund.

Devarappanpatti Panchayat – Athoor Union

Devarappanpatti is a village of moderate size having a population of 5441(1991 census). There are five hamlets including the main village.

Activities Undertaken from the Plan Proposal

Provision of Drinking Water

There are four borewells in the Village Panchayat. In

Chinnagoundanpatti, Vinobaji Nagar and in Meenakshipuram borewells were installed. In Meenakshipuram 10,000 litre OHT was constructed to support the drinking water facilities by providing two public taps additionally. Maintenance work was carried out wherever necessary from the 11th Finance Commission allocation.

Street Light

Six new street lights have been provided with the automatic switch system. Of the above six street lights, three are from Namathu Gramam Fund and the remaining three from the Panchayat Funds.

Road Improvement

There are four works carried out from the SGRY allocation. The approach road to Village Panchayat office is now converted from earthen road to metal road. At Devarappanpatti flood water outlet channel, strengthening of bunds along with the pucca construction of outlet channel were completed. The work is financially supported by the union administration.

Sanitation Activities

In Devarappanpatti main village with regard to solid waste management in 50 houses, two plastic buckets were provided by the Panchayat Administration. Members of these households were oriented in the solid waste management segregation of organic and inorganic waste and also preparation of organic manure. A tri-cycle was purchased for the collection of the segregated waste from the targeted households. The families concerned are very much cooperative in this arrangement. It is proposed to extend this arrangement to other streets in Devarappanpatti and other major hamlets.

Sixty household latrines were constructed and all are in use. It is told that there is no space for the establishment of manure yard due to the non-availability of adequate space for the establishment of manure yard. The President informed that there was a possibility in Odai Poramboke area, where manure yard could be constructed.

The district administration advised the Village Panchayat of Devarappanpatti to install bio-mass gas plant. The President told that he approached the MLA to provide funds for the installation of bio-mass gas plant.

Other Infrastructure Developments

The President informed that he tried his best to get a separate building for VAO, a community hall for Chinnagoundanpatti and a shelter for passengers. The union administration agreed to positively look into these demands.

Health

The Village Panchayat facilitated two eye camps organized at the Devarapanpatti village and Chinnagoundapatti by the union administration and Jaya trust respectively.

The sub-health centre is functioning well. The village health nurse being a local person stays in the village itself and all deliveries are attended to by her. Awareness to adolescent girls and immunization programme for children, pregnant women have been carried out successfully by the nurse with the help of Village Panchayat Administration.

A new building for balwadi was constructed from the union fund allocation. Now it is functioning separately and the child welfare activities are properly undertaken in all five centres, except the Gandhipuram division II *balwadi*, as division I & II are functioning in the same building.

SHG Activities

There are 25 SHGs are functioning in this Village Panchayat. Of which 13 SHGs are engaged in the economic activity of rearing of milch animals. The President informed that the SHG members do not get any orientation the involvement its members in public activities towards as well as Panchayat activities.

Agricutlural Activities

The President told that the AAO has been visiting the villages and renders his assistance to the needy farmers. A farm pond was constructed by three farmers with subsidy from the Government. Desilting work was undertaken in the inlet channel. Steps were taken for the eviction of encroachment in Pothankulam.

Welfare of the Marginalized

House site pattas for 13 poor families have been demanded. Under the two-girl children scheme three eligible families were identified and applications were made to avail economic assistance from the government.

NILAKOTTAI PANCHAYAT UNION

Noothulapuram Panchayat – Nilakkottai Block

Noothulapuram Village Panchayat have 11 hamlets with 1050 acres of land area. The population is 2365 males and 2320 females. 50 per cent of the people belong to Dalit community. It is economically backward. People depend on agriculture and allied activities.

Activities Undertaken in Rural Housing

Planning exercises are carried out in the village with the help of Gandhigram officials. Total houses of the village Panchayat is 1210, out of which 265 belong to eligible patta holders in the Dalit community who will get house from the Government after the planning exercise PMGY scheme. 19 beneficiaries constructed houses (SC – 19), from IAY 8 houses (SC – 5, BC – 3) were constructed. Six *Kutcha* houses (SC – 3, BC – 3) were provided.

The Panchayat President took efforts to survey the Panchayat poromboke land and give land to 40 Dalit members for housing. The President took efforts to get IAY scheme for the 40 dalit beneficiaries.

Drinking Water Facilities Carried out in the Panchayat

After the planning exercise in five villages a borewell was installed and sintex tanks were provided to give water to the people from the union councellor fund. In Utheepatti Village one borewell was installed under the drought relief scheme.

Street lights

Under Namathu Gramam scheme three solar lamps were erected in Noothulapuram S.Thammalapatti and Chinnamanaickenpatti villages. The Panchayat President has taken steps to put up one light in Achanampatti Village and approached the EB office to take steps. The President approached district officials like Project Officer DRDA, District Councellor to get funds for putting up lights in Chinnamanaickenpatti and S.Thummalapatti Village. An attempt for the installation of Bio-mass production plant has been sanctioned the Panchayat. The Panchayat President approached the local Member of Parliament, Dindigul Parliamentary Constituency but she could not mobilize funds from the M.P. for project.

Road Facilities

The Panchayat President has taken steps to repair the Kulathupatti—North Viralipatti road. Under MLA Fund, S.Thummalapatti to Thoppupatti road (5 kms) block top road work was carried out. Panchayat Administration approached the District Collector for this, District Councillor is also the district chairman to construct the bridge nearby Seethapuram village. This bridge is useful for farmers, school going children, business people and gives linkage to three villages. But this work has not yet been completed due to the unavailability of funds.

Disposal of Garbage

In the first period (1996 – 2001) Panchayat purchased garbage cart iron, Chatti and Manvetti for the disposal of garbage. Now bio and non-bio degradable waste thotti has been installed in Noothulapuram village. In the Gram Sabha meeting, people were advised to put their garbages in the thotti. The garbage cart collects the garbage from Kullathupatti and Bangalowpatti villages.

Toilet Facilities

Totally 250 household latrines were constructed in three villages, namely Kulathupatti (80 numbers), Bangalapatti (70 numbers) and Noothulapuram (100 numbers). Panchayat administration has taken steps to construct household latrines in other villages with the help of the NGO under TSRP scheme one toilet for women was constructed in S.Thumlapatti Village.

Public Distribution System

The President has taken steps to construct its own building for S.Thumlapatti village ration shop. Now it is functioning in a rented building. The ration shop supplies materials properly.

Educational Facilities

In all the schools PTA functions well. Under Black Board Scheme (SSA Scheme) school latrine was constructed in Kulathupatti, Seethapuram. Drinking water supply provided to all the five schools. Five students have discontinued their, studies since they have migrated to Tirupur with their parents.

Noothulapuram *Balwadi* is now functioning in the community hall because the *Balwadi* building has to be repaired. The President explained the need for a Balwadi building for S.Thumlapatti and N.Gothupatti village. Latrine in *Balwadis* should be constructed for N.Thumlapatti, Seethapuram, Chinnanaickenpatti, Kulathupatti, Bangalapatti, Noothulapuram and South Viralipatti villages. They are taking necessary steps to construct a toilet for the *Balwadi*.

SHG

In Noothulapuram Panchayat nearly 25 SHGs groups are functioniong. All the SHGs get milch animals with the help of ASEFA and NGO. Two groups are involved in making *agarbathi*, tooth powder and soap making business. The NGO ASEFA and CETIDA are involved in the SHG activities and give loans to the SHGs.

Agricultural Development

According to the revenue records, there is 284.49.5 hectors of waste land. It is proposed to plant saplings in the waste land of about 279.70.0 hectares. The Panchayat Administration takes necessary steps to plant trees in the waste lands.

The Assistant Agriculture Officer (AAO) supplied Cholam, Cumbu and Sunflower seeds to the farmers at a subsidised rate. He gave advice to farmers about new cultivation methods to increase productivity.

Kodanginayakkanpatti Panchayat – Nilakkottai Union

There are 7 hamlets in this Village Panchayat of which Kodanginayakkanpatti and Kokkupatti hamlets have Dalit community as the predominant group.

Rural Housing

Though there is a large number of poor families who are in need of *pucca* housing it was told that there are several hurdles in providing housing to them. The President shared that majority of the poor families divided their living space but the patta is in one name. Further according to the government scheme the beneficiaries themselves had to spend money and it could be claimed only after inspection and checking of measurements by the concerned officials. Poor families do not have any finance to undertake housing if they have been selected as beneficiaries. In one of the hamlets the poor families are residing in the site which is owned by a temple and so they could not get patta for their residence. In this context the Village Panchayat Administration did not take any steps in providing rural housing to the poor.

Improvement of the Water Supply

At Appinayakkanpatti and Thoppupatti hamlets new borewell and mini power pump scheme was implemented by the Union administration. Mini power pump and four of public taps were provided in the above hamlets. By TWAD under the Peranai Comprehensive Water Supply Scheme a sump was constructed at Thoppupatti hamlet. The construction of OHT with the capacity of 30,000 litres is yet to be commenced. Except during rainy season, water supply is inadequate especially during summer as the water table is about 600 feet depth, the President shared.

With regard to the provision of street lights, three new street lights have been provided (with a technology of automatic switch on when the natural light is closed and switch-off when the natural light comes).

Road Improvement Activities

At Kodankinayakkanpatti, Thambinayakkanpatti and Thottampatti hamlet CC road work was undertaken under SGRY allocation. A small bridge was constructed at Kodankinayakkanpatti under SGRY scheme. The retaining wall proposed in the plan at Thoppampatti hamlet will be completed as the Union Councellor came forward to get allocation for the same during the current financial year.

At Kokkupatti under SGRY, the Village Panchayat administration constructed a *pucca* drainage for 80 metres. Now the street is kept clean.

Public Sanitation

Sanitary complex located at Kodankinayakkanpatti is functioning well. About 200 families are using the complex. The President told that each family is contributing Rs.5 for the maintenance of the complex. With regard to the construction of individual household latrine, she told that the fund under TRSP is not available at present. She met the Councillor in this regard and he promised to look into the matter. The President is one of the members in the district level committee constituted under Namathu Gramam Scheme. A sub-health centre is very much needed here. The concerned officials advised the villages to earmark sufficient space for the same. A villager donated 7 cents in this regard, the President informed.

Under Public Distribution System, the Village Panchayat administration assisted 120 eligible families to avail ration cards.

Educational Development Activity

There are three primary schools. Under SSA scheme toilets were provided and now in utility as water supply is provided by the Village Panchayat administration. At Thoppupatti primary school flooring work was undertaken by the union administration. The construction of a kitchen shed prioritized in the plan has been taken up by the Union Councillor. Teaching aids and other planning materials are procured from the SSA allocation. PTA and the VEC (Village Education Committee) are functioning well.

Other Infrastructural Facilities

At Appinayakkanpatti a thrashing floor was provided under SGRY scheme. Open-air theatre was demanded for Kokkupatti and Thoppupatti because during the village temple festival, drama and other cultural events have been organized at Kokkupatti. In the meantime the villagers from Appavoopillaipatti met the MLA and got sanction for the construction of an open-air theatre at Appavoopillaipatti. The President informed that when she contacted the MLA in this regard she was told that the villagers from Appavoopillaipatti came to him personally and persuaded him. The President felt bad about the mind-set of the MLA in spite of a copy of the plan document of Kodankinayakkanpatti was submitted to him so that he could prioritize the fund allocation.

At Kodankinayakkanpatti both Muslim and Hindu communities are commonly using burial/funeral ground. From the public contribution belonging to members of both religions, compound wall, borewell and OHT facilities have been provided by the Village Panchayat administration. Adjacent to this site a Panchayat poramboke of five cent is earmarked for the establishment of a grove. Tamarind, Mango, Neem and Punga tree saplings will be planted in this site, the President shared. Another five cent is earmarked in this village where accessories and tools for physical exercise for youths will be provided, she added.

Improvement of the Anganwadi Centres

There are four *anganwadis* functioning in four hamlets, namely

Thoppupatti, Thambinayakkanpatti, Kokkupatti and Kodankinayakanpatti. The *anganwadi* of Thambinyakkanpatti has been functioning in the public *chavadi* due to non-availability of a permanent centre. Now, a new building was constructed from the union fund. In all the four *balwadis* toilet and water facilities were provided by the union administration and village administration respectively. Public and village community leaders donated for the purchase of goods like plates, tumblers and mats for *balwadi* children.

Self Help Group Activity

There are 25 women SHGs in this Village Panchayat. Kalangiam, Women Education and Empowerment Trust, ASSEFA and MMS are the non-governmental organizations facilitating these groups. Dairy, candle production, mats and *agarbathi* production, vending of flowers and readymade garments are the major activities of the group members. At Kodankinayakkanpatti, Muslim women are engaged in the production of bamboo die (meant for the weaving of border design in silk sarees).They complained that the raw material – bamboo is not adequately available and the cost is also increasing. Hence the profit margin is limited. But the Muslim women are not ready to switch over to any other enterprise. Floriculture is the major farming activity in this block. Preparation of garlands and flower vending are always a profitable. Majority of the members are involved in these enterprises.

Agricultural Activities

Gopalnayakkanpatti hamlet of this Village Panchayat is in the jurisdiction of Chinnamannayakkankottai watershed area, where waste land development programme is implemented. Afforestation is the main activity in this regard. The Village Panchayat administration is encouraging farmers to make use of the scheme properly.

There are two ponds in this Village Panchayat. During 2003-04 desilting work was undertaken in these ponds. Hence there is no financial allocation to undertake any further work, the President informed.

Welfare of the Marginal Sector

The Village Panchayat administration helped four poor families when the head of these families died, to avail a relief of Rs.10,000 as compensation. Two disabled persons were given tri-cycles.

Observation

The President informed that the plan document is very much useful for "Namathu Gramam" project as required data were already available in the document.

NILAKOTTAI UNION

Sithargalnatham Village Panchayat

Sithargalnatham Village Panchayat is a multi-caste one. There are 10 hamlets in this Village Panchayat. In the Village Panchayat Council there are five wards represented by ten members of which three are women.

The following are the activities carried out by the Village Panchayat as the follow-up of plan implementation:

Housing

Under IAY five group houses were provided to poor families, of which four belong to backward classes. Under Kutcha House Scheme four houses were provided to B.C. families. With regard to housing to the Dalit poor families at Parayapatti, there are 42 patta holders for whom a fullfledged colony was demanded by the community. Village Panchayat administration has taken steps in this regard.

Under drinking water distribution from the allocation of District Councillor Fund a new borewell and a pipeline were established from the river Vaigai as the existing water supply system to Sithargalnatham hamlet from the pipeline meant for Dindigul Municipality will be disconnected.

The proposed new pipeline for Malayampatti in the plan document was executed from the allocation of Union Council Fund.

Further for Parayapatti Dalit habitation, a mini power pump system with a storage of sintex tank was provided by the Union Councillor. In another hamlet Kundalapatti, as the existing water supply from Silukkuvarpatti, comprehensive water supply scheme is inadequate, with the help of District Council financial allocation, a new borewell power pump and pipeline were provided. Further for a remote habitation in Kundalapatti a mini power pump scheme was provided from the MLA Fund.

Road Work

The Village Panchayat Council took up the demand of provision of metal road in S.Vadipatti hamlet. The rural Highways Department sanctioned the work and it was completed successfully. From the incentive of Namathu Gramam Scheme and MLA financial assistance, a CC road was constructed in Sithargalnatham, Parayapatti and Vinayagapuram Colony. At EB Colony, from SGRY fund a metal road was provided. The Panchayat President informed that the officials of rural highways department appreciated the Village Panchayat planning for all the infrastructure development.

Under public sanitation pucca drainage was provided wherever CC work was executed. At Kundalapatti 25 wastebins were provided. A cart was purchased for easy transportation of solid waste. The union administration constructed a manure yard for the separate storage for organic and inorganic waste. Orientation is given to the SHG members in this regard. The women sanitary complex is functioning well at Kundalapatti. Open air defecation was prevented through social control in the big hamlet Kundalapatti. At present the men folk got awareness and demanded separate toilet for men also.

With regard to Public Distribution System at Sirunayakkanpatti the PDS shop which was functioning in a rented building, was replaced with a *pucca* building. The Village Panchayat allotted the space where the new building was constructed. Further the Village Panchayat administration helped the householders to avail new ration cards. Further the Village Panchayat identified 70 numbers of families who are in ultra poverty. Efforts are taken to get benefits from AAY scheme to these poor families.

Education development activities: Toilets for students were constructed in all four schools in the Village Panchayat. The financial assistance for the construction of toilets was given by the union administration. Under SSA scheme, an additional building was constructed in the union primary school of Kundalapatti. Officials of Kallar Reclamation Board was contacted to improve the infrastructure facilities in the Government Kallar Middle School functioning in Sithargalnatham.

The Annual Day and Independence Day celebration are regularly arranged with the involvement of Parent-Teacher Association. Essay competition was organized for school students on the theme of Namathu Gramam and prizes were distributed to the winners.

Other infrastructure development initiatives: Thrashing floor and open-air theatre are the only two components which were fulfilled among the proposed infrastructures. Efforts were taken to establish a weekly market in the Village Panchayat area.

As the Hanuman Temple located on the banks of river Vaigai is famous, it attracts many pilgrims. The aim is to improve the basic amenities to the pilgrims. There is inadequate fund with the Village Panchayat. Hence a resolution was passed to declare the Panchayat as a place of tourist attraction by which new and additional financial resources could be mobilized.

Child Welfare Activities

There are five *balwadis* in this Village Panchayat. One new *balwadi* is established at Kuthilnayakkanpatti. Toilet for the children was constructed by the Village Panchayat as per the plan proposal. With regard to the provision of drinking water supply, except in one *balwadi*, water supply provision is needed in the remaining *balwadi*. Now from the Village Panchayat source water tap connection is provided whenever needed.

SHG Activities

There are 37 SHGs facilitated by the NGOs like Kalanchiyam, CENTREDA and Dhanam Foundation. Apart from rearing of milch animals, jawli clothes and bangles are the main trades in which the

SHG members are involved. In production of coconut thatches, members of a few SHG members who belong to landless labour class are involved.

Common Property Resources

There are five tanks of which two are under minor irrigation classification. Desilting and maintenance works were carried out in four tanks, using the SGRY financial allocation and union funds.

Welfare of the Marginalized

With the help of district administration, ten poor widows have been provided with the financial assistance for rearing of milch animals. Effort was taken to organize a camp for physically challenged persons, the President informed.

Observation

As a plan document is readily available, it induced the people to do something to implement the plan, the Village Panchayat clerk observed.

DINDIGUL PANCHAYAT UNION

Balakrishnapuram Panchayat Dindigul District

The Village Panchayat is very large in respect of population and area. The total population is 22,034. About one-fourth of the population belongs to the Dalit Community.

Activities under Rural Housing

After the planning, the Village Panchayat Council availed 25 houses under IAY scheme benefiting 15 SC families and 10 BC families. Further an additional nine houses under Kutcha House Scheme (3 BC and 6 SC families) were provided.

With regard to provision of five house sites to the poor families it was identified that there are about 125 poor families needed house sites with Pattas. It was told that about 25 of them have been provided house sites as there was adequate land available in the Panchayat itself. For the rest, the authorities informed that acquisition of land from the private individuals was proposed.

Improvement in the Drinking Water Facility

In three hamlets, namely PWD colony, Sasthri Nagar and South Malaipatti additional OHT facilities were provided. A new hand-pump was installed in Ambethkar Nagar from the Panchayat union fund. The pipeline was extended to cater to the needs of the residents, public and household water taps, 16 taps and 12 respectively.

The main village Balakrishnapuram is in the list of Cauvery River Water Distribution System. The TWAD engineers decided to construct two sumps in this regard. Suitable sites were identified and earmarked by the Village Panchayat Council for this purpose.

Road Works

CC road work in Naddumalaipatti, North Maalaipatti, Appinaickenpatti and Anumantha Nagar were provided. The main approach road of Appinaickenpatti is a bitumen road and which needs maintenance. Of the three kilometres only half kilometre distance repair work was completed from the SGRY special fund allocation. The metal road in CTO colony was improved into bitumen road from the block panchayat allocation.

Sanitation

Under sanitation activities, the following works have been completed: 1000 metre *pucca* drainage facility and one small bridge were constructed. Manure yard for the segregation of bio and non-bio degradable waste was constructed in CTO colony.

There are two sanitary complexes functioning well and an additional sanitary complex for Balakrishnapuram was demanded from the M.P. Fund. Two carts were purchased for the transportation of waste.

A new ration shop at Rajiv Gandhi Nagar was demanded by

the people. The block officials, and union chairman were contacted in this regard.

Activities under Education

At the union middle school located in Balakrishnapuram, a compound wall was constructed from block Panchayat allocation. People were oriented to give contribution for the construction of toilets for students. Now they are ready and steps are taken to avail the TRSP (Total Rural Sanitation Scheme) Fund.

Enlistment of membership for the library has begun as the government is ready to sanction building for the library, as of now it is in a rented building.

Anganwadi – Children Welfare

A new Anganwadi was sanctioned for Rajiv Gandhi Nagar and a new building was constructed from SGRY scheme fund. In the second *Balwadi*, there were more number of children enrolled. Hence an additional *balwadi* was constructed under SGRY scheme.

At Malaipati extension there are adequate children available for *balwadi*, but there is no *balwadi*. Hence, demand is made to the authorities to provide a new *balwadi* in this campus.

Welfare of the Marginalized Sector

Claiming of pension for the poor widows and old age persons was initiated.

The Village Panchayat Council approached the officials when they had organized Public Grievances Day at the Balakrishnapuram village itself. The plan document was shown to them and the officials appreciated the efforts taken by the Village Panchayats for registering the details of widows. They have gone through details and recommended 26 poor widows out of 66 listed in the plan. This was possible without any undue delay in availing the eligible pension as the evidence of poverty and eligibility was recorded in the plan document approved in the Gram Sabha.

Augmentation of Panchayat Income

A proposal is in on for the establishment of grove of different income yielding tress at the Panchayat poramboke land which was redeemed recently from the encroachment.

SHG Involvement

During a ten-day camp in Balakrishnapuram by Annamalaiar Girls Higher Secondary School students, SHG members involved in the activities of public sanitation, tree planting and removal of plastic waste.

In the shopping complex earmarked for SHG micro business, due to loss in the enterprise, the shops are not functioning. The Village Panchayat administration is taking efforts to replace with other SHGs who have potential to run their enterprises.

The Village Panchayat is taking steps for fish-culture in the PWD tank. Now the desilting work is going on. After the completion of the work, SHG will be encouraged to do fish-rearing.

Observation

The plan document is available with line departments. This facilitated the understanding between the Panchayat and line department. The works prioritised in the plan is taken for consideration by the line departments like TWAD and social welfare departments.

The plan is available to the public during the Gram Sabha which encouraged people's participation.

M.M. Kovilur Village Panchayat

M.M. Kovilur is a small Village Panchayat having a population of around 3000. There are seven ward members of whom three are women including one SC women member. Vanniapatti and Ottailkulam are the two hamlets of which Ottaikulam is a very small habitat having only 25 households.

Housing Activities

Three houses under IAY were provided to three poor families belonging to BC. Two poor families from SC were selected for *kutcha* house. There are five poor families residing in the poramboke classified as odai porambokku. Hence they are not able to get pattas for the same. The village panchayat passed a resolution to convert the same into Nathamporomboke so that the poor could get pattas for their house site.

The President told that the poor are not able to complete the housing allotted under IAY due to their financial constraints. Further the cost of bricks is always going up.

From the Namathu Gramam incentive money, three street lights have been provided.

Road Works

From the allocation of Rural Highway, 2.5 km distance bitumen road is in progress. Further from the village panchayat fund the earthen road in Vanniyapatti was converted into metal road. At Muslim street and Dalit street CC road were formed.

The President told that the plan document of M.M. Kovilur was shown to the officials of the Rural Highways and to the local minister. They appreciated the efforts of the panchayat in drafting a comprehensive development plan, he added.

Sanitation Activities

To avoid the stagnation of water along the main road, a *pucca* drainage was constructed at a distance of 350 metre from the SGRY allocation to the Village Panchayat.

Steps were taken to repair the old cart meant for the transportation of solid waste. A poster campaign was organized appealing the public and the shop owners to separate the inorganic waste for the easy collection of by the sanitary workers. With the service of the NGO, 27 household latrines were provided to poor families. About 50 percent of the beneficiaries are utilizing the toilet.

The septic tank of women sanitary complex existing in

Vanniapatti is filled with flood water due to rain. Due to paucity of fund, the evacuation of flood water and other minor repair works in the sanitary complex are delayed, the President informed.

Public Distribution System

The President told that 35 ultra poor families were selected for AAY and the list is submitted to the government. Decision is yet to be taken by the government, he informed. The glass panes of the windows in the PDS shop had been broken and the issue was informed to the union administration, as there is no official permission to the village panchayat to take up any repair work in the PDS building, the President added.

Educational Development Activities

Students toilets were provided both in the higher secondary and primary school, by the union administration.

To have a separate primary school at Vanniapatti, efforts were taken and the officials have visited the village in this regard. The President told that he was pursuing the issue seriously as the school-going children of Vanniapatti and nearby villages have to walk nearly 3 km. Moreover they have to cross a river and an odai as the straightway is of 4 km distance.

It is told that the officials who made inspection did not send any communication to the village panchayat administration. We advised the President to personally meet the higher officials with fresh details like number of children going to be benefited, space available for school and the cooperation readily available with the village panchayat administration.

The President proudly said that there were no dropouts from the school.

Other Infrastructure Facilities

The President told that due to paucity of fund, the village panchayat was unable to undertake any new works listed out in the infrastructure development plan. The union administrative and the

AD welfare officials were contacted with regard to the provision of a thrashing floor and burial ground facility.

Television Room need maintenance works. It is proposed to take up these repair works only after the receipt of SGRY fund, the President told.

Child Welfare Activities

There is only one *balwadi* in the main village Kovilur. The toilet facility and the water tap connection were given as proposed in the plan. The *balwadi* teacher requested the village panchayat administration to do repair work on the roof of the *balwadi* as there was a heavy leakage during the rain. The issue was brought to the notice of the officials. The block officials visited and proposed to lay tiles over the roof of the *balwadi* to drain out the rainwater properly, the President told.

Steps are taken to get a new building for the *balwadi* functioning in the Community Hall of Vanniampatti.

Mullipadi Village Panchayat

Activities Carried out under THP Plan

Housing facilities were provided to nine poor families of which, four beneficiaries belong to the Dalit community.

Efforts were taken with the help of the NGOs to avail credit assistance to the SHG members for the construction of housing. As the patta is in the name of the head of the family, the bankers do not come forward to lend money. The issue was taken up to the Project Officer, District Rural Development Agency, and he discussed with the bank officials in this regard for a positive solution.

The Panchayat administration encouraged the beneficiaries of *kutcha* house scheme to make use of the Hallow blocks for the construction of their houses as its is cost effective.

Provision of Drinking Water Supply

It is informed that the existing power supply system through

III Phase is not adequate to pump up sufficient water as the electricity is not available all times through III Phase. Hence the villagers demanded provision of a mini power pump facility which could be operated even in single phase power supply. At Chetiapatti, Kodangipatti and Karuthanampatti mini power pump with sintex tank arrangement was provided. The fund for Chettiapatti is availed from TWAD, and the remaining two works were provided from Village Panchayat Fund.

Street Lights

Three additional street lights were provided in hamlet villages. The scheme of single light for each hut is not now in operation. Hence, poor families in the village are not able to avail the benefit of the scheme.

Road Facilities

At Mullipadi and in Kulanthaipatti road works have been completed with the help of fund allocation by the MLA as well as from own sources of the Village Panchayat Fund. It is proposed to undertake tree plantation along the road side of the recently formed black top road.

The Vice-President, who is residing at Annaipatti hamlet, proposed planting of 50 tree saplings on the banks of Annaipatti tank involving school students and local youths.

Bridge-across the Santhanavarthini river is proposed in the plan. If it is accomplished it will be very useful for two more neighbouring village panchayats also. The President of Mullipadi Village Panchayat informed that she discussed the matter with thc Prcsidcnts of the other two villages and decided to take up the matter with the higher level officials as well as politicians.

A separate manure yard was constructed at Kathiranampatti hamlet, the SHGs of the hamlet are oriented through NGO for the management of solid waste. At Mullipadi a similar manure yard is now under construction. The SHG members of the Mullipadi will be involved in the solid waste management. Step was taken to procure a cart for the transportation of solid waste by the Panchayat administration. It was proposed to involve households in this experiment of the collection of bio and non-bio degradable waste from the houses. Two separate plastic buckets were provided to each household in this regard. Regarding toilet facilities, 600 household toilets were provided. NGO staff are sensitizing the public to make use of household toilets.

PDS Activities

As an additional 600 new ration cards have been obtained by the eligible families, the existing two shops are not adequate to cater to the needs of the villagers. The Villagers of Chettiapatti hamlet requested to make arrangements for the establishment of a separate ration shop at Chettiapatti which may cover about 250 to 300 families. It was proposed to have a part-time ration shop in this hamlet.

School Improvement

Out of seven schools, after the plan initiative, in four schools, toilet facilities were provided except Kulanthaipatti government middle school. At the private school run by the Church management constructions for additional building and toilet facilities are going on. From the contribution of CASA, an NGO to coach the children, a teacher was appointed and special classes were handled by the teacher.

A Rural library was established through the initiative of Union Panchayat Administration. 0.5 cent land site was earmarked by the Panchayat for the construction of a rural library. Life membership is enlisted for this purpose. At present a library is functioning in the SHG building. The district local library authority made efforts for the construction of new building with the help of the district councillor.

Child Welfare Activities

Two new buildings were constructed with toilet facilities. SHG members were contacted for the provision of necessary materials like mats, plates and tumblers at the *balwadi*. NSS camp was organized by the High School Junior Red Cross, Kovilur. They arranged Medical Camps for women and children. ICDS programme meant for children ensured taking weight of children and monitoring of nutrition status among *balwadi*-age group children. The Panchayat decided to mobilize mothers of *balwadi* children for proper weight measurement and nutritional status monitoring.

Linkage with Private Health Centre

It is told that a health centre was run by the management St. Joseph's Hospital, Dindigul. Though there is a cordial relationship between the Panchayat administration and staff of health centre, there is no proper joint approach to delivering the services meant for women and children. It is advised to contact the concerned officials of the St. Joseph's hospital in this regard.

With the help of the private doctor's initiative the village Panchayat was able to make arrangement for the prevention of jaundice. Three doses of medicine through injections prevented the occurrence of Hepatitis-B with subsidized cost of medicine. About 100 children were covered under this programme.

Common Property Resource Improvement

At the big tank of PWD desilting and strengthening of its banks were undertaken. The height of the bank was raised. The inlet channel was cleared for the easy and quick flow of water. The fund was released by NABARD and the farmers committee is involved in the implementation and monitoring work.

Welfare of the Marginalized

Two poor widows and two physically challenged persons were provided with group houses.

Steps to augment Panchayat Income

In the plan proposal it was referred that a shopping complex at Akshaya Nagar would augment income to the Panchayat. In consultation with union officials, a proposal was prepared and district councillor was approached for funding in this regard.

Observation

The Panchayat council informed that the plan document is very much useful, for various references like selection of eligible beneficiaries and selection of prioritized works. Further it is used for the drafting of specific plans on the seven items, namely water, sanitation, education, child welfare, women, social welfare and social problems drafted in "Namathu Gramam" scheme. The President informed that it is only after the plan the Panchayat administration got more orientation and the activities of the SHG. During the drafting of the plan a good rapport was developed between the village Panchayat and the SHG members. This gives strength to the village Panchayat, she added.

The President informed that she needed more facilities with regard to the agricultural development in her Village Panchayat. She sought help from the The Hunger Project, Gandhigram Rural Institute in this regard.

Thottanoothu Panchayat

Rural Housing

Out of 16 hamlets, housing to poor families was undertaken in 4 hamlets. Under IAY programme, 16 group houses were provided, of which 19 beneficiaries belonged to scheduled castes. Under Katcha Scheme, five SC families were benefited. For 25 colony houses which were in damaged condition, repair and renovation work were carried out from the allocation of MLA Local Area Development Fund. Two street lights have been provided at the AD colony.

Road Improvement Work

Under SGRY allocation CC roads have been provided at six hamlets. And in one hamlet work is under progress. Of the above seven, only one work was funded by MLA and the remaining works were executed from the Village Panchayat Fund.

Public Sanitation

A cart was purchased for the safe disposal of solid waste and at Irrandula Parai village, a manure yard was constructed for the separation of organic and inorganic waste. Camp for NSS Students was organized in the village where the students and communities were involved in cleaning the streets. Effort was taken to involve SHG in this village for the production of Vermi- compost. A health camp was organized by the NSS students and private doctors. A case of cancer was detected and immediately was referred. It was told that the patient got treatment and is recovering.

In one of the Sanitary Complexes, water from the source was not adequate to meet the requirements of the user group. Deepening of a bore was demanded. In the meantime water supply from the drinking water connection was provided. Now, the sanitary complex is in full utility.

At Irrandalai Parai hamlet, the Women Sanitary Complex is a small one. SHG members demanded a new big sanitary complex. The Village Panchayat Council approached MLA in this regard.

The household latrines constructed under TRSP scheme are not comfortable, as the superstructure on the toilet platform is an improvised one and Coconut thatched. Out of 200 household latrines constructured under TSRP, only about 50 percentage is in utility. It is proposed to persuade the beneficiary of TRSP to improve the super structure facility at the toilets and to make use of the toilets properly.

Education Development

There are nine schools including one SSA school in this Village Panchayat. Except in one primary school in all the other schools toilet facilities have been provided by the union administration. The Village Panchayat Administration provided water supply in these schools where toilet facilities have also been provided. Steps were taken to upgrade the high school of Nallapanayakanpatti into higher secondary school. It is proposed to collect contribution from the public if the positive order is given by the government. The fund available in SSA is properly utilized. Teaching aids and equipments were purchased from this Fund.

With regard to the establishment of rural library, the local library authorities have visited the village and advised the villagers to enlist members as well as patrons. Awareness was given to the villagers in this regard.

In Thottanoothu Village an individual is rearing pigs which may cause pollution to the environment. The individual concerned was asked to give up the practice of piggery. Efforts were taken to get a Primary Health Centre in the Village Panchayat.

Child Welfare

There are eight *balwadis*, of which three *balwadies* needed new buildings. The Village Panchayat succeeded in its attempt to obtain new buildings for the same. Toilets have been provided in the new buildings. The Village Panchayat provided water supply to all *balwadis*.

Agricultural Activities

It was told that there are two Assistant Agricultural Officers (AAOs) visiting this Village Panchayat area. The service of one AAO is properly available, but the service of another AAO is not properly available. Hence the Village Panchayat administration has taken the issue to the higher officials concerned. From the available AAO benefits like subsidy for construction of a farm pond, coconuts saplings, were availed, the President told. Steps were taken to avail the Drought-Prone Area Development Programme (DPAP), she added.

At the Periyakulam (Irrigation Tank) at Nallamanayakkanpatti and Paraikulam of Rettiapatti, desilting work was carried out from the fund allotted by the MP. Steps were taken to desilt two more tanks in Alagarnayakkanpatti as these tanks are the main source for the drinking water borewell.

Augmenting Panchayat Income

It is proposed in the plan for a shopping complex at Rettiyapatti. The Village Panchayat Administration is negotiating with the MP in this regard.

Welfare of the Marginalized Sector

Housing was provided under IAY to two widows. Old age pension was availed for two elders during the current financial year.

Annaipatti Village Panchayat

Housing

In the year 2005-06, under IAY Scheme the village got 10 colony houses, 7 allocated to SC, 3 allocated to BC respectively. Under Kutcha House Scheme the village got 5 houses, 3 allotted to SC, 2 allotted to BC respectively. Nearly 55 huts are there, of which 15 huts were converted into *pucca* house under IAY and Kutcha House Scheme. The President told that the remaining huts will be changed to *pucca* in coming years.

Drinking Water Facility

Pipeline repairing works were carried out in three streets at the cost of Rs.60,000 from the Panchayat fund. The Panchayat Annaipatti got Rs.5 lakhs from the clean village award. From this fund the Panchayat administration undertook necessary maintenance works in all the pipelines in this Village Panchayat, the cost is 2.40 lakhs. Now the people get drinking water without any problem.

Deepening work in the public well at the cost of 2 lakhs from the District Councillors Fund was carried out and it is very useful for washing and other purposes.

Street Light

Three new lights were provided in the main road under "Namathu Gramam Scheme". A.D. Welfare Officer has promise to give 15 tube lights to the Village Panchayat for SC habitation.

Road Works

Approved road to burial ground a distance of 1 km of metal road at the cost of Rs.1 lakh from the Panchayat fund and another metal road work were carried out from Perumal temple to Eswaran temple.

One small bridge was constructed near Bhagawathiamman temple from SGRY scheme at the cost of Rs.30,000. For the remaining nine bridge works the Panchayat President approached the MLA, District Councillor and Union Councillor.

Public Sanitation Activities

The Panchayat constructed a yard for the storing of organic and inorganic waste. Annai Indira self-help group took care of the sold waste management work.

All the houses having a household latrine, and the public toilet were taken care by Annai Therasa self-help group.

The IAY beneficiaries use the household toilets properly. Smokeless *choolahs* are also provided in the colony houses.

Agricultural Development

The AAO visited this Village Panchayat properly and guided the farmers in preparation and application of natural manure.

Madurai agricultural sub-division office constructed a building at the cost of Rs.2 lakh. This building is proposed for the use of storing foodgrains and for training farmers.

Education

The Panchayat administration provided drinking water and toilet facilities to the school. The Panchayat President visits the school to supervise the noon-meal programme.

Self-Help Groups

In this Village Panchayat there are 7 SHGs. All the SHGs got skill training like toys making, kitchen gardening, tailoring, coconut thatch production, candle and incense stick making. Two SHG groups were involved in the waste management and toilet maintenance. Members of SHG groups attended Gram Sabha and availed benefits. The SHG building construction is completed, with the help of Union Councillor Fund at the cost of Rs. 1.75 lakhs.

The President approached the local MLA for construction of community hall in the village and the local MP has assured to provide a library building.

Health

The VHN stays in Palam Rajakkapatti, one kilometre away from Annaipatti. Every Thursday she visits Annaipatti village and conducts adolescence girl awareness camp, ANC and PNC care, supply of iron tablets, check up and immunization to children. She conducts delivery in the centre.

Anganwadi

For *balwadi*, a new building was constructed with toilet facilities and water facilities under Panchayat Union Councillor Fund were provided at the cost of Rs.2 lakh.

Common Property Resources

Pramma Samuthira Tank was desilted by PWD Department. The bund is in damaged condition, due to rain. Now the bunds of the Pramma Samuthira was strengthened to prevent breaching. The Village Panchayat spent money for this from its own source.

Clean Village Award

With the help of the self-help group members, village elders, nearly 4500 tree saplings like teak, silk cotton, *neem*, banyan and *babul* trees on road side, school compound, funeral ground and village porambokes. The Panchayat took necessary steps to clean the streets and segregation of the organic and inorganic wastes with the help of the SHG groups.

All the houses have household toilet and they are in proper utilization. They are:

- There are no school dropouts,
- No child labour in the Panchayat,
- Along the road side tree saplings were planned and protected by fencing and work.

In this regard the Village Panchayat got the Clean Village Award.

REDDIARCHATRAM PANCHAYAT UNION

Karisalpatti Panchayat

Under The Hunger Project in Dindigul District, 16 village Panchayats spread over four Panchayat union have been taken for drafting of the village development plans involving the local community. The draft was approved in the Gram Sabha in October 2004. Now a period of one year is over and a review is made to understand the follow-up activities on the implementation of plan in the target villages.

1. The data available in the plan document are very much useful for furnishing relevant details to the various departments like Medical Department, Revenue Department and Department of Animal Husbandry.
2. Selection of works on priority basis was easily done by referring to the plan document.
3. It was useful to the local villagers to understand the plan and its components as during the Gram Sabha four or five copies of the plan document were made available to the participants of the Gram Sabha meetings.
   Further, the plan document copies were submitted to the various departments. When the Village Panchayat approached the line departments, they received a good response as the priorities of the community have been properly projected in the plan document.
4. Involvement of local NGO(KKSSR). The local NGO came forward to assist the Village Panchayat in implementing the same plans envisaged in the plan. A teaching staff is engaged by the NGO to supplement the coaching of the students in the Government High School.

The repair and maintenance work of the Health Sub-Centre

building was undertaken by the NGO. It is ready for the use of the village health nurse.

A *pucca* building is constructed for the *Balwadi* which is run by the NGO. The NGO workers during their field visits created awareness among the public about the role of the community in maintaining and promoting public health and sanitation.

The Panchayat Ward Members especially SC-Ward members took much interest in the follow-up activities of the implementation of the plan.

Public is extending their cooperation in maintaining cleanliness around the public taps.

The Village Panchayat administration is sensitized in the activities of various standing committees.

The VAO is helping to get house site pattas to those families who have already constructed houses in the Natham Poramboke.

Strategy

The following questions were used as guideline :

1. How far is the plan document useful to the village Panchayat?
2. What are the programmes which were planned and undertaken by the Village Panchayat?
3. What are the steps taken to achieve the programme implementation in the context of financial limitation in the Village Panchayat own sources?
4. How effective was the participation of the Ward Members and community based organisations in the follow-up?

Observation

(a) In the approach road to Karisalpatti via old Kannivadi still open defecation is done.

(b) Panchayat office campus needs a face lift such as proper fencing and additional income generating plantation (Banana Trees).

(c) *Balwadi* in Karisalpatti : There is no mal nutrition among the children. Children's nails are cut and kept clean.
(d) The church priest who is the Secretary of the aided primary school informed that he has taken efforts to undertake repair works and additional buildings in the schools.
(e) In the Government Higher Secondary School, new committee for Parent-Teacher Association was constituted. There is a proposal to conduct a meeting to discuss the over all improvement of the school.
(f) It is proposed to monitor the sports ability among the students, so that proper motivation and special practice could be arranged for the deserving students.
(g) The Head Master insisted that from The Hunger Project, a teacher could be sponsored for the supplementary coaching of social science subject.
(h) The computer facilities available at the Village Panchayat office are not functioning well.
(i) The computer given to the SHG federation is yet to be put into use.
(j) At the community toilets meant for men, there should be a separate drainage to drain out waste water. Otherwise it would go to the septic tank. It is advised to construct a provision to drain the waste water and a garden could be planned.
(k) There is a space at Karamadai extension area along the small pond where a small shopping complex may be constructed to generate income to the Village Panchayat. This will prevent an attempt to encroach the area by some individuals.

T. Pannaipatti Village Panchayat

T.Pannaipatti has seven hamlets with a population of 6930. There are nine Panchayat members (4 – female, 5 – male).

Housing

Under IAY scheme five group houses have been allotted to three SC and two BC families. From the allocation of the kutcha houses seven SC families and two BC families were benefited. 18 very poor families were identified for further allocation.

Drinking Water Facilities

Extension of pipeline and maintenance of pipeline were the important works carried out after planning. Due to this, the extension areas in the hamlets like Pannaipatti, Kombai and Kuttikaradu have been provided with public taps.

Street Lights

Four new street lights were provided, three in the extension area Puthoor Colony and Kuttikaradu and remaining one in Pannaipatti from the Namathu Gramam incentive fund.

Road Facilities

Under the union councellor fund T. Pannaipatti-Vellanservakaran Patti road maintenance works were carried out and CC road for two streets in T. Panniapatti Village was provided.

Health Centre

The ANM is not staying in the health sub-centre building. She comes from Dindigul everyday. She distributes Iron tablets, polio drops and takes the weight details of the pregnant women and children regularly. For the last one year all deliveries are done either in the ANM centre or in the hospital only. Every month, she conducts awareness meeting in the centre for the eligible couples. With the help of a NGO (Darwin, Nilakottai), a medical camp was conducted on 30-09-2005.

The President informed that the Panchayat Administration facilitated the NGO, namely Darwin in its promotion of alternative medicine — Herbal plants. Further the NGO encourages the villagers to understand and make use of the medicinal plants, namely Tulasi, Thuthuvalai, Malaguthakkali, Puthina, alluva, cumid etc. These plants are planted in the school campus involving students and in the backyard of the households involving SHG members. The NGO is receiving the yield of the medicinal crop from the community. There is a scope of income generation from the practice of alternative medicine by the community itself.

Toilet Facilities

With the help of the NGO, the Panchayat Administration constructed 42 household latrines in Kuttikaradu and D. Kombai Villages. Already one woman sanitary complex is being used in T. Pannaipatti village.

Public Distribution System

There are two ration shops functioning in the rented building. Now the Panchayat administration has taken steps to construct a ration shop in T. Pannaipatti from the union councillor fund. Nearly 200 new ration cards were issued by the government. People receive the ration items regularly.

Education

There are two primary schools and one middle school in the T.Pannaipatti village. Now a new additional school building is constructed under SSA scheme. From the MLA Fund a compound wall was constructed at the cost of Rs.2.70 lakhs. The President of Pannaipatti frequently visits the schools and enquires about the children's educational standard and looks after the environmental cleanliness, also checks noon meal centre, kitchen and quality of the meal. He helped two differently-abled students to get disability certificates, and he also sought financial support or any other form of support for the students/children for their higher education from us.

Observation

1. When the researchers enquired about the particulars, two ladies contacted them to get hospital address, another one enquired about the ration shop.
2. The President presented the Namathu Gramam symbol in

a different way so that the people easily understand its seven components.

3. The Vice-President of this Panchayat is having a good relationship with the President.
4. The President is having a good rapport with the NGO, and they conducted medical camp, in which nearly five women with HIV were identified. The Panchayat decided to help these women in their rehabilitation and treatments.

Kamatchipuram Panchayat

I. *Activities carried out after the Hunger Project Planning*

1. Mini power pump at Kamatchipuram was provided and the GLR repair work at Kottaipatti A.D. Colony was carried out.
2. In another hamlet, namely Ramalingampatti A.D. Colony new borewells were constructed, 19 new public taps and 9 house service connections were provided.
3. At Eranampatti a borewell and sintex tank were provided
4. In Pangarupuram hamlet a borewell was erected.

It is observed that out of 16 activities planned to ensure sustainable drinking water supply, five prioritized works were completed.

II. With regard to street lights under Namathu Gramam Scheme Fund, three new tube lights have been provided.

III. Under road facilities 59 works have been planned of which 12 works were completed. Among these, five works were of upgradation of earthen road into cement concrete road.

With regard to the roads under other line department's jurisdiction, highways department authorities have been contacted.

Other Important Works Carried Out

1. A bridge is demanded in the plan across the Mangarayaru in Ellaipatti to Muthunampatti road. It is a link road between the two revenue villages which is very useful. But there

was no fund allocation from the PWD. The Member of Parliament was approached in this regard.

2. The proposal of making the Gobinathuswamimalai as a tourist centre was duly presented to the government through the local minister.
3. The proposal of upgradation of union primary school into Middle school was dropped as there was inadequate students strength.
4. Government approved for the provision of a Police Station at Reddiarchatram.
5. There was a demand for three small bridges of which two were constructed under Namathu Gramam scheme at Ellaipatti hamlet.

With regard to improvement in public sanitation, drainage facility was provided at Ellaipatti and about 120 individual household latrines were also provided. For the solid waste management, a provision was made for the storing of organic and inorganic waste. A Sidha medical camp was organized for which there was a good response from the public.

IV. Under public distribution system, 140 new family cards were obtained with the help of Village Panchayat Administration.

V. Under educational development, in the primary school of Ramalingampatti under SSA scheme, a new additional building was constructed and under TRSP, a toilet for students were provided.

VI. The necessity of repair work at Health Sub-centre was discussed in the Gram Sabha meeting. The higher officials were contacted in this regard. There has been no still birth or infant mortality in this Village Panchayat area.

VII. With regard to Dalit welfare, under MLA local area development scheme fund, repair and maintenance work in 21 old houses belonging to SC were undertaken. 13 poor families among the BC community have been provided with housing facilities and house site patta provision was demanded for 140 SC families.

VIII. 20 poor farmers have been enlisted in government new venture for the welfare of the farmers. Farmers have been organized and started a demonstration demanding to fix minimum support prize for corn.

IX. Six new SHGs have been formed. NGOs have been asked to take steps for obtaining economic assistance.

X. The possibility of small scale production of concentrated cattle feed was discussed at the Gram Sabha meeting. Government authorities have been contacted in this regard.

XI. For the welfare of the physically challenged persons, a camp was organized at the union office Village Panchayat which helped the families of physically challenged to make use of the camp.

XII. An additional school building and a sintex tank, toilet for students and a kitchen have been provided in Kamatchipuram school.

XIII. The injustifiable practice of untouchability ie, a separate tumblers for SC at tea shops existed in this village was done away after a struggle unitedly carried out by the Dalit Community. The Panchayat administration supported the struggle.

XIV. Under the infrastructure development in the Village Panchayat of Kamatchipuram a new building for PDS, one women sanitary complex, SHG buildings have been constructed.

Silvarpatti Village Panchayat

Plan Activities Carried Out

There are 22 hamlets in this Village Panchayat. In the plan in seven hamlets improvement in water supply provision was proposed of which in three hamlets, mini power pumps were provided. Priority has been given to Dalit habitation. The fund was received from TWAD as well as union administration. House electric service connection was given to 12 houses.

Three new street lights have been provided, utilizing the fund from "Namathu Gramam" allocation.

Road Improvement

Under SGRY scheme, 610 metre CC road was provided. The repair and maintenance works were carried out on the BT road from the MLA Fund.

Efforts were taken to get funds for the construction of two small bridges for Sukkampatti and Kathirayankulam hamlets.

Waste Management

A manure yard with the arrangement for separation of bio-degradation and non-bio degradable waste was constructed. Awareness was given to the SHG members to separate the non-bio degradable waste. There are 80 petty shops in this Village Panchayat. The shopkeepers are advised to provide a waste box at the entrance of their establishments to collect polythene based wastes.

Under Public Sanitation

Awareness is generated among the public. 390 individual household latrines have been constructed. The rate of utility of these latrines is improved from 30 percentage to 50 percentage.

Pucca drainage facility was provided at the Silvarpatti and Kathirayankulam AD colony. The maintenance of Women Sanitary Complex located at Silvarpatti is improved.

Educational Development Activities

The additional school building projected in the plan was achieved through Sarva Siksha Abhiyan (SSA) Scheme. And provision of one more building at the union primary school located at S.Vadipatti is also commenced. Further, out of total six schools, in four schools, toilet facilities for boys and girls were completed. To take necessary steps to provide sports goods are taken by the Village Panchayat administration through Parent-Teacher Association.

There are five *Balwadis* functioning in the Village Panchayat of Silvarpatti. Two buildings have been provided in two hamlets. Out of six *Balwadis*, toilet facility has been provided in four *Balwadis*. Public tap facility was provided inside the *Balwadis*.

SHG activities are encouraged by the Village Panchayat. So far seven new groups have been formed to include the left out poor families. NGOs are contacted to get economic assistance to the eligible groups.

With regard to the welfare of the physically-challenged persons, identity card for seven physically-challenged persons were obtained. Tri-cycle was provided to two individuals.

Agricultural Development

The inlet channel and outlet channels and deepening work at one tank were carried out from the fund allocation of the district councillor.

Open Air Theatre facility was provided at Kathirayan Kulam under MP Fund allocation.

Observation

The plan document is very useful to identify the prioriotized works by the ward members. The BPL list is useful to furnish the details collected on the BPL families.

The Viilage Panchayat administration has proposed to conduct household survey with more details on each family. From MLA Fund repair and maintenance work have been taken in ten old group houses occupied by Dalits.

LESSONS LEARNT

Dindigul District

1. Due to the absence of Statutory Committees several activities planned in the Development Plan is attempted all alone by the President.
2. The Village Panchayat clerks are not capacitated enough to do follow-up with line departments with regard to the implementation of plan activities of line department concerned.
3. The union administration and the District Panchayat do not give due recognition to the works prioritized in the plan. As routine, these councils used to carry out activities as they proposed or as per the specification of the government.

4. The mindset of the Government is yet to be transformed with regard to grassroots planning. Namathu Gramam is an innovative scheme to sensitize the village community to involve in the accomplishment of the 7 basic components of social development. The State Government earmarked incentives to the Village Panchayats whenever they achieve target under this scheme. It is learnt that the Village Panchayats after achieving the target are given incentive money with a condition that the money should be spent on the items specified by the government. Where is the concept of 'Namathu Gramam' when the incentive money is not permitted to be utilized for the works prioritized by the Gram Sabha?
5. A system of intervention through facilitating those Village Panchayats targeted under The Hunger Project Development Planning exercise by a professional has not been attempted. Due to this, the Village Panchayats could not convert the plan into project proposals for easy lobbying by themselves.
6. In general the Union Councillor and the District Councillor have not been involved in the plan preparation. Though the involvement of community was taken at the stage of initiative, sufficient for drafting plan, the power and position of conditions to facilitate the Village Panchayat in the following up of the plan with line departments, was not taken into serious consideration.
7. In general the strength of SHG and other CBOs is not properly utilized by the Presidents of the target villages. It is found that some women Presidents made use of the SHG members in the activities of the Village Panchayat.
8. It is observed that invariably, all the targeted Village Panchayat Presidents gave weightage to the activities like improvement in the provision of water supply, improvement in the infrastructure facilities in schools and *Balwadis*, extended assistance for the smooth functioning of Public Distribution System shop, and assisted the marginalized sections to get their entitlement.
9. It is observed that the officials of the department like

TWAD, THADCO, Rural Highways, gave their consent when the plan document of Village Panchayats were shown to them as a proof of community's felt need.

10. Higher representatives like MLAs and MPs recognized the attempt of the Village Panchayat in the preparation of the village plan.
11. It is felt that at least a quarterly meet for review by The Hunger Project—Gandhigram Rural Institute project team as follow-up would make the difference.
12. Due to the existence of more number of hamlets, it is a challenge to fulfil more demands proposed in the plan.
13. It is felt that the Ward Members did not get proper orientation in the plan/follow-up of plan activities. There are a few exceptions. Some Presidents used to brief the Ward Members that what they demanded was taken in the plan and how it was pursued. And so these Presidents were able to mobilize the support of Ward Members in the follow-up activities of the plan.
14. The Block Administration needed proper orientation to extend their support in this experiment so that their orientation would be useful for replicability.
15. In addition to the preliminary orientation to the President and Ward Members concerned, it is felt that specific orientations in preparation of sectoral projects, in building alliance with NGOs and other developmental agencies, and in collaboration with local CBOs including SHGs are needed.
16. The Hunger Project—Gandhigram Rural Institute and the district administration must come together to influence the MPs and MLAs to extend their support and assistance in the implementation of the innovative scheme highlighted in the plan.
17. There is a scope for involving the corporate sector in the fulfilment of village plan by emphasizing their social responsibility (e.g. mills and other business concerns functioning in and around the target villages).
18. The Hunger Project—Gandhigram Rural Institute should have periodical extension works with the targeted Village Panchayats for effective follow-up.

19. A mass sensitization is needed before and after the plan initiative to ensure public awareness and involvement.
20. The major/significant/innovative proposal highlighted in the development plan should be widely disseminated in order to create a mass sensitization which could make an impact on the follow-up.
21. There should be a Village Plan Implementation Committee duly represented apart from the elected representatives, which includes community leaders, proactive political leaders, NGO representatives and representatives from CBOs.

To strengthen the implementation of the development plans, it is realized that the following interventions are needed :

1. Athoor Panchayat Union

In Kalikkampatti Village Panchayat

(i) Strengthening of SHG activities by facilitating a meaningful interface between the NGO concerned and the Village Panchayat Administration.
(ii) Renovation of old colony houses. Assistance to avail fund from the MLA.
(iii) In the *Balwadi* run by Gandhigram Trust, a toilet should be provided.
(iv) Assistance to mobilize eligible widows and elderly persons to avail pension scheme.

2. Panjampatti Village Panchayat

(i) Assistance to sensitize the community especially near the bazar and the main roads for the scientific solid waste management.
(ii) Assistance to contact the MLA to have an additional sanitary complex for women.
(iii) Assistance to get funds from the AD welfare officials to improve the SC Burial Ground.
(iv) A new building for *Balwadi*, to be received from the Union Councillors Fund.

3. Athoor Panchayat

(i) Help to organize mass awareness of the community in sanitation and public health.
(ii) A new building for *Balwadi* — to be received from the MLA Fund allocation.
(iii) To assist the Village Panchayat avail the services of AAO properly.

4. Devarappanpatti Panchayat

(i) Help to extend the solid waste collection in other streets and hamlets in this Panchayat where it is not carried out.
(ii) Assistance for effective and successful solid waste management.
(iii) Orientation to SHG in the maintenance of women sanitary complex.
(iv) Helping to find source for the establishment of Bio-mass gas plant.

NILAKOTTAI PANCHAYAT UNION

1. Noothulapuram Village Panchayat

(i) The Panchayat President took efforts to survey the Panchayat poramboke land and has arranged to distribute land to 40 Dalit members for housing.
(ii) The Panchayat President approached the area M.P. for installing a Bio-Mass gas plant.
(iii) Assist to get fund for construction of a bridge constructed near Seethapuram.
(iv) Give awareness on the use of household toilet and its importance, in all the villages of this Panchayat (Household latrine use is less in the Panchayat Villages).

2. Kodanginaickenpatti Village Panchayat

(i) Poor people need house, but the problem is that they are not able to get land patta from government. The Panchayat administration should take steps to get patta from the government.

(ii) Assist in the efforts taken by the Village Panchayat in the establishment of a sub-helath centre as the land is readily available.

(iii) Assist to get union councillor fund to construct a kitchen-shed in the primary school.

(iv) Assist the village Panchayat administration to get the fund for open air theatre from MLA Fund.

(v) Assist to formulate a project for the establishment of a garden in the Panchayat poromboke.

(vi) Assist to establish a physical exercise centre for the youth.

3. Sithargal Nattham Village Panchayat

(i) Assistance to establish a Dalit colony of 42 families as patta land was available with them.

(ii) Assist in the solid waste management.

(iii) Assist to mobilize fund for constructing for a community toilet for men.

(iv) Assist to improve the infrastructure facility in the Kallar Middle School.

(v) Assist to establish a weekly market place.

(vi) Assist in drafting a proposal to improve the "Hanuman Temple" as a tourist and pilgrim attraction.

(vii) Assist to organize a medical camp for physically challenged persons.

DINDIGUL PANCHAYAT UNION

1. Balakrishnapuram Village Panchayat

(i) Assist the Village Panchayat administration in its attempt to provide house-sites to poor families by acquisition of land from the private individuals.

(ii) Assist to get allocation for the construction of a new ration shop at Rajiv Gandhi Nagar in the Village Panchayat.

(iii) Assist to mobilize public contribution for the construction of a toilet for students in the middle school.

(iv) Assist to get sanction for the establishment of a new *Balwadi* at Mallipatti extension area.

(v) Assist to have own building for the public library.
(vi) Assist to strengthen the SHG activities. Proper utilization of shopping complex.
(vii) Fish rearing and other activities.

2. M.M. Kovilur Village Panchayat

(i) To assist to acquire land for house sites to the poor.
(ii) Assist to sensitise villagers in solid waste management.
(iii) Assist to mobilise fund to undertake repair works in Women Sanitary Complex.
(iv) To assist in getting sanction for a new primary school at Vanniyapatti.
(v) To assist to get sanction to undertake repair work in the *Balwadi.*
(vi) Assist to get a new building for Vanniyapatti *Balwadi.*

3. Mullipadi Village Panchayat

(i) Assist in creating awareness among the SHG members in low cost housing techniques.
(ii) Assist to mobilise public support to undertake tree planting.
(iii) Assist to get sanction for a new bridge across the Santhanavarthini River.
(iv) Assist in orienting SHG members involving NGO in the solid waste management activities.
(v) Assist to get sanction for a separate rationshop at Chettiapatti Hamlet.
(vi) Assist to establish proper linkage with the private aided health centre.
(vii) Assist to get fund for the establishment of a shopping complex.

4. Thottanoothu Village Panchayat

(i) Assist to involve SHG in Vermi-composit production.
(ii) Assist to get a new sanitary complex at Erandalaiparai hamlet.
(iii) Assist to persuade the beneficiaries of TRS programme to make use of the toilet facilities.

(iv) Assist to get sanction for the establishment of rural literacy.
(v) Assist to get a primary health centre.
(vi) Assist to have linkage with the agriculture department and to avail a project from (DPAP) (Drought Prone Area Development Programme).
(vii) Assist to sanction for desilting of tanks.
(viii) Assist to get fund from MP to construct a shopping complex.

5. Anaipatti Village Panchayat

(i) Assist to get more number of allocations under Kutcha House Scheme.
(ii) Assist to properly make use of the service of the agriculture sub-division office.
(iii) Assist to get fund from MLA and MP for construction of a community hall and library respectively.
(iv) Assist to get fund for strengthening the banks of the village tank.
(v) Assist to sustain the status achieved under clean village activities.

REDDIARCHATRAM PANCHAYAT UNION

1. Karisalpatti Village Panchayat

(i) Assist to sensitise villagers in old Kannivadi hamlet with regard to maintenance of public sanitation.
(ii) Assist to improve the Panchayat Office campus.
(iii) Assist to influence the authorities to undertake necessary improvement in the primary school.
(iv) Assist to conduct parent-teacher association meeting to chalk out plan for students personality development and sports and games activities.
(v) Assist to fully utilize the computer facilities available in the Village Panchayat Office.
(vi) Assist to the SHG federation to put into use the computer provided to them.

(vii) Assist to make improvement in the drainage in the community toilet meant for men.

(viii) Assist to mobilize fund for the construction of a shopping complex.

2. T. Pannaipatti Village Panchayat

(i) Assist to strengthen the tie up arrangement with NGOs to improve the SHG activities.

(ii) Assist to follow-up the proposal submitted to the government with regard to promotion of tourist activities in Gobinathaswamimalai.

(iii) Assist to get fund for the repair work at the health sub-centre.

(iv) Assist to have linkage with the NGOs to avail economic assistance to the newly formed Self Help Groups.

3. Silvarpatti Village Panchayat

(i) Assist to get fund for the improvement in water supply provision in the remaining four hamlets.

(ii) Assist to sensitize villagers in solid waste management.

(iii) Assist to organise Parent-Teacher Association to mobilize fund for school improvement activities.

(iv) Assist to avail scheme fund for construction of a toilet each in the two schools and two Balwadies.

(v) Assist to strengthen SHG activities.

Success Stories

In Panjampatti planning exercise helped them introduce innovative concept to their Panchayat. Panchayat introduced a new way to distribute water evenly to all households with a concept called 'water audit'. The Panchayat had very cordial relationship with all SHG members with the help of the SHG members, the Panchayat was able to sensitize all households to construct toilets. SHGs are maintaining women sanitary complex properly. The Panchayat is concentrating on sanitation and water issues. It works closely with M.S. Swaminathan Foundation, Chennai. They are facilitating Panchayats to run ICT Centre, and make Panchayat a 'bio-village'.

Evaluation Report on the Process of Implementation of the Village Development Plan in Dindigul District

Sl. No.	Name of the Panchayat	Activities Undertaken by the Panchayat								
		Housing	*Drinking Water*	*Street Light*	*Road*	*Sanitation*	*PDS*	*Education System*	*Others*	*Observation*
1.	Kalikkampatti	2 SC families got houses	1 Borewell with 5 HP power pump, 1 OHT with 1000 litres capacity	3	3 road works	—	—	Toilet in the primary school in Kalikkampatti and Kottaipatti	1. VHN very active 2. Creation of AIDS awareness and gender discrimination 3. Construction of new *balwadi* building 4. Three SHGs formed 5. Asst Agriculture Officer visiting regularly 6. Pension for widows and old people 7. Management of CPR	1. Strengthening of SHGs are important 2. Renovation of old colonies is needed
1.	N.Panjampatti	Constructed 5 houses	2 Pipeline works	2 Street lights	8 Road works	325 Household latrines, pucca	—	Toilets constructed	—	1. Sensitization of community

(*Contd...*)

(Contd...)

		for widows	completed management		2 small bridges	maintenance by women complex	sanitary	in the primary school premises, secondary school, the two additional buildings were constructed for classrooms	- wall for higher	for scientific solid waste 2. Additional women sanitary complex
3.	Athoor	5 Houses	1 New borewell and sintex tanks	3 Street lights	500 Metre road, 2 small bridges	Manure Yard	400 new ration cards the distri- buted	Toilets in primary school, 1 additional classroom building	1. Special medical camp 2. Proper distribution of pension for widows and old age people	1. Need to organize mass awareness on sanitation and public health 2. AAO service should be properly utilized
4.	Devarappanpatti	—	4 Borewells, 10000 OHT	6 Street lights	4 Road works	Separate buckets for degradable and non-degradable wastes, tricycle was purchased for collection of waste, 60 household latrines were constructed	-	-	1. 2 eye camps organized. 2. Sub-Health centre functioning well. 3. Awareness campaign on immunization. 4. New building for balwadi	1. Solid waste management for entire Panchayat 2. Establishment of bio-mass gas plants

(Contd...)

(Contd...)

5.	Noothulapuram	19 New houses, 6 *kutcha* houses upgraded	5 Borewell and a sintex tank	3 Solar lamps	5 km black top road	Separate bucket for degradable and non-degradable wastes, 250 Household latrines were constructed	Construction of own building	School latrine was constructed, *Balwadis* functioning well	Surveying of poramboke land and patta for 40 Dalit families for housing	1. Should install bio-mass gas plant 2. Should construct bridge near Seethapuram 3. Awareness creation on household toilet
6.	Kodankinayakkanpatti	—	1 Borewell and mini power pump was installed	3 New street lights	A small bridge, retaining wall	—	120 Eligible families got ration card	Toilets in primary school, flooring in primary school, construction of kitchen shed	—	1. Land patta for poor 2. Establishment of sub-health centre 3. Establishment of physical exercise centre
7.	Sithargalnatham	5 Houses for BC	New pipe line, mini power pump, storage sintex tank, new borewell provided	—	1 Metal road, 1 CC Road constructed	*Pucca* drainage system, separate manure yard, prevention of open air defecation	Construction of new building, providing AAY scheme for 70 ultra poor families	Toilet in four schools, additional building	1. New *Balwadis* 2. Maintenance of CPRs	1. More assistance for solid waste management 2. Mobilizing fund for community toilet 3. Improvement infrastructure facilities for middle school

(Contd...)

(Contd...)

										4. Organizing medical camps for physically challenged
8.	Balakrishna-puram	25 New houses, and upgradation of 9 kutcha houses	1 OHT, 1 new hand-pump, and extension of pipeline	—	4 CC Road	1000 metre *pucca* drainage facility, 1 small bridge, manure yard	-	Compound wall for middle school, Enlistment of membership for the library	1. One new *anganwadi* 2. Claiming of pension for the poor widows	1. Housing sites for poor families 2. Need to have own building for public library 3. Proper utilization of shopping complex 4. Micro-financing
9.	M.M.Kovilur	3 AAY houses, 2 *kutcha* houses	—	—	2.5 km Bitumen Road	Pucca drainage for 350 metre; 27 household latrines	Selection of 35 ultra poor families for AAY	Toilets in secondary and higher secondary school	—	1. Sensitization of solid waste management 2. Assist to get new primary school 3. Assist to get sanction for the repair of *Balwadi*.
10.	Mullipadi	9 Houses	Mini power pump with	3 Street lights	—	—	600 New ration cards	Toilet facilities for 4 schools		1. Creating awareness on low-cost housing

(Contd...)

(Contec...)

		sintex tank							2. Mobilizing public for tree planting 3. Solid waste management 4. Establishing linkage with private aided health centre
11. Thottanoothu	16 Group Houses	—	—	CC Road for 6 hamlets	A cart purchased for disposal of solid wastes	—	Toilet facilities for all the schools	1. AAO visiting regularly. 2. Augmentation of Panchayat resources	1. Involving SHGs in vermi-compost 2. New sanitary complex 3. Desilting of tanks
12. Anaipatti	10 Colony houses, upgradation of 15 *kutcha* houses	—	3 Street lights	1 km metal road and small bridge	Separate storing of organic and inorganic waste, individual household latrines for all families, smokeless chula for colony houses	—	Drinking water and toilets to schools	1. Clean village award	1. More allocation under *kutcha* houses 2. Should properly use agriculture sub-division office

(Contd...)

(Contd...)

13. Karisalpatti							PTA functioning well	1. Pucca Panchayat office 2. Nail-cutters for Balwadi 3. Encourage of sports activ-ities	1. Computer facility in Panchayat is not functioning well.
14. T.Pannapatti	5 group houses	Extension of pipeline	4 new street lights	Maintenance of CC road	42 house-hold latrines	200 new ration cards distributed	New additional building	1. ANM staying at sub-health centre itself.	1. SHG should be strengthened 2. Tourism activities should be promoted for Gopinatha Swamikoi
15. Kamatchipuram	—	Mini power pump and borewell, 19 new public taps and 9 in house water	3 New street lights	12 Road works	—	New building for PDS shop, 140 new ration cards	Toilet and new buildings for schools	—	—
16. Silvarpatti	—	—	3 New street lights	610 mt CC Road	390 indi-vidual household latrines, improvement 30% to 50%	Additional school building		—	1. Assist to improve water supply provision 2. Sensitize villages of sold waste

TUTICORIN DISTRICT

Gram Panchayat Development Plan – Follow up
Name of the Gram Panchayats Targeted

Sl. No.	*Union and Gram Panchayat*	*Name of the President*	*Sex*	*Category*			
				G	*SC G*	*SC Women*	*G Women*
I.	**Ottapidaram Panchayat Union**						
1.	Ottanatham	S.Jayabarathi	F	–	–	–	P
2.	Puthiamputhur	P.Jebaraj	M	P	–	–	–
3.	Kodiyankulam	A.Yakammal	F	–	–	P	–
4.	Pattinamaruthur	Marakatchi Beevi	F	–	–	–	P
5.	Tharuvaikulam	Anthony Jayapal	M	P	–	–	–
II.	**Sirivaikundam Panchayat Union**						
1.	Sriparangusanallur	Juliet Suseela	F	–	–	–	P
2.	Sirithondanallur	Chandrikasarvesan	F	–	–	–	P
3.	Thirupanichettikulam	A. Hepsi	F	–	–	–	P
4.	Parakiramapandi	S. Kanakaraj	M	–	P	–	–
5.	Mukkani	A. Subbiah	M	P	–	–	–
III.	**Pudur Panchayat Union**						
1.	Mettilpatti	S. Jeyarani @ Jayamani	F	–	–	–	P
2.	Mathalapuram	C. Shanmugalakshmi	F	–	–	–	P
3.	Kadalkudi	V. Velusamy	M	–	P	–	–
4.	Thaapathi	Amudha	F	–	–	P	–
5.	Ayyanrajakkapatti	R. Mumoorthy	M	P	–	–	–

PLAN IMPLEMENTATION – THOOTHUKUDI DISTRICT

Mettilpatti Village Panchayat – Pudur Union

In Mettilpatti Village Panchayat, a lot of improvements have been made possible due to the cooperation from the people and guidances from the officials, the President explained. She referred to The Hunger Project—Plan exercises which had created an expectation from the Panchayat administration as well as the community leaders, SHGs and youths. It has become a source of strength to the Village Panchayat administration, she added.

Rural Housing

Under the IAY 7 houses (one SC beneficiary and six beneficiaries from other backward classes) have been constructed. Further six houses were also availed under Katcha House Scheme. Altogether 13 poor families were able to improve their housing condition.

Water Supply

As there is insufficiency of ground water, water scarcity issue could not be solved inspite of digging new borewells. With the financial assistance of block and TWAD officials, among the existing hand pumps, three hand pumps were identified where the ground water source was adequate for pumping up through motor pump. 3 sintex tanks were provided along with three hand pumps. Now from these three mini power pump systems water supply is properly ensured in all the three hamlets, the President explained.

Other Infrastructure

With the financial help from the union, five new street lights were provided at Mettilpatti and Surappanayakkanpatti.

Four road improvement works have been projected in the plan. The Highways Department has completed the improvement work in the link road between Alagapuri and Muthuswamypuram. Under the special SGRY, a cart road was improved with *pucca* earthen road. The improvement on the approach road to the burial ground was taken up from the union allocation. Sanction was availed to convert the metal road linking Mettilpatti with Vempur into bitumen road and a CC road work was executed at the distance of 500 metre from the Union assistance.

Under DPAP, one retaining wall was constructed. And one small bridge was constructed from public contribution.

Public Sanitation

Forty-one household latrines have been constructed by individual householders from their own contribution. 379 toilets were provided under Total Rural Sanitation Programme. The sanitary complex so far unutilized has been brought for utilization. There is a total change in the overall mindset and practice among the villagers in respect of public sanitation and personal hygiene, the President explained. She acknowledged that due to the cooperation of the public in this regard, she was able to move further in achieving other activities with the support of government officials and attained 'A' grade under Namathu Gramam.

Further to improve the public sanitation at four places where a quiet number of householders do not possess adequate space for the construction of individual latrine, a mini community toilet facility with public contribution was constructed as the special fund of Rs.1.20 lakh is not adequate to meet the construction of 4 mini-community toilets the President explained. The householders themselves demanded this need as the sanitary complex situated at Mettilpatti is not easily accessible to all hamlets.

Welfare of the Marginalized

About 102 ultra poor families were enlisted for Annapoorna *Antyodaya* Yozana Scheme. 4 poor widows and four elderly persons have been selected to avail monthly pension. With regard to the welfare of the disabled, all have been mobilized to attend the camp and identified for benefits. Free bus pass to eligible persons was demanded. Arrangement is made to utilize facilities at the physiotherapy centre by the deserving disabled persons. Five disabled persons joined themselves and formed into a self-help group, and their demand of providing training was brought to the notice of the district officials, the President explained.

Welfare of Women and Children

Attention is given to the welfare of children. Mothers are asked to bring their children to *Balwadi* and to extend cooperation to the *balwadi* teacher for measuring weight/nutritional status of their children. Repair work on the floor of *Balwadi* was completed. The *Balwadi* building was whitewashed. A toilet was provided.

Self-Help groups were properly oriented to undertake economic activities. Rearing of milch animals, production of vermi-compost, and match box production are the major activities of the members of SHGs. To ensure regular marketing of milk and vermi-compost, the guidance and assistance of NGOs have been arranged. District Industries Centre has come forward to give training to entrepreneurs. Twenty-three potential entrepreneurs (seventeen women and six-men) have been identified for the training.

A private business constructed a spinning mill at Mettilpatti. The general manager was contacted to provide employment to the local persons.

Agricultural Development Activities

Activities under DPAP were properly carried out. All channels were maintained. Tanks have been desilted. With regard to the construction of a retaining wall at Chennurettipatti, which was suggested in the plan proposal, the levelling has to be done before the construction so that the flood water would be easily drained into the channel which leads to Mettilpatti. The officials concerned were approached in this regard.

Animal Husbandry activities have been improved. Assolo, the plant for cattle feed is cultivated by three farmers. It is rich in protein, very much needed for lactating cows. A veterinary camp was organized at Perumal Nayakkanpatti hamlet.

To augment income to the Village Panchayat, tree planting was undertaken. Apart from Neem and Pungan trees, 50 number of Tamarind tree saplings have been planted on the roadside and poramboke lands.

The President informed that they have been preparing themselves to contest for the national clean village award.

Thirupparanchettikulam Village Panchayat – Pudur Union

Thirupparanchettikulam Village Panchayat is a thinly populated village in which there are three number of small hamlets apart from the main village T.P. Chettikulam. There are only 28 huts in this Village Panchayat. About 27 families are living in poramboke lands, of which during 2005-06, 16 house site pattas were distributed to 16 poor families. Further under IAY 5 houses (4 numbers to SC and 1 house to BC) were provided to eligible families.

With regard to the drinking water. It is projected to construct one new OHT as the existing one is very old. But in consultation with the TWAD officials the same was repaired during 2005-06. Moreover, the existing pipeline system was replaced with a new one and gatevalves were fitted wherever necessary to ensure equal supply to all habitations. Further, permission for 13 new house service connections have been obtained as specified in the plan. The expenditure in this regard was met from the allocation of fund from the union administration during the year 2005-06 resulting in the improvement in the basic amenities.

Seventeen new street lights have been installed from the fund allocated under MLA Local Area Development Programme.

Road Improvement Works

In the plan about 15 number of works have been identified under the road improvement. During 2005-06 six works have been completed. For one work administrative sanction is granted to undertake the work during 2006-07. The incentive availed for the achievement in Namathu Gramam was very useful to replace one *kutcha* road as well as one pucca concrete road. Union Fund was released to form bitumen road. Sampoorna Rojgar Yojana Fund was also utilized for the improvement of earthern roads in two hamlets.

Bridge works have not been attempted due to lack of fund the President explained.

Economic Activities

A private entrepreneur has been operating an export trade on flowers. Dry flowers are produced in the village jurisdiction in which about sixty women have been employed. About twenty women from T.P. Chettikulam are regularly getting employment in this venture.

Agricultural and Animal Husbandry Activities

At the initiative of the IOB, Sayarpuram Branch, a Farmers Forum has been formed by three farmers through the guidance of Agricultural Engineering Department officials with a subsidy from the Government.

The avocation of animal husbandry is now-a-days has decreased due to want of grazing lands. As a strict control is exercised with regard to stray animals by the farmers, a quiet number of rearers of milch animals stopped their rearing. Self-Help Groups contacted the government officials with a request to help them for the establishment of fodder crop plantations in a scientific manner.

Maintenance of Water Bodies

Pumari Chettikulam is the only water body available in this Village Panchayat. Cleaning of thorny and wild bushes which grow thickly inside the tank has to be removed along with the desilting so that the water storage capacity could be improved, the President explained. She approached the Project Officer and who has positively agreed to consider the proposal. The channel of the Pumari Chettikulam was maintained under DPAP scheme which was implemented by the nearby Village Panchayat, namely Nattathi.

Public Sanitation

About 8 dustbins were provided in the main village Thuppani-chettikulam. Public are very much cooperative in the maintenance of streets and roads. They segregate the plastic solid wastes and put them into the dustbins.

To improve the road side and to make the village green, steps have been taken to clean all thorny bushes/weeds along the road side, where flowering and shady trees would be proposed to plant. Rs.50,000 is earmarked from the Namathu Gramam incentive of Rs.3.0 lakh rewarded for the achievement of Grade 'A' by the Tharuppanichettikulam Village Panchayat during the year 2005-06. The President acknowledged the guidance provided by Gandhigram Rural Institute and The Hunger Project as they learned the art of mobilizing of public for grassroots planning through The Hunger Project exercises.

Educational Development Activities

SSA scheme is properly implemented. PTA meetings, Village Education Committee meetings are periodically convened. Students are encouraged to perform well in extra curricular activities also, the President explained.

Public Distribution System

A new site is identified for the construction of own building for the Public Distribution System. The District Panchayat Ward Members have agreed to allocate fund for the same. 35 ultra poor have been identified and the list is submitted for the free rice scheme.

Other Infrastructure Facilities

One more SHG building has been constructed at Valasakkaramvillari hamlet. District authorities were contacted with regard to the financing of the construction of a community hall.

Welfare of Women/Children

The Village Panchayat administration is closely linked with the VHN who facilitates activities, the President explained. Special awareness programmes were organized to educate the lactating mothers with regard to the nutritional care of their babies. The chimney at the Balwadi was repaired as projected in the plan. Materials like mats, tumbler and plates have also been provided for the children in Balwadi. The repair works demanded at the VHN centre has been attended to.

The SHG activities are intensified through frequent interface with them. A new SHG among men is formed recently. Out of 9 women SHGs five SHGs had been already availed been given fund. During 2005-06, three more groups availed the fund. One SHG proposed to undergo training in the production of napkins and another SHG proposed to undergo training in hollow bricks manufacturing, the President informed.

Welfare of the Marginalized

Provision of house site pattas enlistment in the free rice scheme and provision of IAY group housing are the activities carried out for the welfare of families of ultra poor. Pension for two widows identified in the plan was arranged. With regard to the welfare of the disabled, credit assistance was availed for 4 persons. Tools and equipments were provided to two persons. Further, the Village Panchayat administration has helped the government officials when they convened a health camp for the disabled.

Augmenting Village Panchayat Income

As there is no other source of income, there is a proposal to enhance the house tax during the year 2006-07, the President informed.

Parakiramapandi Village Panchayat – Srivaikundam Union

Parakiramapandi is a small village surrounded with agricultural lands. The income of the Village Panchayat is very limited. As there are six hamlets including Parakiramapandi, provision of basic amenities in these six habitations is a challenge the President observed.

THP-Plan Activities Carried Out During 2005-06

(a) Infrastructure Development

The link road between the hamlets, namely Pottal and the nearby Village Panchayats Sivakalai has been executed from the union fund. Further the road work linking Ayyathurai with Pottal was also completed.

Out of eleven small bridges projected in the plan, two have been constructed by the Highways Department.

One women sanitary complex has been constructed at Samayathur hamlet and the same is in use. The Balwadi of Samiyathu is at present functioning in the SHG building and the old Balwadi needs proper facilities and maintenance. Union officials have been approached in this regard.

In respect of promotion of SHG activities, steps have been taken to avail revolving fund to all eligible SHGs. Now all eight SHGs availed revolving fund. Earlier only one SHG had availed the revolving fund. The SHG members do not show any interest in self-employment activities or any other business endeavours. As wage employment opportunities are available in the village and in neighbouring area. Some women members learned the skill of stiching but many of them preferred to work in the field whenever there were agricultural activities, the President explained. In spite of these handicaps, an entrepreneur from outside of the village identified women who had real interest and attitude in self-employment through tailoring, arranged 10 sewing machines to manufacture readymade garments. This would create a new impact on the mindset of the womenfolk, the President observed.

Welfare of the Disabled

When the national camp for disabled was organized at the Panchayat Union, the disabled persons were mobilized to attend. Identity cards for all disabled have been obtained.

With regard to the welfare of the marginalized, about 30 ultra poor have been included under Annapoorna *Antyodaya* Scheme, and availed free rice from the scheme.

Step was taken to get financial assistance to the village craftsmen—potters. It is told that the two potter families who have already availed loan and they are yet to repay. Hence the banker did not come forward to assist the other potters.

As projected under agricultural development activities, meetings were organized to disseminate the information on the vegetable cultivation and natural way of agriculture.

The President observed that the government must review the financial allocation to the Village Panchayat on the basis of population. Provision of minimum basic necessities is very essential in all hamlets. Hence he appealed to the government to identify the gap in the provision of infrastructure and allocate funds accordingly.

Ayan Rajapatti Village Panchayat – Pudur Union

Ayan Rajapatti is a small Village Panchayat with a single hamlet, namely Kailasapuram apart from the main village, Ayan Rajapatti. During the year 2002-2003, there was a revenue of Rs.65 lakh from the auction of small mines (sand). During that period the Village Panchayat Council did not have any plan for its development activities. But the THP plan initiatives triggered the mind of villagers during the focus group discussion sessions. The felt needs of the various sections of the community have been projected in the plan document. Due to availability of funds in the Village Panchayat account, a number of works identified in the plan were successfully executed.

There are 19 works projected in the plan document of Ayan Rajapatti. Of which several works have been completed during the plan implementation period 2005-06. The major works are under the following category:

(1) Improvement of water supply,
(2) Infrastructure Development – Community-cum-Marriage Hall,
(3) CC Road Formation,
(4) Bitumen in Union Road,
(5) Threshing Floor.

Apart from the above works, a new office building for the Village Panchayat has been constructed at the cost of 3 lakhs.

The remaining works like improvement to approach road to burial grounds, retaining walls along the side of Ooranis and tree planting at the Village Natham would be taken up in the ensuing year, the President informed.

Economic Development of Ultra Poor

Out of nine members identified as very very poor, for two people loan was arranged for the purchase of milch animal; to one person under *katcha* house scheme, one *katcha* house was provided; deserving persons have been included in the IAY list. To one poor, person housing was sanctioned under IAY group house.

Out of 12 women, two widows have been included in the SHG and two have been given monthly pension from social security scheme.

Housing to poor is yet to be done. Locating of sites for more house pattas is initiated with the help of Village Administrative Officer.

Improvement in the Common Property Resources

There are eleven ooranis of which in five ooranis desilting work was completed.

Formation of a grove in the poramboke site along the river has been proposed. Further a bio-mass plant for production of electricity was established there.

From 2004-05 DPAP scheme, activities were implemented in the Village Panchayat area.

SHG Activities

The expected water for irrigation from the Irukkankudi Dam had been released. About 100 acres of land filled with karuvel trees have been reclaimed. Karuvel trees have been uprooted and cultivation of crops like, paddy, ragi, chilly, and onion has been undertaken by the farmers.

The President observed that earlier the officials delayed to give administrative sanction to carry out activities from the Village Panchayat Fund. Now there is a plan document, framed by the people themselves. And so, the officials responded positively to spend the Village Panchayat Fund for the needs identified by the villagers in the plan document.

Kodiyankulam Village Panchayat – Ottapidaram Union

It is a small Village Panchayat where the population of Dalits is more than 90 per cent. There are only 17 huts and during 2005-06 10 huts have been replaced with tiled houses.

With regard to the provision of drinking water from the river source in the habitation of new colony and Mettur, the district authority is yet to sanction the required money to make extension of the pipeline. As there is a lack of finance in Village Panchayat account, the President approached the district administration to extend its financial support.

With regard to road improvement, four works have been projected in the plan of which one road work namely Kodiyankulam to community hall, the earthern road has been improved as metal road. And in the category of bridges, four small bridges have been proposed at the new colony. During 2005-06 two small bridges were constructed. The President informed that though the plan document was given to the Councillors of Union and District Panchayat, they do not give priority to those works proposed in the plan. Usually they prefer works like formation of CC road, thar road, building construction by which their names could be remembered.

With regard to the improvement works in school building, nothing has been done about the paucity of fund, in the Village Panchayat, the President told. At the *balwadi*, a toilet for children has been constructed, at the SHG building electricity supply connection was provided, and an approach road to burial ground. These were the activities undertaken in the year 2005-06 from the Village Panchayat Fund.

From the Namathu Gramam incentive money of Rs.10,000 3 street lights have been provided at Kodiyankulam Panchayat.

In the year 2004-05, from the Village Panchayat Fund desilting of channels, desilting of ooranis, water storage facility for cattle in two places, and a retaining wall have been provided to the community.

From the allocation of the Local Area Development Fund of the Assembly Member Rs.1,00,000 has been spent for the laying of a CC road.

The President is of the opinion that the Planning Committee should be oriented in the plan implementation so that their active cooperation and involvement will be ensured and more schemes from the sectoral departments could be availed for the Panchayat.

Parakiramapandi Village Panchayat – Srivaikundam Union

Parakiramapandi is a small village surrounded with agricultural lands. The income of the Village Panchayat is very limited. As there are six hamlets including Parakiramapandi, provision of basic amenities in these six habitations is a challenge, the President observed.

The Hunger Project-Plan Activities carried out during 2005-06

Infrastructure development: The link road between Pottal and the nearby Village Panchayat Sivakalai has been executed from the union fund. Further yet another road work linking Ayathurai with Pottal was also undertaken.

Out of eleven small bridges projected in the plan, two have been constructed by the Highways Department.

One woman sanitary complex has been constructed at Samaythu hamlet and it is in use. The *Balwadi* of Samiyathur is at present functioning in the SHG building as the old *Balwadi* needs proper facilities and maintenance. Union officials have been approached in this regard.

In respect of promotion of SHG activities, steps have been taken to avail revolving fund to all eligible SHGs. Now all eight SHGs availed revolving fund. Earlier only one SHG had availed it. The SHG members do not show any interest in self-employment activities or any other business endeavour, as employment opportunities are available in the village and in the neighbouring area. Some women members learned the skill of stitching, but many of them preferred to work in the field whenever there were agricultural activities, the President explained. In spite of these handicaps, an entrepreneur from outside of the village identified women who had real interest and attitude in self-employment through tailoring, arranged 10 sewing machines to manufacture ready-made garments. This would create a new impact on the mindset of village womenfolk, the President observed.

Welfare of the Disabled

When the national camp for the disabled was organized at the Panchayat Union, the disabled persons were mobilized to attend. Identity Cards for all disabled persons have been obtained.

With regard to the welfare of marginalized people about 30

ultra poor have been included under Annapoorna Antyodaya scheme and availed the free rice.

Steps were taken to get financial assistance for the village craftsmen, namely the potters. Two families engaged in pottery work have been already given loan but they could not repay the loan. Hence the bankers did not come forward to assist the other potters.

As projected under agricultural developmental activities, meetings were organized to disseminate the information on the vegetable cultivation and natural way of agriculture.

The President observed that the government must review the financial allocation to the Village Panchayats on the basis of population. Provision of minimum basic necessities is very essential in all hamlets in respect of the population. Hence he appealed to the government to identify the gap in the provision of infrastructure and allocation of funds accordingly.

Siruthondanallur Village Panchayat – Srivaikundam Union

Siruthondanallur Village Panchayat has eight hamlets including the main village Siruthondanallur. There are 14 activities under various heads projected for the plan period 2004-05. Out of 14, 8 works have been successfully executed, the President informed. 3 cement concrete road works were completed from the Village Panchayat Fund. The Highways Department has put up the bitumen road at a distance of 5 km between Aral to Subramaniapuram. This work was proposed in the plan. The plan document was submitted to the Highways Department, they earmarked the work in their plan and so the work was executed, she added. Yet another projected work, construction of a retaining wall and replacing of the two small bridges with big bridges on the Siruthondanallur link road was also taken for implementation by the Highways and the union administration.

The improvement in the water supply was possible with the help of TWAD. Now the drinking water source is at the Thamaraipadi river site.

Provision of additional street lights in Kottaikadu hamlet was completed from the incentive money of Namathu Gramam Scheme. Further, in the Mottathathamvillai as well as Sakkammalpuram hamlet, 11 new street lights were provided from the allocation made by the MLA.

The work proposed under PWD was the desilting/removal of wild weeds and provision of fencing around Perunkulam. The authorities of PWD have been contacted in this regard. In the mean time, with the participation of the public, the wild weeds were removed from the tank.

Implementation of Plan during 2005-06

1. 5 group houses were constructed under IAY.
2. The Village Panchayat assisted 25 families to get new ration cards.
3. 4 disabled persons have been assisted with tools/ equipments and credit facility for self-employment.
4. 15 ultra poor families have been enlisted for the free rice scheme.
5. Water supply has been provided to the *Balwadi* at Sakkamalpuram and Manalur.
6. At the union primary school, toilet facility for students was provided.
7. Students have been encouraged to participate in the competitions under Namathu Gramam and prizes were distributed to them.
8. CC road work was completed in Siruthondanallur.
9. Bitumen road was provided under union scheme at Manalur hamlet.
10. The District Councillor was approached for the construction of retaining wall at the Manalur hamlet.
11. At three places rain water harvest structures were provided. Soak pits were provided at 3 public taps where the environmental sanitation was very bad. Now the waste water is filled into the soak pits. The site around the public tap is kept neat.
12. Awareness programme were convened in respect of public sanitation. The public extended their cooperation and the Village Panchayat secured a 'B' grade under Namathu Gramam.

13. The MP was contacted for the construction of a community hall.
14. To establish library, a site was identified at Kothalari hamlet. Fund is earmarked from the Namathu Gramam incentive assistance.
15. Under SSA two additional buildings have been constructed in the higher secondary school. MLA agreed to get a computer centre for the school.
16. Drinking water supply is provided by the Village Panchayat in the higher secondary school.
17. Members from 4 SHGs were mobilized to undergo entrepreneurship training with the assistance from District Industries Centre.

The President said that the plan prepared in the Village Panchayat was very useful to contact various sectoral departments like PWD, Highways, Health and also the higher officials like District Councillor, MLA, MP have come forward to give weightage to the plan activities when they allocate fund under Local Area Development Programme, she added.

THAPPATHI VILLAGE PANCHAYAT

Rural Housing

There are about fifty huts in the Village Panchayat. The President was able to avail financial support for the construction of 10 *pucca* houses to SC under IAY scheme as well as *katcha* house scheme. The poor among the caste Hindus also needed *pucca* housing. Six poor families from the caste Hindus will get *pucca* housing.

The President said that improvement in the rural housing should be attempted through many agencies. Bank loans with a marginal subsidy to the eligible poor should also be encouraged. She suggested that the SHG members should be properly oriented since many of them use the saving and credit money to purchase jewels and other household utensils. If they are properly oriented about the importance of *pucca* housing, and if bank assistance with marginal subsidy is extended to them, the rural housing scheme will succeed the President added.

Among the plan activities projected for the period 2004-05, the following works have been completed successfully: The President informed that many of the activities projected in the plan were executed from the Village Panchayat's own fund. Construction of a retaining wall, provision of CC road, shelter to the passenger and manure yard were provided. Cart to carry out the dead body is proposed in the plan. Permission was sought from the district administration to procure cart from the Village Panchayat's own fund. The President informed that demand like this had been put forth by the villagers when the need assessment was done through focus group discussions, initiated at the early stage of the planning process. Otherwise these demands are never expressed by the villagers even during Gram Sabha meetings, she observed.

Provision of a compound wall was taken up but the work was yet to be completed for want of fund. The President demanded the union administration to allocate fund under the scheme to improve the basic amenities. But the Union Councillor did not allocated any fund during 2004-05 under this head.

One of the activities identified under plan for the period 2004-05 was, mobilizing loan assistance for the poor individuals. The President helped 25 poor families to avail loan for the purchase of milch animals.

Activities like improvement of water bodies, planting of trees, and maintenance of irrigation channels have been proposed and the fund allocation for the same was subject to the sanction of the scheme, namely Drought Prone Area Development Programme to the Village Panchayat Thappathy. The President had taken initiative since 2002. But she was able to avail funds only in the year 2005-06. This was possible as it was shown in the plan document and also she persuaded the authorities to sanction the DPAP scheme to Thappathy Village Panchayat.

During 2005-06, under DPAP, desilting works in two tanks, maintenance work in two channels and construction of two check dams were the major activities undertaken in Thappathy Village Panchayat. The period of the operation of the scheme is three years.

Hence all the activities under Common Property Resource Management (CPRM) could be covered.

During 2005-06, as per the plan, the pipeline was extended to the needy areas and 8 new public taps were provided to the community in these areas. Maintenance work in the *Balwadi* building was proposed in the plan. When the collector visited the village to inspect the ration shop, the issue was brought to his notice. The Collector advised the block official to allocate the needed fund from the Panchayat Union general fund. Accordingly Rs.20,000 was obtained and the repair work in the *balwadi* building was completed.

There was a need to provide an automatic switch at the Borewell and the pump meant for water supply. The borewell/pump room is located at a distance of 4 km. To switch off the power pump, the operator has to travel the long distance. Hence the provision of automatic switch system was proposed, the President explained.

Permission was sought to spend the Village Panchayat fund for the erection of one hand pump, proposed in the plan, she added. With regard to the construction of community-cum-marriage hall, she approached the Member of Parliament as proposed in the plan.

The President Mrs.Amutha opined that in order to ensure cooperation and the participation of the officials from the various developments, the plan should be drafted in all Village Panchayats and the consolidation of Panchayat plan into block plan could ensure the involvement of all sectoral officials, she pointed out.

The first step of drafting a model plan in five Village Panchayats in Pudur Block of Thoothukudi was a trend setter, she claimed. When the Namathu Gramam scheme was introduced in the Village Panchayats, the experiences of The Hunger Project's model villages have been a learning experience to all other Village Panchayats, she explained. Due to the availability of a plan through The Hunger Project-Gandhigram Rural Institute initiative, the potentials of the Village Panchayat and the community were known to the higher officials who positively considered the plan proposals.

Mrs. Amutha pointed out that in Melakaranthai, the Panchayat President experienced hardship in collecting data when a programme was proposed from the district administration, whereas the details have been immediately furnished in The Hunger Project plan villages. The Panchayat was able to project the number of works be completed to the State Government referring to the plan documents. Since the priority was accepted by The Hunger Project plan for the villages.

Sri Parangusanallur Village Panchayat – Sri Vaikundam Union

In Sri Parangusanallur Village Panchayat there are two hamlets, namely Kila Alwarthoppu and Mela Alwarthoppu. In this Village Panchayat there are no SC people. It has only BC population, and out of 760 households only 34 are huts. Activities Projected in the Plan carried out during the year 2005-06 are:

Water Supply and Rural Electrification

There is only one activity of digging of one new borewell/ construction of OHT and extension of pipeline for the Mela Alwar Thoppu residents projected in the plan. This need was fulfilled. Now five new public taps have been provided in Mela Alwar Thoppu where equal water supply to all habitants is ensured.

With regard to the provision of street lights from the grant given under Namathu Gramam, 3 street lights were given to the Mela Alwar Thoppu. For the residents of other two hamlets Kila Alwar Thoppu and Sri Parangusanallur, 15 street lights were demanded along with a demand for an *anganwadi.* 7 solar lights were fitted and the expenditure was met from the Village Panchayat fund. Two hutment dwellers were benefited under one light scheme.

Road Improvement

During the implementation of road works, the encroachment existing along the link road between Mela Alwar Thoppu and the Hindu Middle School have been removed.

2 CC road works and 3 metal road works have been executed as projected in the plan. The Highways Department positively considered the demand of providing a metal road linking Srivaikundam and Alwar Thoppu bitumen road. A retaining wall has been erected to prevent the damage caused during floods. About

Rs.1.0 lakh was spent from the Village Panchayat Fund for this.

15 families were assisted to avail new ration cards.

Educational Development

There are two primary schools and one middle school in the jurisdiction of the Village Panchayat. The Village Education Committee is functioning effectively. Provision of drinking water supply and toilet facilities were completed in two schools. Further the kitchen-shed repair works were also attended to.

With regard to the improvement in the two *Balwadis*, toilets facility was given to one centre. From the public contribution, utensils needed for this centre were also provided.

New building was demanded for Keela Alwar Thoppu *Balwadi* centre. A suitable site was identified and survey work was completed. The construction of new *Balwadi* building would be commenced soon.

The monitoring of nutritional status of children below five years is periodically done and follow-up work with concern mothers when the level of nutritional status of children decreased, was also carried out properly, the President explained.

Women Development Activities

A new economic activity, namely production of bio-gas from the wood/plant wastages was commenced. A building complex at a cost of Rs.2 lakh and equipment and machineries at a total cost of Rs.3 lakh has been established. Members of SHG are getting wage income by the selling of fire wood to produce gas from the gasifier plant. The plant operators are women. They get the necessary training in this regard, the President explained.

It is learnt that the NGO responsible for the strengthening of SHG does not give much attention in its activities. Hence a lack of interest among the member was noticed, the President explained. A new NGO has been encouraged to involve with the self-help groups, she added.

Additional toilet has been provided at Sri Paragusanallur. Two hundred household latrines were provided in the Village Panchayat area.

With assistance of VHN, motivation/awareness was given to adolescent girls in respect of personal hygiene and practice of good health habit and maintenance of public sanitation.

A new tank was constructed at a cost of Rs.0.50 lakh. It has been serving as the rainwater harvest structure also.

To augment income to the Village Panchayat, construction of a commercial complex and community-cum-marriage hall was proposed. The building design is yet to be finalized. Exposure has been given to study various designs, the President informed. The projected cost for the commercial complex is Rs.2.0 lakh and Rs.15.0 lakh is estimated for the marriage hall. The expenditure will be met from the fund given from the revenue share of income from small sand mines.

Other Activities

Two shelter facilities for passengers were provided; the activities of Kamaraj Youth Association have been properly guided by the Panchayat Administration. Encouragement was given to these youths in their sports and recreational activities. They showed interest in the activities of the Village Panchayat, especially in the maintenance of public sanitation.

Welfare of the Marginalized

Hearing aid, identity card and monthly cash assistance have been arranged for the deserving persons among the disabled.

Widow pension and old age pension were given for 7 persons.

25 persons were selected to avail free rice under AAY.

Agriculture Development

Awareness is given in the natural farming to the farmers with the guidance of the agricultural department. Planting of more tamarind trees is suggested as sales of tamarind is a good revenue for farmers.

The economy of animal husbandry is explained to the members of SHGs as the cattle rearers did not give much attention to increase the milch yield.

The President observed that the activities of her Village Panchayat have been strengthened due to the plan. The officials understood the felt needs listed out in the plan and so necessary delay in the process of availing administrative-cum-technical sanction was reduced to a considerable extent, she added.

The plan document is very useful when the Namathu Gramam Scheme was introduced, she observed. And so they could achieve a 'B' grade and availed the incentive money of Rs.1.0 lakh. Provision of a CC road was proposed from this fund so that the environmental sanitation would improve in her village, she remarked.

SHG members are encouraged to use the computer facilities established under 'RASSI' scheme.

Pattinamaruthur Village Panchayat

- As proposed in the plan, construction of a ground level reservoir at the capacity of 10,000 litre was undertaken under Eleventh Finance Commission grant.
- At Palarpatti, the maintenance work in the BT road has been taken up by the union administration. Further, as per the plan proposal provision of two retaining walls was completed.
- Efforts were taken to provide individual household toilets under TRSP in hundred houses.
- Under public distribution system plan activities, fifty new ration cards have to be obtained for fifty families. But only thirty cards were obtained.
- Higher authorities were contacted in connection with the provision of additional building to the primary school of Pattimaruthur village.
- Shelter for passengers was provided. And under Tsunami special relief fund, fish auction centre work at Pattimaruthur was taken up at a cost of two lakh rupees.

- Under SHG activities, four new groups among women were formed, enlisting the left out poor families. Out of 12 SHGs, eleven got revolving fund. Credit assistance for economic activities was demanded by three groups. The Panchayat administration has contacted the concerned NGO in this regard. Further, men SHGs are also formed at the instance of NGOs and Nehru Yuva Kendra.
- Under IAY, three houses were provided to three poor families belonging to the Most Backward Community. There are about 15 poor families who needed patta site for their dwelling unit. Revenue officials have been contacted in this regard.
- Identity cards were obtained for five persons among the physically challenged individuals.
- From the Village Panchayat Fund, provision of CC road was completed as planned. Further under Namathu Gramam incentive, two CC roads and three street lights were provided.
- Desilting of a fish pond was taken up by the union at the cost of Rs.75,000.
- To augment income to the Village Panchayat tree planting was undertaken on the tank bund.

Ottanatham Village Panchayat

Observation

The Woman President is completely dependent upon her father-in-law for advice and support. Though she is educated and also oriented in the plan process, it was observed that her father-in-law who is a retired teacher also a lead farmer is virtually handling the Village Panchayat administration.

Accomplishment of Plan Activities

Formation of a park-cum-play centre was successfully executed after removing all encroachments. Courts for the outdoor game like tenniguoit, volley ball and ball badminton have been provided.

Toilets were provided in the two *balwadis* and also one CC road was provided as proposed in the plan.

Extension of water supply was proposed in the plan. But it was dropped as there was sufficient water supply in all borewells. With regard to solid waste management, it was proposed to procure a tricycle with a motor. But due to paucity of fund, a tricycle was purchased to transport the solid waste. Further it was proposed to procure equipments like sprayer and other sanitary tools. Effort has been made in this regard.

A marriage-cum-community hall was proposed in the plan and the sitting member of the Parliament was contacted and after verifying the plan document, he sanctioned five lakh rupees and the work is in the completion stage.

Puthiamputhur Village Panchayat

A number of activities proposed in the plan were carried out by the Village Panchayat. Drainage facilities, four CC roads, mini power pump and gravel roads were the major works carried out under SGRY fund, Namathu Gramam incentive, besides the Village Panchayat Fund.

Provision of roof and basic amenities like water, approach road, and light facility were proposed in the graveyard of all communities. The Village Panchayat Administration had approached the district administration in this regard.

The repair and maintenance work in the water supply system was carried out as proposed in the plan. It was planned to provide twenty street lights but only eight streetlights were provided.

In all three *Balwadis*, toilets were provided. Further the vessels needed for cooking were also purchased from the contribution of the public.

There was a proposal to streamline the disposal of solid wastes especially plastic/polythene items as a number of readymade garments production units were functioning in the jurisdiction of Puthiamputhur Village Panchayats. The President informed that the collection of solid waste was undertaken by engaging labourers periodically. But the President informed that it was not feasible as the wage expenses was higher than the sales proceedings of the plastic waste. He further told that he was interacting with the Traders Association for creating a common fund in this regard.

Tharuvaikulam Village Panchayat

Tharuvaikulam is a coastal Village Panchayat. In the plan proposal, activities like desilting of ponds and tanks to augment ground water were listed out. Accordingly in two tanks and twelve ponds, desilting work was undertaken. Further the extension of nine pipelines to fishermen colony was also executed.

In respect of road improvement work, the approach roads to sea-shore and fishermen colony needed maintenance. When the special fund for Tsunami relief was sanctioned, as per the plan, the approach roads to sea-shore, street roads, and the approach road to Annathamadampacheri hamlet were completed. Now step has been taken to avail fund for the maintenance of approach road to graveyard.

With regard to solid waste management, fifteen dustbins were provided in bazaar street at Tharuvaikulam main village. The efforts taken for the improvement of sanitation were yielded dividend. Individual toilets were constructed in hundred houses.

Under public distribution system, fifty-five poor were enlisted under Annapoorna Antyodaya Scheme (free rice distribution).

In the educational sector, an additional building was provided in the government high school.

SHG activities were strengthened when two SHGs availed revolving fund. For the remaining seven groups the assistance of NGOs was sought by the Village Panchayat administration. Among the men SHG, one SHG at Tharuvaikulam which was affiliated with NYK had also availed revolving fund.

Out of hundred housing units proposed under plan for fishermen families, twenty-five was availed.

The President informed that after Tsunami, the district administration came forward to undertake needed repair/ maintenance works in addition to fulfil the unattended felt need if shown to the district administration and the officials selected the activities identified in the plan without any delay whereas in other coastal villages the selection process was delayed. The President acknowledged the facilitation extended by The Hunger Project-Gandhigram Rural Institute team in the plan process as the tsunami relief fund at the cost of one crore was availed without any delay.

Observations made by the Presidents on the Impact of Planning

1. The issues in the equal provision of water supply to all hamlets and to all habitations came to be debated and so planning has been done to overcome the problem. After planning as priorities, efforts have been taken to improve the water supply system. In these initiatives, sources of fund were identified and the Village Panchayat Council by showing the plan document was able to influence various sources and availed fund assistance to improve water supply to the villages.
2. Further the activities which have to be executed from the Village Panchayat's own fund were also listed out in consultation with the Gram Sabha. Accordingly, based on the availability of Village Panchayat Fund, activities projected in the plan have been executed one by one. Due to this plan, there is no hue and cry from the ward members as the activities listed out would be carried out in a phased manner. The habitants of the concerned ward and its member were also aware of these problems. This created a healthy atmosphere in many of the target Village Panchayats where THP-GRI plan exercise was undertaken. Provision of solar light, small bridges, overhead tank, CC road, street lights etc. were the major activities in this regard.
3. Activities planned under the jurisdiction of other sectoral departments were brought to the notice of the concerned officials and frequent reminders/contact resulted in the accomplishment of these proposals.

   Departments like highways, health and family welfare, agriculture, public work department THADCO, Revenue and social welfare extended their support to the execution of important activities projected in the plan. The plan document facilitated the interface between these sectoral departments and the Model Village Panchayats.

4. Villagers realised the limitation of the Village Panchayat as well as the actual financial position. Hence in many model villages, the public came forward for voluntary activities like desilting of tanks, removal of thorny bushes/ wild weeds in water bodies. Moreover, the villages realised the significance of prioritizing the needs in the context of financial crunch as well as the system and procedure of financing. Hence there is no unnecessary demand/pressure over the implementation of works. The public have developed confidence in the ability of Village Panchayat as they witnessed the execution of activities one by one through the hard efforts of the council.
5. The GRI-THP-Plan initiative has been undertaken prior to the announcement of innovative social development scheme namely "Namathu Gramam". The experience of GRI-THP Planning helped a lot to the Village Panchayats when they worked for 'Namathu Gramam'. Due to this experience, many of the GRI-THP plan villages have gained progress in planning and implementation of activities under 'Namathu Gramam' and achieved grades to avail incentives in this regard. In the district of Thoothukudi, there were only 3 village Panchayats which have been adjudged as the 'A' grade. Out of the three two Village Panchayats, namely (1) Mettilpatti, (2) Thirupanichettikulam are the The Hunger Project-plan villages. Further in the 'B' grade out of six Village Panchayats two villages, namely Sriparangusanallur and Siruthondanallur are the GRI-THP Plan villages.

   During the ceremony of the prize distribution held at the district headquarters, the above GRI-THP Plan village Panchayat Presidents acknowledged the THP-GRI contribution in orienting the Village Panchayat Council as well as the village community in the concept and practice of village level planning.

6. The welfare of marginalized section of the community is focused in the plan. The social welfare department, the district disabled rehabilitation society and the revenue officials provided necessary input to the village plan activities in this regard.

The clerks of GRI-THP Plan Village Panchayats made the following observation as impact of the plan exercise:

(a) Furnishing of data/details with regard to village planning is very easy.
(b) The other sectoral department officials made note on the needs projected in the plan and positively responded.
(c) Villagers realised the prioritized works.
(d) As ward members were provided with the plan document, they instead of making demands, came forward to facilitate plan implementation. They showed interest to visit other departments. They themselves met union councillors/ district councillors during their visit to the village functions/ Gram Sabha meetings.
(e) The villagers gained knowledge and practice with regard to the scope of 29 subject activities.
(f) Interest is created to probe financial sources and in this attempt many new information/ways were found to improve the village conditions.
(g) Served as a precursor to the innovative scheme 'Namathu Gramam'. Block officials advised other Village Panchayats to refer the GRI-The Hunger Project Plan document for preparing plan under Namathu Gramam. The clerks of the THP plan villages have been asked to facilitate the needs of the other Village Panchayats in this regard.
Comparison with other villages GRI-THP plan villages, gained many improvements under Namathu Gramam activities.

- GRI-THP plan exercise created awareness among the villagers. Especially the SHG members, village elders and community leaders extended their cooperation in Village Panchayat activities.
- The attendance of the participants from SHG has increased

when various meetings have been convened in the Village Panchayat.

- The concept and practice of transparency in administration was learnt and a considerable progress was attained in GRI-THP Plan Village Panchayat, administration in this regard.

Observation Made by Block Officials on THP-plan initiatives

1. From the data, the real felty needs of the villagers have been identified through the grassroots planning under The Hunger Project.
2. Efficiency and the utilization of fund is improved as the activities projected already have to be executed. Earlier the Village Panchayat Council did not have vision in proper utilization of funds.
3. A new attempt/initiative is made to dovetail schemes/ allocations to fulfil the plan needs.
4. An opportunity was created to have official interface with various departments/sources of financial assistance through the plan document. This facilitated the sustainable linkage between the Village Panchayat and sectoral departments.
5. A vision is created with regard to the development. A road map is now framed. In the case of any additional need pointed out by the villagers, the same may be added to the existing plan. Thus a continuity of developmental activities is ensured in spite of changes of leadership/membership in the Panchayat Council.
6. The plan document is an inducing instrument to activate Village Panchayat Council, as well as stakeholders which command their interest and attention to make necessary follow up.
7. Government officials positively reacted to the plan, and showed considerable flexibility at their end in deciding necessary allocation to the fulfilment of identified needs in the plan in spite of other activities which have been advised by the higher officials/government order.
8. Organization of other activities like 'rural sports' are easily done in the THP-Plan villages where a conducive atmosphere is created through the plan exercise.

Evaluation Report on the Process of Implementation of the Village Development Plan in Thoothukudi District

Sl. No.	Name of the Panchayat	Activities Undertaken by the Panchayat								
		Housing	*Drinking Water*	*Street light*	*Road*	*Sanitation*	*PDS*	*Education System*	*Others*	*Observation*
1.	Mettilpatti	7 IAY houses, 13 houses improved	3 Hand pumps 3 Sintex tanks, 3 mini power pump systems	5	–	41 Household latrines, individual contribution, 379 total rural sanitation mini community total – public contribution Rs.1.20 lakh funds	–	–	AAY – 102 families, camp for differently abled persons, channels provided	Plan is source of strength for Panchayat, It mobilized community for Panchayat work
2.	Thirupani-chettikulam	Patta for house sites	1 OHT	17	15 number of works	8 dustbins, clearing thorny bushes weeds	AAY – 35 families own building	PTA, meetings, village education, committee system	–	Welfare of marginalized concentrated
3.	Parakirama-pandi	–	–	–	–	1 Women sanitary complex	AAY 30 families	–	Balwadi improvement, promotion of SHG activities	Welfare of differently abled concentrated, 65 lakhs from auctioning of small sand mines

(Contd...)

(Contd...)

4. Ayan Rajakkapatti	–	Improvement of water supply, retaining wall to ooranis	–	Improvement of approach road to burial ground, CC road for all streets, bitumen in union road	-	–	–	Threshing community floor, hall of marriage, new office building, tree planting	–
5. Kodiyan-kulam	17 Houses	Providing drinking water from river source	–	CC road, Thar road	*Balwadi* toilet	–	–	Community hall, bridges, electrification of SHG buildings, desilting of tanks	Planning committee should be oriented, sectoral departments should be sensitized
6. Siruthonda-nallur	5 Group houses	Water supply to *Balwadi* and higher secondary school	–	CC road, bitumen road,	Primary school toilet facility, rainwater harvesting structure, soak pits near public taps	25 families, new ration cards, 15 ultra poor families for AAY scheme	2 additional buildings for higher secondary school, computer centre	–	Plan document helped to contact sectoral departments, District Councillor, MLA, MP

(Contd...)

7.	Thappathi	10 No. of *pucca* houses	8 new public taps, automatic switch at bore well, 1 hand-pump	–	1 CC road	–	–	–	Manure yard, planting trees, irrigation channel maintenance	Consolidation of village plan should become a block level plan
8.	Sriparangu-sanallur	–	1 new bore well, OHT and extension of pipelines	18 street lights, 7 solar lights	Removal of encroachment, 22 CC roads, 3 metal roads	–	–	Active functioning of Education Committee Monitoring nutritional status of children	Production of bio-gas by SHG, strengthening of SHGs, shelter facilities, hearing aid, natural farming	Plan helped to strengthen the Village Panchayats, felt need realized, useful for Namathu Gramam Scheme

5

INTEGRATED ANALYSIS

This planning exercise was carried out in a phased manner. First it was initiated in Sivagangai district and later it was continued in Pudukkottai district. Subsequently the planning was done at micro level in Dindigul and Tuticorin districts. While doing this exercise, we learnt the process and necessary improvement was made. But in the whole exercise we made a few principles non-negotiable. First, the District Administration has to involve itself in the process as a partner. Secondly, the leader should have commitment and honesty. Thirdly, the community should support the Panchayat and there will not be any social conflict. Fourthly, involvement of women and dalits is ensured.

Each district has its own district characters in evolving the village development plan.

Before commencing the actual work, an intensive training was organised for three days to build the capacity of the leaders including men and women who were all committed to this exercise. The training programme was organised from 27 to 31 May 2002 in Gandhigram Rural Institute as a fully residential programme. Experts were drawn from different institutions including the government to conduct the training programme (G. Palanithurai, 2002). All the ten Gram Panchayat Presidents initially selected wanted to have a common workshop to sensitize the Panchayat Ward Members, community leaders, SHG leaders, members of the youth groups and opinion-makers on the importance and the implications of grassroots planning. The lead NGO, Rural Welfare Trust, agreed to help the Panchayats to organise the workshop and assist in the process of planning also. The Hunger Council of Tamil Nadu agreed to hold some of the responsibilities. As a result on 17 August 2002, a workshop was organised at Tirupathur for all the six Panchayats and around 210 members from all the Panchayats participated in the programme (G.Palanithurai, 2002). The whole exercise focused on planning at the Gram Panchayat level and the discussion was on the steps to be followed in the planning. It was agreed that the planning exercise would be completed before October 2002 and that the Panchayats and the NGO would take up the responsibility. Further it was decided to identify what could be done by the leaders and the people of the respective Panchayats. What could not be done by the Panchayats would be done by The Hunger Project.

Table 5.1 presents some details of the Panchayats selected for the pilot exercise in Sivagangai District.

PLANNING EXERCISE IN PHASE I

Table 5.1 : Model Panchayats for Community-Based Micro-Level Planning in Sivagangai District

Sl. No.	*Union*	*Panchayat*	*Name of the Panchayat President*
1.	Kallal	1. Veppangulam	Veera Kalaiarasi (SC)
		2. Nerpugapatti	A. Pushpam (BC)
		3. Kalipuli	S. Gandhimathi (SC)*
2.	Thirupathoor	4. Velangudi	A.Alphonsamary (BC)*
3.	Sigampunari	5. Vaduvanpatti	R.Rakku (SC)
		6. Sevalpatti	S.Poongothai (BC)*
		7. Kozhikudipatti	Nagajothi (BC)
4.	S.Pudur	8. Urathupatti	C. Chinnammal (SC)
		9. Manaloor	S. Gomathi (BC)
		10. Keelavayal	S. Sumathi (MBC)*

* The above Panchayats were included in this pilot exercise only at a later stage as per the suggestion of the District Collcctor.

A total of 10 Gram Panchayats headed by women were selected in four Unions of Sivagangai District, Tamil Nadu. Out of the 10 Panchayat leaders, 4 belonged to the scheduled caste.

The next step was to collect basic data about the people and their conditions. This could be done by the Panchayats. Before starting the exercise the statutory seven committees had to be constituted so that the number of members in the orbit of governance would be increased. For the data collection a well developed schedule prepared by the State Planning Commission was used. After collecting the data from each village a PRA exercise was carried out with the help of the staff of the Kottayam based NGO, Centre for Rural Management (CRM) to assess the needs of the people and to prioritise the needs. This exercise was done extensively and the staff of the CRM prepared a plan. Simultaneously the representatives of the people in the Panchayats also prepared a plan based on the PRA exercise. Finally, both the plans were synthesized and brought out in the form of a document. In the whole process the concept of development was critiqued, the role of the Government was criticized and people expressed their willingness to participate in the whole process as the Panchayat leaders provided ample scope for people to participate in the planning exercise. When the document was ready for presentation in any forum for critical evaluation, The Hunger Project of Tamil Nadu organised a development seminar with a set of objectives, namely, of making this document legitimate, to sensitize the Government on planning at the grassroots and to motivate other Panchayat Presidents to start this kind of exercise in their Panchayats. On 26 and 27 October, 2002, the development seminar was organised in Gandhigram Rural Institute, inviting the State Minister for Local Bodies, secretaries, directors, planning officials, experts, representatives from the media, MLAs, community leaders, Panchayat leaders and women and youth groups from the six Gram Panchayats and Women Gram Panchayat Presidents from all over Tamil Nadu numbering around six hundred.

The perspective plan document of the ten Gram Panchayats contained a brief history of the Panchayats, details about the former Panchayat Presidents who held office during the pre-73rd Amendment era, basic data about agriculture, source of irrigation, veterinary facilities, land utilization, land ownership, landless families with social background, facilities available in schools, admission in schools, dropouts in schools, status of women and children, energy utilization, non-conventional energy sources, environmental conditions, skills available in the village, housing facilities etc. After projecting all these, the document projected the needs and prioritized them. Further it stated how these prioritized needs are to be met (Veerakalaiarasi 2002; A. Pushpam 2002; K. Rakku 2002; V. Nagajothi 2002; C.Chinnammal 2002 and S.Gomathi 2002).

Responsibilities were fixed on individuals and groups to take steps to meet the needs indicated in the plan document. Achievable indicators were fixed to monitor the activities of the Panchayats. It was stated unequivocally that the Panchayat would concentrate on 100 per cent school admission, ensure the normal weight of new born babies, institutional delivery, pre-natal and post-natal care, malnutrition, family welfare etc. Thus this plan document became a vision document. Responsibility was not fixed on the Government alone. Activities were classified and accordingly responsibilities were fixed by which partners were identified for administering development and social justice.

Reactions and Responses to Plan Document

Officials from the State Planning Commission and the Project Office of the District Rural Development Agency of Sivaganga District first examined the document and offered their comments. They found certain deficiencies in the process of data collection. Apart from the basic data all other data were collected through PRA exercises and prioritization was also done through the same exercise. This was not approved by the officials. The activities envisaged in the plan document could not be carried out under the available schemes of the Government. The Panchayats had not identified the individual beneficiaries for the government schemes. While entering the activities in the plan document, the Panchayats had to indicate the source of funding to carry out all the activities. Further they questioned the legitimacy of the plan document in the absence of a planning exercise at the Block level and the District level. On certain issues such as agriculture, veterinary care, non-conventional energy and environment, the people in the villages had not consulted the government departments while projecting activities in the plan document. These subjects were highly technical in nature, but the Panchayats had taken the opinion of the people in deciding upon the activities. On the whole it was an expression of cynicism. It is to be noted here that, in the inaugural function, the Minister for Panchayati Raj and Rural Development, Government of Tamil Nadu, paid encomium on the women leaders for their exercise and he said that despite the implementation of a variety of schemes and programmes of the Central and State Governments, people's felt needs could not be met and that this kind of micro-level plan would reverse the trend and the felt needs would be met and thereby wasteful expenditure could be avoided. He further said that this kind of exercise would trigger a movement for people's planning. He even appealed that in each district this kind of exercise should be initiated.

Despite the remark of the Minister, the officials recorded their negative remarks about the whole exercise. Following the reaction and response of the officials, some of the experts from the audience came forward to express their opinion. Prominent among them were B.S. Raghavan, retired Chief Secretary of West Bengal and adviser to the FAO, A.K. Venkatasubramanian, retired civil servant specializing in Public Distribution System, Dr. Rajagopalan of the M.S.Swaminathan Foundation, Mr.Vallinayagam, retired Additional Director of Rural Development, and Mr. N.S. Chidambaram, retired Additional Director of Rural Development. These experts appreciated the effort expended in taking up this cause and facing all the problems in collecting data and putting them in a plan proposal and getting the approval of the people in the Gram Sabha and the Panchayat Council. It is a plan of the people prepared by the people and not a plan prepared by officials. It is their vision. They have chalked out their activities on the basis of their felt needs. It is true that they have not chalked out activities to implement the schemes of the government and hence there will be a gap between the available schemes and the activities envisaged in the plan document of the Panchayats. The plan document is not a petition prepared by them to get sanction from the government. It is their plan and they seek to be partners in governance to administer development. They have indicated the possibilities to generate employment opportunities with the resources and skills available in their respective Panchayats. Further it is to be noted that social development issues have been projected in the plan document and it is indicated that they would take up the responsibility to achieve sustainable results in development in the social sector. While appreciating the efforts of the Gram Panchayat leaders, they addressed a few questions to the government officials and a few suggestions to the Gram Panchayat leaders.

In fifty years of democratic governance in India, no such document was prepared for village development by the government. Even after the introduction of the 73rd Amendment and the constitution of the District Planning Committee, no systematic effort was made at the micro-level, despite planning officials working at the district level. Having failed miserably in discharging their duties and responsibilities at the government level, it was unfair on the part of the officials to criticize the efforts made by the women leaders for their small technical lapses. Further it was characteristic on the part of the officials to denigrate the people's efforts as unscientific. Since the officials have been oriented to act in the supply driven mode of development activities, they look at everything from the supply side and not from the demand side. While evaluating the proposal, officials had looked for proposals for the government schemes and programmes and that was why they were not in a position to suggest ways and means to meet the demands which could not be fulfilled by the government schemes and programmes. The experts said that the officials could have offered their suggestions rather than criticizing the plan. Even the model plan prepared by the officials in some of the villages in Tamil Nadu did not include social development issues. The model plans prepared by the officials have not seen the light of day.

It is a unique exercise in fifty years of governance because every segment of the rural community has been involved in this exercise to make a declaration that their destinies are going to be decided by their efforts only. Now stakeholders have been found for the rural development activities. They have realistically projected their needs as felt by the community without looking into the supply side of it. Hence, it is the responsibility of the officials to help in identifying the institutions to be involved in the process of fulfilling the needs of the people. The existing schemes of the government could be utilized for many of the demands and for some of the demands a slight modification is necessary in implementing the existing government schemes for which the District Collector as Chairman of the DRDA and Inspector of Panchayats can make use of his discretionary powers. Demands which could not be met through government schemes could be taken to various financial institutions for financial support with a viable action proposal prepared by professionals for which the Panchayats have to seek the support of NGOs. It is fortunate that the Rural Welfare Trust is working with all these six Panchayats. The same organization can be involved in preparing such proposals and approaching CAPART, DST, NABARD and other agencies. For the social development issues targeted, achievable and quantifiable indicators have to be fixed. For instance school enrolment of students, birth weight of newly born babies, institutional delivery, reduction of school dropouts, providing safe drinking water supply to all families, ensuring sanitation facilities to all families, eradication of plastics and so on have been identified as activities and responsibilities have also been fixed in the case all the above said activities. The seven statutory committees in the villages have to be activated to involve themselves in all these activities. What the Gram Panchayats now require is partners to carry this task further.

After making these observations, the experts again requested the officials directly dealing with planning at the grassroots to give their feedback again. The officials from the State Planning Commission and the District Rural Development Agency informed the audience and more specifically the Panchayat Presidents of the possibility of making use of many of the Central and State Government schemes and programmes to meet many of the issues projected in the plan document. For other issues and demands the nodal agency, the NGO, Rural Welfare Trust, was to prepare and send proposals to NABARD, CAPART and other agencies. Achievable indicators have to be explicitly entrusted to the committees of the Panchayats and their activities have to be monitored every year. This was the assurance given to the Panchayats by the officials.

Finally, the Panchayat Presidents concluded their presentation by assuring the officials that they would take up the responsibility to achieve many of the achievable indicators on social development. Further they informed that they would meet all the sectoral departments to seek their help to fulfil all the demands of the people mentioned in the PRA meetings while preparing the plan for the Gram Panchayats. The women leaders, while expressing their gratitude to the officials, explained their struggle to make use of the power devolved to them.

The whole exercise and the presentation of the plan in the development seminar provoked the women leaders assembled in the seminar to think on the social issues highlighted by the Women Presidents of the six Gram Panchayats. The Women Presidents who assembled in the seminar from all over Tamil Nadu under the banner of the Tamil Nadu Federation of Women Leaders prepared a charter of activities and declared it a charter of activities for the next year. The charter is presented hereunder.

Declaration

We, the elected women representatives who are gathered here at Gandhigram Rural Institute on this 27th day of October 2002, declare that we will address the following issues in the next one year :

(1) All the eligible children (girls and boys) will be enrolled in schools.

(2) We will strive to remove malnourishment amongst children in the age group of 0-5 years. As elected representatives we shall ensure that no underweight babies are born in our villages. The mothers will be given proper nourishment before and after delivery.

(3) Better anti-natal and post-natal care will be provided for all the women in our Panchayats.

(4) Any injustice against women in our Panchayats will be dealt with firmly. As a collective we will fight against

domestic violence and also any other form of violence against any women in our Panchayat.

(5) We will ensure that child labour is abolished in our Panchayats.

(6) We will ensure equitable access to and distribution of Panchayat resources among all the people in the Panchayats and guarantee at least the provision of the basic minimum requirements for the poorest. The PDS system will be improved with our intervention.

(7) Problems faced by the Women Panchayat leaders and women in general will be addressed collectively by making alliance with supportive institutions and organizations.

(8) The newly implemented sanitary complexes meant for women will be effectively managed by women's groups with the support of the Panchayats.

(9) Our Panchayats will not suffer from lack of drinking water. Everyone will be entitled to safe drinking water.

(10) We will ensure that Gram Sabhas meet regularly and more people take part in these meetings. We will ensure that a minimum of 50 per cent of the total women in the Panchayat attend the meetings and that their issues are properly heard.

(11) We commit ourselves to the implementation of the 15-point programme prepared by the Tamil Nadu Government and request the state government to devolve necessary powers to the Panchayats and local bodies for the same.

Following the presentation of reports and the declaration of the charter of activities for Women Panchayat Presidents, the Pudukkottai District Project Officer, DRDA, representing the Pudukkottai District Administration, pleaded that this kind of exercise be undertaken in the whole of Pudukkottai District for which he sought the help of NGOs and Gandhigram Rural Institute. Women leaders from Pudukkottai District who attended the development seminar expressed their willingness to undertake this kind of exercise in their Panchayats. Thus the micro-plan exercise done in six Gram Panchayats and the presentation of all the six plans in the development seminar in the presence of the Minister for Panchayati Raj and Rural Development, Government of Tamil Nadu, officials of the State Government, experts in Micro Level Planning and six hundred Gram Panchayat Women Presidents created an awareness among the Minister, the officials and the local body leaders on the importance of micro-level planning and, as a result, the State Planning Commission started the exercise of giving training to the local body leaders on planning exercises to be done at the grassroots.

Analysis of I Phase Efforts

Primarily, though it is a constitutional mandate that the planning exercise has to be initiated at the grassroots, beyond the State Governments and the Central Government producing documents on decentralized planning, nothing has been done on the ground in the 9th and the 10th Plans. These ten Panchayats, under the leadership of women, have sensitized the Minister and the higher officials to the implications of micro-level planning.

Secondly, while carrying out this exercise, it could be seen at what level devolution of powers has taken place in the state as the Panchayats faced problems in getting the support of the sectoral departments. Empirically this proved the extent to which powers have been devolved to the Panchayats.

Thirdly, in the process of interacting with the officials and hearing views of the officials on the plan proposals of the Panchayats, the official attitude to this new dispensation and the exercise has been exposed and they have been sensitized to the legal and social implications of micro-level planning.

Fourthly, the other Women Presidents have gained confidence that this kind of exercise could be done in their Panchayats also as they learned the methodology adopted in the ten Gram Panchayats for planning at the micro-level.

Fifthly, social development issues came to the limelight because of the micro plans of the ten Gram Panchayats. These ten Gram Panchayat leaders gained this insight while they were in self-help groups and thereby they quickly grasped the social development issues and fixed achievable indicators for the Panchayats. This kind of exercise motivated the other Panchayat leaders to take up this issue. As a result the women Panchayat leaders published a charter of activities to be undertaken by the Panchayats in the social development sector.

Sixthly, in the recent past people have been mobilized by various agencies for participation in the implementation of various schemes and programmes brought from above. But the stance "we govern you receive" has not altered. By undertaking the planning exercise by the people, people's demands and priorities have been prominently projected in the plan document and thereby the old position "we govern you participate" has been replaced by "you govern and you participate".

Seventhly, the ten Panchayat Presidents have started negotiations with officials, representatives of the people like MLAs and MPs and NGOs for fulfilling the requirements of the plan. They have developed skills of negotiation.

Eighthly, the hidden potential of the leadership has been displayed through this process. Class, caste and political organizations have their own roles in the activities of the rural society. While mobilizing all the groups cutting across these differences, the women leaders have exhibited a high degree of democratic leadership. Even the traditional Panchayat leaders have extended their fullest cooperation to the efforts of these Panchayat Presidents.

Ninthly, the conventional mode of looking at issues and demands from the supply mode has been done away with and instead issues are being looked at from the perspective of the people and thereby a sense of ownership has been cultivated among the people for the development of the community.

Tenthly, so far the Panchayats negotiated for schemes and programmes of the government. Now the trend has been reversed and they ask for the government's participation in their schemes and programmes. Petitioners have changed their role to that of negotiators because of this new exercise.

Eleventhly, the Panchayats have started mobilizing partners for their development activities. They have gathered many organizations to their support in implementing their schemes.

Twelfthly, the leaders have built a vision document through this exercise. They have gained rich input on vision building from the training undergone elsewhere by the Presidents. While doing so they are critiquing the very concept of development. They move around the skills and the resources available at their disposal.

Though they are women and, that too, three of them are of the Backward Class and another three are Dalits, their leadership is recognized, appreciated and supported even by the traditional Panchayat leaders. The women leaders, by their performance, have won the recognition of the community. Since initiatives are taken jointly by the leaders, the administration becomes transparent and it reduces corruption to the maximum extent. The planning exercise has made the people volunteers in the development initiative.

Summing up of Phase I

Planning at the grassroots for administering development and social justice has long range implications in the paradigm of development. It alters the entire process of development. The roles of the government and the community have been reversed. All the loopholes in the development process in the existing paradigm have been exposed and people have developed a new perspective to look at issues and now plans of activities are chalked out on the basis of their demands and needs as prioritized by the people and not on the basis of the available schemes and programmes of the government. The concept of "we govern you receive" is gone and the new concept "you govern and you participate" has ushered in. Social development issues have drawn the attention of the people because of this exercise and achievable indicators have been fixed for these issues and people have taken up the responsibility of achieving the target. People have also developed a sense of ownership as this plan document carries the demands of the people as schemes and programmes. Now the government finds itself in a tight spot as to whether this is to be allowed or not. There is no other option but to allow and continue the new practice. Over and above, at the earliest, the entire state has to take the initiative to plan for development from the Gram Panchayat to the District Planning Committee. The new paradigm will gain momentum and it will ultimately end in a movement for decentralized governance for development and social justice.

PLANNING EXERCISE IN PHASE II

Based on the exercise undertaken in Sivagangai District micro level planning was started in Pudukkottai District. Pudukkottai District offered three advantages for undertaking this exercise. They were: the District Collector is pro-Panchayat and he believes in the potentialities of the Panchayats and the community; the link between Panchayats and the communities is strong; and, the capacity of the leaders is very high as periodical orientations apart from training were given to the Panchayat leaders. As the District Collector invited The Hunger Project, it was decided to work with the Panchayats. The district administration provided office space for The Hunger Project in the District Panchayat office. Thirteen Gram Panchayats were selected from all the 13 Blocks. The main criteria adopted in the selection process is that the Panchayat leader should have commitment and honesty, the link between the leader and the community should be so strong, and there should not be any communal and political conflict between and among the collectivities. By adopting the criteria, the following Gram Panchayats were selected in a meeting held in the Collectorate with the participation of The Hunger Project staff, the District Collector, the Project Officer, DRDA, of Pudukkottai District. Table 5.2 presents the list of the selected Panchayats.

Out of the 13 Gram Panchayat Presidents, 6 are men and 7 are women.

Planning Methodology in Phase II

After getting consent from the Panchayat leaders, the President was asked to constitute the statutory Panchayat committees along with the Panchayat Planning Committee. In all the committees it should be mandatory that women and Dalit representatives should

Table 5.2 : Model Panchayats for Community Based Micro Level Planning in Pudukkottai District

Sl. No.	*Name of the Panchayat*	*Panchayat Union*	*Name of the Panchayat President*
1.	Merpanaikadu	Aranthangi	Ms. Bhavani Ilango
2.	Poovalur	Avudayarkoil	Mr. Sarvana Perumal
3.	Melathur	Thiruvarankulam	Mr. Saravanan
4.	Edaiyathimangalam	Manamelkudi	Mr. Arumugam
5.	Elaikadaividuthi	Karambakudi	Ms. J.Manjula
6.	Melaputhuvayal	Kunandarkoil	Ms. Dhanalakshmi
7.	Parambur	Annavasal	Mr. Abdulwaheed
8.	Nerinjikudi	Ponnamaravathy	Mr. P.Ramnu
9.	Punalkulam	Gandarvakottai	Mr. Shanmugam
10.	Mookampatti	Pudukkottai	Ms. V.Mangalam
11.	Meenaveli	Viralimalai	Mr. Alagiri
12.	Virachilai	Tirumayam	Ms. Devi
13.	K.Rayavaram	Arimalam	Ms. Rani Sathappan

find a place. Panchayat President, Vice-Presidents, Panchayat clerk, committee members, traditional Panchayat leaders, SHG leaders, youth leaders, retired officials of the Panchayat areas were drawn for training. A three-day training in planning at the village level was offered. It was a residential training programme and it was conducted in Gandhigram Rural Institute. In the training exercise, emphasis was laid on the participation of people, especially women and Dalits, and social development issues. Following the training in each Gram Panchayat, a sensitization exercise was conducted to prepare the people for evolving a perspective plan for socio-economic development of the Gram Panchayat area. To change the mindset of the people, this exercise continued till the draft plan was approved in the Gram Sabha. Sensitization was also done on social development issues. When the training was over, responsibilities were fixed as to how the needed data have to be collected from both primary and secondary sources. After collecting the data, a neat profile of the village was developed which was termed a development report. After consolidation of the report a Participatory Rural Appraisal for every Panchayat was to be conducted to prioritize the works that were to be undertaken in the Panchayat.

After prioritizing the activities, The Hunger Project staff, with the help of the Panchayat leader and the clerk identified the vulnerable families and gave numbers to the families. A list of the disabled was made for constant monitoring. Schools, *anganwadi*, primary health centre service would be assessed by the staff of The Hunger Project. Thus social development activities became the primary concern of the Panchayat. A manual, listing out the activities related to social development to be carried out in the Panchayat area by the Panchayats in partnership with other agencies was supplied to all the Panchayat leaders (activity chart). Malnourished children, pregnant women affected by anemia and poor women stricken with diseases would be identified and all the lists would be appended to the plan document. Finally, responsibilities were fixed as to how these prioritized activities were going to be carried out and with whose partnerships. All the needs identified and prioritized through the PRA were to be matched with the schemes and programmes of the Central and State Governments that were being operated through sectoral departments. For unmatched issues Panchayats were to seek the help of MLAs and MPs and to get substantial funds from their Local Area Development Fund. The whole plan document was to be placed before the Gram Sabha for evaluation, suggestion and approval. After getting the approval, with modifications if any, the plan document was to be printed.

The printed plan document would be circulated to all the sectoral departments. The District Collector as Inspector of Panchayats would give necessary instructions to the sectoral department heads to carry out activities in the Panchayats based on their needs. The Panchayats with the help of the Planning Committee and the representative of The Hunger Project should do the follow-up activities.

Lessons Learnt in Phase II

It is not a State driven planning activity. It is initiated from below. Though it was initiated by the leader of the Panchayat in the process of mobilization, people have been made to participate in the process of preparation of the development plan. Panchayat leaders and the members of various committees have developed negotiating skills in the process of the preparation of the plan. They negotiate with the sectoral departments, MLAs and MPs. Further they negotiate with Union Councillors and District Ward Members to make use of the funds available in the Block and District Panchayats. Since there was no initiating from the State Government and the Central Government for planning from below with the participation of people, these Gram Panchayat leaders took the initiative and followed the guidelines provided by the State Planning Commission for planning at the micro-level, especially at the Gram Panchayat level. Because of these initiatives, even the State Planning Committee has started doing this exercise in 250 Gram Panchayats throughout Tamil Nadu. It is not planning as such but preparing a development report.

While engaged in this exercise, it could be visualized at what level devolution of powers has taken place in the State as the Panchayats faced problems in getting the support of the sectoral departments. Empirically, this proved the extent to which powers have been devolved to the Panchayats. Further, while interacting with officials in the process of plan preparation, the attitude of the officials towards planning could be seen. Thanks to this exercise the officials are exposed and sensitized towards planning and social development. The grassroots leaders have exhibited an extraordinary commitment towards communities for social development. The micro-level plan experience made the Panchayat leaders enhance their capacity and use the full potentiality of leadership. Panchayat Presidents and the people have prepared the plan. Now they have reversed the process of development activities from supply driven to demand driven mode. Realistically speaking the plan is a vision document and the activities listed in the plan document are only their wish list when there is no conducive atmosphere for micro- level planning.

Summing up of Phase II

The new dispensation of micro-level planning with the participation of the people to administer economic development and social justice envisioned in the Constitution through the 73rd and the 74th Amendments has far reaching implications in the development paradigm in the context of redefining the concept of the governance against the backdrop of democratic decentralization of powers and globalization of economy. This new initiative has reversed the process from supply driven to demand driven activities. The old practice of the government providing and the people receiving has been reversed. Now people plan and participate and the government just supports. The whole development exercise moves in a different mode which is totally different from that of the government. People's wishes and vision have been projected as a major set of activities and people have taken up responsibilities.

There is yet another striking feature in the micro-level planning process. In all such previous exercises only infrastructural facilities were projected as the major set of activities. But now people have focused more on social development activities because of the continuous sensitization and conscientization programme. This kind of people's initiatives in a few Panchayats has put the Government in a tight spot. As a result the State Planning Commission has taken efforts to prepare a development report in about 250 Gram Panchayat as a pilot project. Thus this new paradigm will gain momentum and it will ultimately end in a movement for decentralized governance for development and social justice.

LESSONS LEARNT IN PHASE III

Dindigul district and Tuticorin district Gram Panchayats are coming under the third phase. In the third phase external support to the Panchayats has been reduced. The whole responsibility was fixed with Gram Panchayat elected representatives and the functionaries working with Gram Panchayats. As a result, the Gram Panchayat Presidents and the Panchayat Clerks played a key role in the whole process in collection, consolidation, and validation of data. For focus group discussion enough input was given to the Panchayat leaders and they have conducted the focus group discussions on their own. In the same way while implementing the Panchayat plan the responsibility fell on the shoulders of the Gram Panchayat leaders.

By using their negotiating skill, they managed to carry out many works prioritized by the people. Blaming the others is eliminated in these Panchayats as Panchayat Presidents are strong and their leadership quality is high.

It has been tested in the process of planning at grassroots that planning can be possible even without much power and the cooperation of the government departments. By initiating the process the gap between the Panchayat leaders and the community is bridged. People are mobilized constantly and conscientised on social development activities. Ownership is being developed among the people for many of the development activities. In the process of interaction with Panchayat leaders and officials, Gram Sabha members have established a grip over the Panchayat administration. While the Panchayat Presidents are organizing meetings with various committee members the Panchayat administration becomes transparent and corruption-free. Planning initiative at the grassroots involves the women, and thereby women's issues have been dealt with. Slowly Panchayat leaders, Ward Members and Committee Members are sensitized towards gender issues. Committee formation is a process by which women members and representatives from the Dalit community are inducted and their participation in the meetings has created sensitiveness among all towards the issues of Dalits. Panchayat leaders have started bargaining with other representatives of the people namely, MLA, MP, Ward Members of Block Panchayats and District Panchayats. The leaders have developed bargaining capacity to deal with officials. Panchayat leaders have developed a vision for the development of the community. Panchayat leaders and the people have realized the fact that for most of the social development activities money requirement is minimum and that to accomplish the same what is needed is commitment on the part of the Panchayat leaders and the community. The District Collector and his team of officials have evinced interest in Panchayat activities as they have faith in the Panchayat's potential. Along with Panchayats, the officials also claim credit in achieving the target of all development activities. Without the cooperation of the Panchayats and the community, officials cannot achieve the target successfully and hence they now bank on the Panchayats. Further, the quality of the works carried out by the Panchayats with the participation of the people is better, compared to the work of the contractors. Each and every Panchayat is having a plan document which is regarded as its pride.

By developing a plan document at the village level, indirectly a compulsion has been placed on the sectoral departments to work in the villages with their allocation of resources restricted to the activities indicated in the plan document of the respective Gram Panchayats.

In the given context, however, poor devolution of powers of functions and of finances in Tamil Nadu, planning at grassroots will compel the government to devolve the same. Administration has become transparent and involvement of women and Dalits is remarkable in the activities of the communities. Both people and their leaders are sensitive towards the social development issues. Every Village Panchayat has a legitimate vision document which prevents the sectoral departments spending unilaterally. It bridges the gap between the people and the government. Now the entire state and later the entire nation can replicate it.

6

CONCLUSION

The two historic constitutional amendments (73rd and 74th) have come with full of promises and hopes to bring socio-economic transformations at the grassroots. But to realize the full potentials of the amendments an array of steps have to be taken from the below and the above. While evaluating the implications of two amendments one would find the dismal outcome as the stakeholders had not realized the potentials. Of the mandatory provisions, planning from below with the participation of people is one and important. The planning from below is the key in the devolution process which will turn the supply driven activities into demand driven and in the whole process this planning exercise will empower people and reduce wastage of money. Micro-plan is only in paper since the enactment of 73rd and 74th Amendments. To translate the concept into action, with the support of The Hunger Project planning was done in a few Panchayats in Tamil Nadu as an experiment.

If any one says that a Gram Panchayat is developing a micro plan, immediately questions are raised about they resources to carry out activities as per the plan document. Normally, people forget the fact that all the government departments are working in the villages and spending huge money to carry out their activities. The sectoral departments have earmarked budget and they will be sent on activities whether people demand or not. The very purpose of developing a plan for Gram Panchayat is to make the Government departments to work on the demand of the people. It is a peoples plan ard Government Departments have to participate in it. On an average, District Rural Development Agency alone through different schemes spends more than hundred crore annually. But the entire amount is to be spent on schemes whether people have needs or not. Religiously, huge money is spent but needs of the people are unattended. As a result there is always a pressure on district administration.

For a realistic planning at grassroots, scientific data base is an imperative. There is yet another issue namely working on the scientific data base for each and every issue, which is totally absent at the grassroots. In the absence of a scientific data base whatever activities are planned and carried out in the rural development sectors which cannot attack the real issues and as a result we continue to struggle in the dark and we could not show much progress. This micro-plan provides a new opportunity to the Gram Panchayats to work on scientific data base. Even the higher level officials are relying on the data generated by the Panchayat and confirmed by the people through Gram Sabha.

By doing the entire exercise through a scientific survey people have an opportunity to look at their life, conditions and facilities available to lead a decent human life. It is a collective exercise and every segment of the society is looking at their conditions of life in the village. This process makes them conscious of their problems. It provides an opportunity to build their vision for a common and collective living. While this process is being facilitated by external agencies, requested information input is given people have started tracking the resource line. People have begun to locate the resource pools in the government departments and try to link it to their plan activities. While working in partnership with the Government Departments, people start negotiating with sectoral departments for assistance to fulfil their demands. Thus a new synergy is found which is lacking so far in development activities. Panchayats have moved over to systemic actions due to this plan exercises. Panchayat Presidents go with a scientific database and convincing arguments to track funds for development activities. In this process demand determines the supply. Panchayat Presidents, functionaries and others are conscientized on the issues of Dalits, women and marginalized. They internalized on the social development issues. They are serious about the issues of exclusion.

To implement the activities of the plan, Panchayat Presidents and the individuals who are involved in the process get closer to the District administration. The fear of approaching a government officer has gone. They get information on many matters akin to governance while interacting with government officials frequently. Till planning exercise was initiated Panchayat activities were considered as the activities of the President not the entire Panchayat. Ward Members did not know what Panchayat is doing. But this planning initiative made every one to involve himself or herself in the planning process. As a result a participative culture is developed.

Even in Gram Sabha meeting, Panchayat Presidents used to dominate in the whole process. But in the planning exercise, voicing of voiceless is happening. Dalits, women, labourers, farmers and marginalized have raised their voices as they are all concerned with their life and infrastructure. A new culture of listening to the voice of others has emerged. While carrying out this planning exercise, one could easily identify to what extent devolution of powers has taken place in a particular state. Gram Panchayat Presidents have developed skill to negotiate with MLAs and MPs apart from the officials. In the whole process leadership potential is unleashed.

In the process of enabling the Panchayats to plan for the development people had been oriented to look at their conditions of life. They build vision for their development. Even they had the practice of jointly looking at their life conditions. This is the first time in their life they did exercises. Developmental issues are not their priority. They always harp on infrastructure. After attending the training programme, the Panchayat leaders moved over to some of the issues of social development. Beneficiary selection is a major contentious issue in every village. In the villages where planning was done people have planned and adopted a strategy and by which they had ranked the people. Poorest of the poor has been given priority. As a result they fixed the ranks of the people on the basis of the intensity of poverty. People are in a fixed mindset. People believe that development work is the sole responsibility of the government. People have to put their demands to the government. Government is spending three crore rupees on an average on every Gram Panchayat in a period of five years. Yet the basic demands of the people are not met. But now they have started searching for resources for the activities.

Panchayat leaders seek partners for carrying out development works of the villages. Panchayat leaders have developed working relationship with traditional Panchayat leaders. Normally the constitutional Panchayat leaders will get clashed with traditional Panchayat leaders. The planning exercise brings them closer and together to carry out the activities of the plan. There is yet another major issue in the process of governance, namely "we govern you participate syndrome". State Government through its bureaucracy wants to govern the people and at the same time they ask the people to participate in governance and development activities. People did not evince interest in participation. Wherever people are allowed to govern themselves, they actively participate in governance and development activities. Micro plan exercises provided such opportunity for the people to decide things on their own. The Panchayat leaders tried their level best to carry out the development activities as prioritized by the people in the plan document. When the plan activities are implemented, people will gain confidence and develop faith in themselves.

There are improvements in planning methodology over a period of time. In the first phase more number of days were taken, external agencies were involved. In the second phase, the external agencies had not been involved. Panchayat leaders had been facilitated to carry out the exercises with the help of some of the researchers of the Gandhigram Rural Institute.

In the third phase totally responsibility had been fixed with the Panchayat leaders. In the third phase adequate training was given to the Panchayat leaders. In the last phase it is proved that Panchayats with a little support of external agencies, can develop a plan. Tsunami had made the people look for external assistance for everything. But the planning exercise made the people to realize their potentials and worth. It builds the capacity and capability of stakeholders to manage their affairs on their own. Thus planning at grassroots is an instrument by which Panchayats can be strengthened and people can be empowered. It touches upon many vital issues of social development. Issues of exclusion and marginalized are addressed.

Appendix

GOOD GOVERNANCE AND SOCIAL DEVELOPMENT IN GRAM PANCHAYAT INDICATORS

Sl. No.	Activities	Responsibility	Outcome
1.	100 per cent enrolment of eligible children	President, Vice-President, Ward Members, PTA, SHG Members, Youth Clubs, NGO, Retired Officials	Increase in literacy, Human Resource Development
2.	Reduction of school Dropouts	President, Vice-President, Ward Members, PTA, SHG Members, Youth Clubs, NGO, Retired Officials	Increase in Educational Standard
3.	Ensuring protected Drinking Water Supply to School	President, Vice-President, Ward Members, School Teachers	Improvement of students' Health, reduction of absenteeism of students
4.	Providing toilets to school	President, Vice-President, Ward Members, School Teachers	Increase in health of children
5.	Utilizing the toilets by the school students	President, other members of the Panchayat Council Teachers	Toilet Culture Developed
6.	Cutting the nails of the students every Monday in *Balwadi* and School	Youth Club, SHG, Panchayat Ward Members, School teachers	Health education, reduction of diseases, improvement of nutrition
7.	Planting of saplings in the school premises	President, teachers, agriculture departments	Environment awareness eco development, income to school
8.	Creating a school garden	President, teachers PTA, Youth clubs	Education, increase in nutrition
9.	Keeping the *Balwadi* clean and neat	*Balwadi* teacher, President, Vice-President, Ward Members	Health education, increase in status of health

(Contd...)

(Contd...)

10.	Providing a toilet in the *Balwadi*	President, Vice President, Ward Members	Education, increase in health status
11.	Bringing a toilet culture among the kids	*Balwadi* teacher	Health education, increase in health status
12.	Adding vegetables to the noon meal by getting donations and getting the vegetables from the school garden	President, Vice-President, *Balwadi* teacher	Nutritive food for students
13.	Taking steps to prevent the practice of child labour	President, Vice-President, Ward Members, School teachers, PTA, NGO, SHG, Youth Club	School enrolment, literacy, HRD
14.	Cleaning over head tanks	OHT operators, under the instruction of panchayat regularly	Health status, productivity Enhancing
15.	Creating awareness among the people about the consequence of alcohol and stop brewing and selling the same in the panchayat area	President, Vice-President, Ward Member, Health Committee, SHG, Youth Club, NGO	Enhancing economic status of poor, status of women and children, health of individuals and reduction of social problems
16.	Creating Awareness among the people about family welfare	PHC Staff, President, Vice-President, Ward Members, Health Committee, SHG, Youth	Livelihood security, family welfare
17.	Identify the vulnerable families and ensure food security to them and constantly monitor them with the help of government schemes	President, Vice-President, Ward Members, SHGs	Income generation, reduction of poverty, status of women
18.	Developing the skills of the women through training	Presidents, Vice-President, Ward Members, Training institution, Social Welfare Department at the District Women Development Corporation	Income generation, reduction of poverty, status of women
19.	Establish link between the skilled persons and banking sector for the establishment of business ventures by women	President, Vice-President, Ward Members, Planning Committee Members, NGO, Banks,	SHG Development of rural economy, and status of women

(Contd...)

(Contd...)

20.	Developing the skills of the youth through training	President, Vice-President, Ward Members, Training institutions, NYK	Human Resource Development, Economic Development
21.	Establish link between the skilled persons and Banking sector for the establishment of business ventures by the youth	President, Vice-President, Ward Member, Planning Committee Members, NGOs, Banks, NYKs	Development of Rural Economy
22.	Ensuring proper functioning of PDS	President, Vice-President, Ward Members and SHG, officials of Civil Supply	Food Security
23.	Prevent open defecation in the villages by creating awareness and constructing toilets in each and every house	President, Vice-President, Ward Members, SHG, Youth Club, NGO, Project Staff, TRSP, Retired Employees	IImprovement in Health, Sanitation Environment
24.	Creating awareness about RCH by printing a card and giving it to every family	President, Vice-President, Ward Members, Health Committee, NGO, Staff	Improvement in women and children's, health, economic status
25.	Ensure the delivery of services from sub centre and PHC to the people through the schemes available for prenatal and post natal care	PHC Staff, President, Vice-President, Ward Members, SHG, NGO, Health Committee	Increase in health status and economic status
26.	Creating awareness about growing medicinal plants and make it a business by involving SHG and youth clubs	President, Vice-President, Ward Members, SHG, Planning Committee, Youth Club, NGO	Increase in health, income generation productivity
27.	Creating awareness among the importance of water management	President, Vice-President, Ward Members, Community leaders, Planning Committee Members, NGO	Rational Utilization of Water

(Contd...)

(Contd...)

28.	Creating a common burial ground/ grave yard in the villages	President, Vice-President, Ward Members, SHG, Youth Club	Social justice
29.	Taking steps to manage solid waste and earn money from it for panchayats	President, Vice-President, Ward Members, Planning Committee, NGO, SHG	Environment development, income generation, better agricultural practices
30.	Organise workshop for pregnant women to disseminate the needed information akin to ANC PNC	PHC Staff, SHG, President	Increase of health awareness, health status, economic status, Reduction of infant mortality; new born babies are in exact weight
31.	Conducting medical camps for poor and school children	President, Vice-President, Ward Members, NGOs, SHG, nearby Rotary and Lions Club	Improved health status
32.	Make the SHG and Youth Clubs take up Panchayat works instead of employing contractors	President, Vice-President, Ward Members, SHG Youth club, NGO	Employment opportunity, quality of work, reduction of expenditure, meeting local needs
33.	Regularly conducting Gram Sabha meetings.	President, Vice-President, Ward Members	People's participation, Good Governance
34.	Ensuring 60 per cent attendance in Gram Sabha meeting.	President, Vice-President, Ward Members, all eligible members, SHG members, NGOs working in the Panchayats.	Transparency, accountability of panchayats
35.	Ensuring Women / Dalit participation 50 per cent of attendance	President, Vice-President, Ward Members, SHG, NGO	Social justice, status of weaker section
36.	Information disseminations ❖ Income/Expenditure display ❖ Report on schemes implemented display ❖ List of schemes proposed to be implemented ❖ List of beneficiaries	President and Panchayat Clerk	Transparency, accountability credibility of Panchayat, Better participation

(Contd...)

(Contd...)

37.	Participatory decision making ※ Opportunities for discussion to all communities ※ Equal status to all in seating ※ Developing consensus	President, Ward Members, community leaders/ retired government officials, school teachers, Planning Committee Members, Dalit Leaders, NGOs and other association members	Generation of collective wisdom, social justice
38.	Develop a system of communication to give information about Gram Sabha meeting	President, Clerk, Ward Member, SHG, Youth Clubs, NGOs	Transparency, accountability
39.	Provision of water supply to Dalit hamlets	President and the concerned Ward Members, Committee for water supply	Communal harmony, status of Dalit, productivity of Dalits
40.	Removal of untouchability by ❖ Eliminating the two tumbler system ❖ Participating in temple festivals	President, Ward Members, SHG, Youth Clubs, Community Leaders.	Social justice, communal harmony
41.	Training to Dalit Youths in skill development	President, Youth Clubs, NGOs, Education Institutions	Economic development, social justice
42.	Availing THADCO schemes	President, NGOs, Vice-President and Ward Members	Economic development of Dalits, social harmony
43.	Identification of all CPR verifying the status of encroachment details	Panchayat President, Vice-President, Ward Members, Government Officials, Police Department	Environment development social justice, income generation
44.	Removal of encroachments	Panchayat President, Vice-President, (Revenue and Police Department)	Productive use of resources, equity, income generation
45.	Utilizing the Common Properties and developing the same	Panchayat President, Ward Members, NGO, SHG, Youth groups	Environment development, income generation

(Contd...)

(Contd...)

46.	100 percent house tax collection	President, Clerk, Vice-President, Ward Members, SHG, Youth	Financial status of Panchayat more government funds
47.	Panchayat functioning as a system	President, Clerk, Vice-President, Ward Members	Integrated development
48.	Records maintenance / transparency	President and Clerk	Good Governance
49.	Preparing a perspective plan through village planning forum	President, Ward Members, Planning Committee	Planned development better use of resources
50.	Formation of Statutory Committees	President	Efficiency of Panchayats, accountability
51.	Old age, Physically and Mentally disabled, destitute, orphan and other vulnerable sections	President, Ward Members, SHG, NGO, Government, and Planning Committee	Social security, social harmony

Key Assumptions

- Harmony prevails in Panchayat.
- Panchayat is perceived as development space.
- Community supports the Panchayats.
- Panchayat leader has got commitment.
- Panchayat leader has vision.
- Panchayat leader has got skill and capacity.
- Panchayat is not leader-centric.
- Panchayat is people and system-centric.

BIBLIOGRAPHY

Ali Sofi and Rao Anita, "Reinventing Public Administration for 21st Century", *The Indian Journal of Public Administration*, Vol.XLVI: No.2 April-June 2000.

Banerjee, Ajit M., and Chidambaram, K.A., (eds) *Renewing Governance: Issues and Options,* New Delhi: Tata McGraw Hill Publishing Company, 1996.

Chambers, Robert, *Rural Development: Putting the Last First,* Harlow: Longman Scientific and Technical, 1983.

Chinnammal, C., *Perspective Plan for Development of Urathupatti*, Thirupathur: Grama Iyakkam, 2002.

Ghosh, Jayati, "Development Strategy in India: A Political Economy Perspective" in *Nationalism, Democracy and Development: State and Politics in India* (Eds), Sugata Bose and Ayesha Jalal, New Delhi: Oxford University Press, 1998, pp.165-83.

Gomathy, S., *Perspective Plan for Development of Manalur*, Thirupathur: Grama Iyakkam, 2002.

International Commission on Peace and Food, *Developing Human Resourcefulness: Strategies to Eradicate Poverty in the 1990s*. Draft Working Paper, California: ICPE, 1989.

Issac Thomas, T.M., and W. Franke, Richard, *Local Democracy and Development,* New Delhi: Left Word, 2000, pp.16-32.

Manor James, *The Political Economy of Democratic Decentralization*, Washington DC: The World Bank, 1999, p.1.

Nagajothi, Y., Perspective Plan for Development of Kozhikudipatti, Thirupathur: Grama Iyakkam, 2002.

Palanithurai, G., *Development Roles Reversed: People's Initiatives and Governments Participation,* (monograph), Gandhigram, Rajiv Gandhi Chair for Panchayati Raj Studies, 2003.

Palanithurai, G., *From Participation to Self-Governance: An Agenda for Restructuring Tamil Nadu Panchayat Act, 1994*, Gandhi-gram: Department of Political Science and Development Administration, 1998.

Palanithurai, G., *Grassroots Democracy in Indian Society,* New Delhi: Concept Publishing Company, 2000.

Palanithurai, G., *New Panchayati Raj System at Work: An Evaluation,* New Delhi: Concept Publishing Company, 1999.

Palanithurai, G., *Panchayati Raj System in Tamil Nadu: With Original Act,* New Delhi: Concept Publishing Company, 2003.

Palanithurai, G., *Report of the Training Programme on Training of Trainers in Multi Level Planning Conducted for DRDA Officials,* Gandhigram: Rajiv Gandhi Chair for Panchayati Raj Studies, 2000.

Palanithurai, G., *Report of the Workshop on "Panchayati Raj: Trials and Triumphs",* Gandhigram: The Hunger Project, 2003.

Palanithurai, G., *Report of the Training on Multilevel Planning*, Gandhigram: Tamil Nadu Council for Sustainable Livelihood, 2002.

Palanithurai, G., *Report of the Workshop on Multilevel Planning*, Gandhigram: Tamil Nadu Council for Sustainable Livelihood, 2002.

Pushpam, Y., *Perspective Plan for Development of P. Nerpuhapatti*, Thirupathur: Grama Iyakkam, 2002.

Raj, K.N., *Some Thoughts on Decentralization of Development Planning and Implications,* keynote paper presented at Seminar on Decentralized Planning and Implementation, Nov. 29–1 Dec. 1984, ISEC, Bangalore.

Rakku, K., *Perspective Plan for Development of Vadavanpatti*, Thirupathur: Grama Iyakkam, 2002.

Sivaramakrishnan, K.C., *Power to the People?: The Politics and Progress of Decentralization*, New Delhi: Konark Publishers Pvt. Ltd., 2000, pp. 95-96.

State Planning Commission, *Report of the Working Group on Decentralized Planning and Panchayati Raj,* Chennai: Government of Tamil Nadu, 1997.

Sundaram, K.V., *Decentralized Multi Level Planning*, New Delhi: Concept Publishing Company, 1997.

Tandon, Rajesh and Mohanty, Ranjita, *Civil Society and Governance,* New Delhi: Sanskriti, 2002.

The World Bank, *World Development Report, 2004: Making Services Work for Poor People*, Washington DC: The World Bank, 2003.

Tornquist, Olle, *Politics and Development: A Critical Introduction*, New Delhi: Sage Publications, 1999.

Veerakalaiarasi, *Perspective Plan for Development of Veppankulam*, Thirupathur: Grama Iyakkam, 2002.

Index